The Survival of Poetry

A Contemporary Survey

The Survival of Poetry

A Contemporary Survey
by
Donald Davie, Martin Dodsworth,
Barbara Hardy, Derwent May,
Gabriel Pearson and Anthony Thwaite

EDITED BY
MARTIN DODSWORTH

FABER AND FABER
London

First published in 1970
by Faber and Faber Limited
24 Russell Square London WC1
Printed in Great Britain
by Ebenezer Baylis and Son, Limited
The Trinity Press, Worcester, and London
All rights reserved

ISBN 0 571 09057 5

Contents

Prefatory Note

THIS book began life as a series of lectures on recent poetry in England and America which I organized for the Department of Extra-Mural Studies of the University of London early in 1968. I would like to thank Miss Winifred Bamforth, of the Department, both for her invitation to plan the series, and for her unfailing helpfulness and efficiency in all that concerned it, as in so much else.

The Survival of Poetry must not be thought to reproduce the lectures of 1968, however. It did not seem feasible to reproduce the discussion on 'Poetry Today' between Peter Porter and Barry Cole which concluded the series, although I would have liked to do so, and am very grateful to them for their contribution to the lecture series; the introductory piece on 'The Survival of Poetry' was devised especially for this book; and in general the contributors have used their lectures as starting-off points for further thought.

Two other points are worth making. First, the poets discussed here are those who can be said to have matured as poets only since about 1950. This is not quite true of Lowell, but his style has at least notably changed since then, and this change has coincided with a change in the popular notion of his stature as a poet. Within these limits, I believe that the most interesting poets of our time are discussed. Without those limits, of course, poets like W. H. Auden, Roy Fuller and Austin Clarke should have been included. Second, no attempt has been made here at a uniformity of approach. The writers speak as individuals, and not from some common point of view. It is hoped that this will make the book more interesting, and serve to remind the reader of the diversity of ways in which the reading of poetry can be pleasurable.

I would like to thank for their help the Librarian and staff of Birkbeck College Library, London, where much of my own share of work for this book was done in pleasant and familiar surroundings; Mr Charles Monteith and Mr Frank Pike of Faber and Faber, especially for their patience; and Joanna, my wife, whose greater knowledge of existentialism, and of Sartre in particular, proved invaluable in my work on Thom Gunn.

M.D.

MARTIN DODSWORTH

Introduction: The Survival of Poetry

———————————

THE situation of the poet in England or America at the present time must in many ways seem more fortunate than that of his recent predecessors. He is much better cared for than ever they were; there are now more prizes for distinguished and promising work in poetry than there were ten years ago, and there are more fellowships in poetry in the universities, requiring the poet either to give only a little of his time to helping the young to become, like him, 'creative writers', or simply to grace the academic community by living within it without responsibilities of any specific kind. Even for the young poet just beginning to try for publication things are better; the number of small magazines printing poetry seems to increase daily, and the chances of getting a book of poems published are also improved: in 1968 over 700 books of poetry, of which more than 600 were entirely new, were published in the United Kingdom. Furthermore, paperback series like the Penguin Modern Poets sell to a far larger audience than ever used to be the case. The extensive use of modern poems as the basis for instruction in literature in the schools has also considerably enlarged the potential readership of many poets besides those who have been favourably reviewed in the Sunday newspapers or the weeklies.

There is a sense, too, in which poetry has become more popular; the increasing number of public readings of poetry has brought poets into a far more direct contact with their public than was available to those of the generation before. As poets, Allen Ginsberg and Adrian Mitchell are far better known to their large audience than W. H. Auden has ever been. A leader

11

in *The Times* has noticed this phenomenon and has argued that, despite certain inherent dangers, it is a sign of renewed vigour in the art:

'Yet surely, all things considered, the situation is healthier now for modern poetry than it has been for many years? A sickly, precious minority has been transformed into something robust and vigorous. The maker of verses again has fire in his belly.'

It may be questioned, of course, whether Lord Thomson's *Times* is well qualified to judge the state of health of poetry, or any other art, for that matter; but in any case it was certainly exaggerating the extent to which the audience for poetry has renewed itself. The truth is that in the last few years a new kind of poetry has created a new kind of audience, and both have kept themselves distinct from the old poetry and audience, despite various attempts at *rapprochement*.* The new audience is young and frankly uncritical in any academic sense; it expects its poets to speak boldly, to be unafraid of emotion and to be unsympathetic towards conventional middle-class sentiments. It does not look for intelligence in its poets; nevertheless the kind of poetry it favours varies widely from the obvious simplicities of Adrian Henri or Roger McGough to the sophistication and difficulty of Basil Bunting or Charles Olson. In many cases, one suspects, a poet's personality or aura of sanctity may ease the audience over points of difficulty—this is one of the doubtful advantages of the public reading. The English poets associated with this audience tend to be simpler in style and thought than their American counterparts. Nevertheless the same split between audiences for poetry is evident in America as in Britain. Donald Allen's anthology *The New American Poetry* was for the new audience, *New Poets of England and America* was for the old. *A Controversy of Poets* brought together selections from poets in either camp, but it took two editors to do it, one old-

---

*For an example of such an attempt, and for an interesting, if uncritical, account of the two audiences for contemporary poetry, see Edward Lucie-Smith's review of *Bomb Culture* by Jeff Nuttall, and other books, in the *New Statesman*, 29 November 1968.

style, one new-style, and the reader is rarely, if ever, left in doubt who chose what.

In England, as in America, the split between audiences has come to be felt in publishers' lists. The Fulcrum Press, Cape Goliard and Jonathan Cape now cater largely for the new audience, publishing poets of the new English scene like Tom Pickard or Adrian Mitchell, or American poets associated with it, like Gary Snyder, Allen Ginsberg, Denise Levertov, or the two poets discussed in this book by Donald Davie, Charles Olson and Edward Dorn. Firms like Chatto and Windus and the Oxford University Press, on the other hand, remain true to poets of the old school. It is for them as though the 1965 reading, which filled the Albert Hall with an audience actually paying money to hear poetry, had never been.

The fact that this English trend coexists with an American one may suggest that we have to deal here with something of only ephemeral interest, a fashion that has crossed the Atlantic like others and that will, like them, die. However, the development of a distinctively English style in the work of McGough or Pickard argues against such a dismissal; these new English and American poets share a common situation, not a common style. The creation of two kinds of poetry and audience marks, indeed, a new stage in the transformation of Western literary culture, and brings the poet once more to a point of crisis in relation to his art.

The new audience is primarily young. It is not illiterate. It is conscious of itself as a group. My own first acquaintance with it was at Sunday night sessions of bad jazz interspersed with poetry readings on the first floor of a pub near Liverpool Street station; these sessions took place under the auspices of the Campaign for Nuclear Disarmament's Committee of 100 which had initiated them, though by the time I first went, in about 1963, there was not much sign of commitment to a political cause on the audience's part. The link between jazz and poetry is important; both music and reading were expected to induce a sense of community between audience and performers, and bad readers who could not hold their audience were barely tolerated. The 1965 Albert Hall reading was filmed, and the film was appropriately entitled *Wholly Communion*. The new audience aspires to a total communion with itself and its chosen poets; it wants to create a new community within the community, of a more or less liberal and ideal kind. Almost any number of the London *International Times* will exemplify this point, and there are similar American journals similarly dedicated to the dissemination of simple slogans ('Make Love—Not War') and to campaigning for the extension of personal freedom from restraint—the legalization of marijuana, for example.

Naturally, this mild anarchism is subject to the changes of fashion—Buddhist temple bells one year, gipsy bangles the next. But in its recurrent plea for the extension of individual freedom, no matter how ridiculous or wrong-headed some of the causes are, it is expressive of a total reaction against the conventional organization of society, which must be attractive to the poet.

Whatever the poet's relation to society, the successful practice of his art has always in Western culture been felt to depend on his individual nature. Even the Augustan poet whose verse sought to embody the existing ideals of society felt that he was different from other people, made special by his gift. But it is just this quality of difference that is now threatened by the society which we have evolved, ever less tolerant of difference more than superficial between people or things.

In this essay, I want to consider three of the ways in which poets are responding to the increasing pressures on them to conform; these are what I would term 'academicism', 'international symbolism', and the 'projective verse' of Charles Olson. They do not, of course, exhaust the possible ways of response to the situation for the poet, but do, I think, illuminate that situation and the way in which it has affected the work of the poets discussed in this book.

'Academicism' is a word without very precise content, but I want to use it in order to emphasize the part at present played by the universities and schools in the making or unmaking of an audience for poetry. One notices an increasing emphasis on the study of contemporary or near-contemporary literature at the expense of the great authors of the past, as well as a tendency to avoid judgements of authors in general in favour of discussion of a few particular works, in which historical considerations play only a small part, if they play a part at all. What this means for the student, and perhaps the teacher too, is that it becomes more and more difficult to imagine that a poem (or novel or play) is actually written by a person with individual characteristics, intellectual and emotional, writing in a particular situation which is at once implicit and transcended in the poem itself. Instead, poems are experienced as things ideally self-consistent, whose verbal organization can be considered without reference to any social or historical situation. (In the graduate school, historical circumstances may be taken into account, but it is very rarely that historical knowledge coexists with full respect for an author's imaginative achievements.) Poems come to be regarded as machines which can be taken to pieces and put together again, whose function can be summarized, and whose principles of construction can be methodized. One might hazard, at least, that this is what many students believe that they have learnt about poetry, and that consequently it cannot signify much in their lives. And as John Bayley has acutely observed, this new situation must affect the poet also. John Berryman exemplifies one possible reaction to it—revulsion, and a deliberate and 'unmeaningful' flouting of poetic convention. 'Academicism', however, consists in a conformity to academic demands for a verse that can be easily taken to pieces. Academic verse should be sophisticated in construction and apparently individual in form, but it must be devoid of any feeling that is at once strong and individual, since that will distract the student from the task of grasping the poem intellectually. Its subject-matter should be large, so that the reading of it will seem to be an important activity, but it will nevertheless be easily assimilated to the conventional process of 'analysis'.

Academic verse differs slightly in England and America. The English product tends to a superficial experimentalism, absent on the whole in the American variety, which absorbs a great deal of Yeats, whose dramatic intensities assimilate all too easily to the great simplicities of the American way of life. James Dickey, for example, combines hunting, shooting and fishing with the old bardic certainty; his poetry appeals to the academic by virtue of its amenity to explication, especially in the stunning unsubtlety with which its symbols are deployed, and in the commonplaces few students will dare to question. 'The Ice Skin' is just the thing to give a class in its Junior year:

> All things that go deep enough
> Into rain and cold
> Take on, before they break down,
> A shining in every part.
>
> ...
>
> And the redwoods let sink their branches
> Like arms that try to hold buckets
> Filling slowly with diamonds
>
> Until a cannon goes off
> Somewhere inside the still trunk
> And a limb breaks, just before midnight,
> Plunging houses into the darkness
> And hands into cupboards, all seeking
> Candles, and finding each other.

The theme is clearly stated, and then it is particularized in the description of trees in the grip of ice; the syntax accumulates until the cannon goes off, the *limb* suggests the human as well as the arboreal, the double reference of *plunging* gives a feeling of the instantaneous effect of the limb's breaking, the balance of *candles* and *each other* leaves it suitably ambiguous whether we

are or are not sources of light to our fellows. The cannon comes
back at the end of the poem:

> I am still,
> And my son, doing what he was taught,
> Listening hard for a buried cannon,
> Stands also, calm as glass.

The trouble is that it only makes the hint of human reference in
limb more obvious. The father is only standing because that is
required of him by the implicit likeness to a tree, so that the
scene has no dramatic force or air of reality. *Calm as glass* is
chosen for the poem's last phrase, one supposes, because glass
connotes not only cold and shining but also fragility, which
contrasts effectively with the imperturbability one would naturally associate with *calm*. Like the father-son vignette and the
cannon's reappearance, this metaphor doesn't really come off,
however, because we sense no reason for the comparison other
than that it fits in nicely with the rest of the poem. The whole
thing is clangingly deliberate, an utterance that cannot move us
because it is in an assumed and assuming voice. This is especially
obvious in the three lines omitted from my quotation of the
opening of 'The Ice Skin':

> The necks of slender trees
> Reel under it, too much crowned,
> Like princes dressing as kings . . .

The comparison is only possible because it is assumed that we
will accept the *princes* and *kings*, remote as they are from our
experience and by our imagination still probably overdressed,
for the sake of the pun in *too much crowned* and the chance to
indulge in covert feelings about the sovereignty of nature.

The poem is in this way false throughout. Yet it is the sort of
thing that can be overrated by the use of those very techniques—
attention to ambiguity, syntactical analysis and so on—that

evolved in the effort to discriminate better among poems. It would be easy to overlook the self-contained nature of the poem in the interest of its very literary effects.

'James Dickey, born in Atlanta, Georgia, in 1923, has been called by *Life* magazine "the hottest of emerging US poets". His many honours include fellowships from the *Sewanee Review* and the Guggenheim Foundation; the Melville Cane Award; the National Book Award in Poetry; and for 1966–67, appointment as Consultant in Poetry to the Library of Congress.' (The quotation is from the English publishers' jacket for *Poems 1957–1967*.) Mr Dickey has certainly paid the price for his prizes and fellowships.

An English equivalent would be George MacBeth or Edward Lucie-Smith. Like the American, these are talented poets, but their talents are used merely to fulfil shallow expectations. One might contrast the first part of Mr Lucie-Smith's 'Genesis' (from his book, *Towards Silence*) with 'The Ice Skin' in order to see how wide the taint of academicism extends:

> The apple tasted of flesh. The
> Blood of the apple was salt
> (Though it smelt sweet, like semen).

> Adam's mouth was choked with blood.
> His flesh stiffly erect, like
> The flesh of a hanging man.

> The plan was written in this:
> The superfluous part stood,
> A tall monument to foresight.

One has here the same availability to explication as in the poem by Dickey. There is plenty of room for round-the-table discussion of the meaningful links between *apple, flesh, blood, salt* and *semen*, and of who has best claim to the *plan* and *foresight*.

The Hanged Man comes later. The 'outspokenness' of the sexual references (anaesthetized by their context, of course) acts as a false guarantee that the poem is *not* what it is— academic; just as the choppy line-breaks (*The/blood, like/the*) and the 'wit' of *superfluous part* declare the poet's serious concern with his art. Yet the poem's short lines permit no intensity of feeling equivalent to the poem's intellectual complexity. The short sentences have no terseness or finality to justify their thrusting upon us such large symbolic statements; the parenthesis with which the first stanza ends, the passive tense of *was choked*, the absence of verb altogether in the next two lines, the fact that the last line is in apposition and no integral part of the poem's concluding statement—all these things tell us that the poem is decoration, a fuss about nothing, a trivialization of poetry and its subject-matter. Yet the poem is representative of Mr Lucie-Smith's work, and his pages of acknowledgements are as impressive in their way as Mr Dickey's awards.

Not that the academic is the only kind of vicious poetry that flourishes today. We have to face the possibility of an international style in poetry becoming dominant in the English and American scenes. The craze for concrete poetry is one sign of this, but certainly not the only one. Consider, for example, the amount of translated verse now appearing in such little magazines as *Stand* and *Agenda*, or the interest which Robert Bly's much respected journal, *The Sixties*, has consistently shown in translation. In England at any rate publishers have become noticeably less reluctant to bring out poetry in translation—witness the Penguin Modern European Poets, for example.

In many ways, of course, this new tendency should be welcomed; the culture gains by contact with work from other countries, other cultural situations; its defects, as well as qualities, are brought into relief by comparison with central work from beyond its limits. When a great deal of foreign poetry is being translated, though, dangers arise, principally the probability that poets will be chosen on grounds of translatability rather than of merit. One aspect of a poem's translatability is its language: the more it exploits the particular qualities of its own language, the less available that poem is for translation. This is one reason for the poverty in number and quality of translations of the early Pasternak. Similarly, formal qualities apart from the crudest devices do not go over well into another language: rhyme presents a problem here, and so does the meaningful placing of words in relation to line-endings. Pasternak like other Russians suffers from the disadvantage of using conventional form: some of Donald Davie's versions of the *Zhivago* poems overcome this difficulty, but poets like Yesenin and Tsvetayeva still await adequate English versions. Finally, some tones of voice cannot be translated; they are natural within the social situation which gave rise to them but cannot be assimilated to other conditions. The fact that most translations appear without adequate explanatory comment only makes it more difficult to translate this sort of poetry— Robert Bly and James Wright in their *Twenty Poems by Pablo Neruda* misrepresent Neruda not only by the meagreness with which they have chosen from his work but also in the emphasis thrown on his surrealist poetry at the expense of such original and simply pleasing things as the *Odas Elementales*.

The translatable poem, then, tends not to exploit the particular qualities of its language, not to insist on particular cultural situation. Some positives have to be there as well, of course, but the range of particular qualities is by now necessarily restricted. It is not really enough that a poem's sentiments should be acceptable to a new audience; we are too sophisticated to believe that a poem's force ever lies in what it *says*. (In this we are wrong, of course.) What else, then, can the translatable poem offer? Well—imagist poetry is very translatable, indeed, was deeply influenced in its origins by translated Japanese and Chinese poetry. Translatable poetry can offer the precise images of imagism, and can intensify their emotional effect by letting the relation between them seem obscure. A hint of surrealist mystery overhanging the objects described in a poem which says little but suggests *something*, however hazy: that is very translatable. See, for example, the poems of Johannes Bobrowski, as rendered by Mathew and Ruth Mead; or the translated poems of David Rokeah.

In England, the effects of the new vogue for translated verse have yet to be seen. In America they are already apparent. Louis Simpson, for example, in his *Introduction to Poetry*, an anthology for schools and colleges, writes:

'The poems that, in my opinion, are most interesting are being written by poets who have adapted the ideas of the imagists and surrealists. They have escaped the deadening influence of teachers who can think of nothing better to do with poetry than to turn it into prose, and critics who treat a poem as though it were a machine designed to produce criticism. They are not writing light verse for magazines, or confessions for an audience that is emotionally bankrupt. These poems have an inner life which they express in original images.' (p. 56.)

Simpson's point of view is interesting because he sees the imagist-surrealist line of poetry (which I have associated with the criteria of translatability) as offering an alternative to the poetry written under the 'deadening influence of teachers' (which I would exemplify in the work of James Dickey). And that, it seems to me, is the reason why he overrates it. He has in mind the poetry of James Wright and (one assumes) Robert Bly—the two have collaborated a number of times. They are both poets of undeniable talent and seriousness, but the style of poetry which they have adopted permits the cultivation of an 'inner life', only at the expense of contact with the world outside.

Both poets have tried to remedy this defect, but neither has notably succeeded. 'The Minneapolis Poem', for example, in Wright's latest book, *Shall We Gather at the River*, is about the city as some monstrous, clean, hygienic, policed prison:

There are men in this city who labor dawn after dawn
To sell me my death.

But Wright cannot sustain a tone appropriate to his subject-
matter; something inhibits him from speaking out—perhaps the
fear that he might then be writing 'anti-poetry'. ('Current
poets in the United States seem to be perishing on either side
of a grey division between century-old British formalism on the
one hand and a vandalism of anti-poetry on the other.'*)
Instead he cultivates a deliberate style, obscure yet suggestive,
that reduces tension instead of increasing it:

> The soul of a cop's eyes
> Is an eternity of Sunday daybreak in the suburbs
> Of Juárez, Mexico.

The reference to Juárez, particular but baffling, seems a personal
indulgence, rather than the sign of personal involvement in
what is said, that, no doubt, it hopes to be. As for 'the soul of
a cop's eyes', this strikes one as a pure example of translator's
English, the sort of thing that would never rise spontaneously
to one's lips in any situation. It might, of course, be
thinkable and speakable in a Latin American context such as
César Vallejo's. Wright seems not to be conscious that what
is excellent in one cultural situation may not be so in
another.

Bly does not either. Trakl is a fine poet, but he cannot be
taken over on the large scale attempted in *Silence in the Snowy
Fields* or *The Light around the Body*. Furthermore, the flatness
of language employed only makes the poems seem more, not
less, finicking: the charge of preciosity seems very real when
brought against lines like these:

---

*James Wright, 'A Note on César Vallejo', *Twenty Poems of César Vallejo*,
chosen and translated by John Knoepfle, James Wright, and Robert Bly, Madison,
Minnesota, 1962, p. 10.

We cannot see—
But a paw
Comes out of the dark
To light the road. Suddenly I am flying,
I follow my own fiery traces through the night!*

As yet, this style of poetry has not reached England, partly because the existing 'formalist' tradition has more life in it than in America; I am not sure, in any case, that there are not traces of it in the brief poems which the editor of *The Review* likes to print, especially in the work of the young poets Michael Fried and David Harsent. Both generate a greater intensity than Bly or Wright, but about both there hangs an air of symbolism strained to the point of preciosity.

As alternative models for the serious and gifted poet, neither the well-made nor the translatable poem has much to offer. The well-made poem implies, socially, collusion with the worst tendencies of the academy to turn the experience of literature into a specialization as meaningless and unrewarding as the expert playing of a game of ping-pong; the 'translatable' poem, on the other hand, goes with a cultivation of the inner life at the expense of public concerns, and issues in a poetry that is time-less only in the sense that it seems dissociated from all conceivable place, time or truly human interest.

There is good reason, therefore, that a poet should feel the attraction of such a programme for poetry as Charles Olson's 'Projective Verse', a central document for poets of the 'anti-poetry' so much abhorred by Wright. It is not an easy document to summarize: two of its principal features are opposition to the old-style 'formalism' that Wright too would reject, and a new insistence on the poem as personal utterance:

'Verse now, 1950, if it is to go ahead, if it is to be of *essential* use, must, I take it, catch up and put into itself certain laws and possibilities of the breath, of the breathing of the man who

*Robert Bly, *The Light around the Body*, 1968, p. 50.

writes as well as of his listenings. (The revolution of
the ear, 1910, the trochee's heave, asks it of the younger
poets.)'*

The demand for a new form arises from the new conception
of the poem as utterance—the idea of breathing takes on near-
mystical colouring, for breath is spirit, and the poem is to be
an extension, a projection, of that spirit, not the malleable,
imposed-on nature of the academic poet and his well-made
poems, nor the essentially retiring, sensitive yet timid expression of individual will and the need for self-protection that we
get in Bly or Wright. ('The Minneapolis Poem' ends in this
way:

> I want to be lifted up
> By some great white bird unknown to the police,
> And soar for a thousand miles and be carefully hidden
> Modest and golden as one last corn grain,
> Stored with the secrets of the wheat and the mysterious lives
> Of the unnamed poor.)

Olson's essay seeks to relate the idea of poetry to the idea of
man himself in a manner that is as admirable as it is unexpected
in our days. Without specific ideological bias, he gives the poet
a place in the world that does not require him either to accommodate himself to forces ultimately hostile to the imagination
or to waste himself in a refined but sickly self-protective
aestheticism:

'It comes to this: the use of a man, by himself and thus by
others, lies in how he conceives his relation to nature, that
force to which he owes his somewhat small existence. If he
sprawl, he shall find little to sing but himself, and shall sing,
nature has such paradoxical ways, by way of artificial forms
outside himself. But if he stays inside himself, if he is contained
within his nature as he is participant in the larger force, he will
be able to listen, and his hearing through himself will give him

*Charles Olson, *Human Universe and other Essays*, New York, 1967, p. 51.

24

secrets objects share. And by an inverse law his shapes will make their own way.'*

Olson's poetic individualism is not a cultivation of personality or a simple form of self-expression. Self-knowledge, for him, comes first—the prerequisite for excellence in poetry turns out to be a form of *humilitas* that must cancel out thoughts of display. There must be a 'getting rid of the lyrical interference of the individual as ego, of the "subject" and his soul, that peculiar presumption by which western man has interposed himself between what he is as a creature of nature (with certain instructions to carry out) and those other creations of nature which we may, with no derogation, call objects.'† The self-conscious aesthetics of the translatable poem cannot seem desirable in such a view of the poet's role, which, for one thing, puts such an emphasis on the poet's sense of *locality* and *existence in time* as to give a quite particular and personal stamp on his work of a kind lacking in Bly or Wright.

Donald Davie writes persuasively about the kind of perspective on human activity opened up by Olson, and Dorn, in their poetry. Yet I cannot share his enthusiasm to the full: the sort of objections raised by Gabriel Pearson in what he has to say about them in his essay on Lowell seem too substantial. In their emphasis on 'geography', man's existence as an object among objects, these poets seem to turn away from 'history', the entangling web of relationships with others past and present with which we find ourselves willy-nilly engaged. This is reflected in the air of coterie which hangs about their work; their community-within-the-community is extremely narrow. This would be a trivial objection were it not that their poetry constantly finds itself up against the question of human relationship and, in my opinion, rarely succeeds in dealing with this sort of subject-matter convincingly. *The Maximus Poems* deal largely with the early history of the settlement at Gloucester, Massachusetts, and Olson's recapturing of the historical moment

*Ibid., p. 60.
†Ibid., pp. 59–60.

is often an enthralling process to watch; but it *is* watched. We feel involved *not* in the recreation imaginatively of the experience of community in face of the unknown geography of a new continent, but rather in Olson's train of thought evoked in his readings in the documents of the town's history. When he has to speak of the present society of Gloucester he can do little but turn from it in revulsion; the galumphing pun 'mu-sick' won't do to sum up the music of our present civilization, because it does not suggest how it is tolerated.

> Polis now
> Is a few, is a coherence not even yet new (the island of this
>   city
> is a mainland now of who? who can say who are
> citizens?*

Olson posits an ideal natural expressiveness arising from a poet's properly establishing his relation to the world of objects around him, and this should be the compensatory quality for the lack of faith in any community other than that comprised by a few. Yet again and again in his work one is conscious of a strained heartiness that never quite convinces, a studied kind of spontaneity that almost blushes for itself on the page, as in the first of his *Mayan Letters*:

'Birds, lad: my god what birds. Last evening a thing like our hawk. And that woman of mine (again) most alert to their nature. It happened this way. I was down on the beach bargaining to buy a piece of their best fish here, what sounds like madrigal, only it comes out smedreegal . . .'

Carlyle, Ruskin, Doughty, Burton—Olson's prose has the charm but also the archness of much Victorian prose, and the quality is extended to his verse, as in the final twist of these lines, concluding 'Stiffening in the Master Founders' Wills' from *The Maximus Poems*:†

*Olson. *The Maximus Poems*. New York, 1960, p. 11.
†p. 132.

We pick

a private way
among debris
of common
wealths—Public
fact as sure

as dimensions stay
personal. And one desire,
that the soul
be naked
at the end

of time (the screech
of the tunnel
says
it better be, or
what's all this

for

The weakness of these lines, a wry dogmatism, head cocked to an approving audience of peers, is not so far, after all, from the weakness of the British poets associated with the 'popular' audience, the community-within-the-community purged of academic preconceptions, which we have already discussed. It is a weakness that also lurks at the heart of Dorn's work, I think, though he attempts a more direct confrontation with the issue: what sort of society do we actually have? The weakness is a sentimental evasiveness quite complementary to the emotional preciosity of Bly and Wright. Olson's concept of poetry is theoretically hostile to the display of personality but also allows for it in the notion that where a man is in the right relation to nature, the realm of other objects (man himself being an object), then 'his shapes will make their own way'. All the critical faculties, it seems, are to be exercised on the quality of the poet's life, not his art; the consequence can be a sloppiness with which the poet remains hubristically content because the general quality of his life assures him that all is well. A major indulgence on Olson's part is his curious belief about the typewriter—that 'due to its rigidity and its space precisions, it can, for a poet, indicate exactly the breath, the pauses, the suspensions even of syllables, the juxtapositions even of parts of phrases, which he intends'. The typewriter is 'the personal and instantaneous recorder of the poet's work'—doubtless, but it will only be the best recorder if his life is of the quality Olson requires. The machine is hardly an adequate instrument to carry the modulations of human speech in all their variety, and the examples he gives (in 'Projective Verse') of the way in which it can be used are noticeably unsuitable, even superfluous, for example, the use of the oblique stroke to represent a pause lighter than a comma: 'What does not change/is the will to change.' The argument about breath here seems to be perverted in the interests of a personal and instantaneous medium; the unsatisfactoriness of Olson's account should be evident.

Olson's view of the personal is strictly limited: at his best he can make us aware of the limitations of consciousness centred entirely in human affairs, but at his worst he exhibits an empty kind of personality-display. The hostility of his point of view to the human life and the poetic act as both fully committed to the sort of society we actually have is something that tends to reduce the scope and relevance of his work. For the writing and reading of poetry are both *social* acts: they take place in the context of history and the preconceptions of generations. Even in denying preconceptions poetry is engaged with a historical and social context that Olson prefers to miss out, or is actually incapable of offering us. He often reminds one of Whitman, but in his 'Song of the Open Road', for example, Whitman is able to make exactly the kind of qualification to his openness to experience that one misses so direly in Olson:

Still here, I carry my old delicious burdens,
I carry them, men and women, I carry them with me
   wherever I go,
I swear it is impossible for me to get rid of them,
I am fill'd with them: and I will fill them in return.

The poem is a social act, not merely in the sense that it is
an act of communication, from one person to another, but also
in that the way in which the message is taken is determined by
the way in which the reader has previously understood poems
and by the way in which poems have been read and valued in the
centuries before this reader or that came across them. 'I carry
them, men and women, I carry them with me wherever I go';
Whitman's line holds good for any poet in that the way in which
he writes, as well as the way in which he will be read, is determined partly by the poetic tradition in which he realizes himself
and partly by the existing social context for all his actions.
That is not to say that the poet himself has nothing to say in
the ultimate shape of his poetry—far from it. But the poet who
turns away from the facts about his craft deprives himself of the
full authority to speak that belongs to one who writes from
within a society and in full consciousness of his historical role,
involving the preservation, as much as the propagation, of
certain kinds of feeling held by him to be valuable. Olson's
work suffers from the effects of his withdrawal from the society
around him. His view of the human past reconstructs the experience not of a community but of individuals. Fitfully he illu-
minates: there is never a sense of the picture as a whole being
equally surveyed. This is true as much of his account of literary
history ('verse here and in England dropped this secret [of the
syllable] from the late Elizabethans to Ezra Pound'—'Projective Verse') as of the historical reconstruction in *The Maximus
Poems*.

   The kind of total repudiation of existing society that we find
in Olson has, then, its dangers, though these may seem less than
those entailed in bowing to such social pressures as do the

makers of the academic or the translatable poem. In writing of *The Present Age* (and that age is still in essentials ours) Kierkegaard concluded that in it a man must learn to be content 'as priest to be his own audience, and as author his own reader'; Olson and Dorn demonstrate this possibility for the future of poetry, and for this reason Donald Davie's essay on them gives this book on poetry in the present age an appropriate, if not for all of us hopeful, conclusion.

The other poets discussed here speak from within society to a more or less degree. They seem to me to be the poets of the present day, that is, who have found their style in the post-war world, who are most aware, though not always obviously, of the social and historical context in which they write. The selection is not exclusive. (Had I inclined to a longer book, I would certainly have wished to include something on Donald Davie, Geoffrey Hill and Thomas Kinsella.) If there is one tradition rather than, simply, 'tradition', then these poets, often desperately, seem to continue it, and in doing so, to proclaim their own individuality to a world increasingly indifferent to the idea of the individual. None of them is 'translatable' in the precious way of Bly or Wright, none writes poems merely academic; all of them make us conscious of individual tones of voice. Larkin and Hughes are immediately recognizable without one's feeling that they simply indulge personal idiosyncrasy; in reading them one is reminded once more of the pertinence of Kierkegaard's antithesis of the 'public' and the individual, although many of us would read him in a secular fashion the adequacy of which he would not accept.

This individual tone of voice has to be maintained against social pressures, which have been most recently examined by A. Alvarez in the introduction to his anthology *The New Poetry*. His argument is that the course of English poetry in the last forty years has been determined by a series of negative feedbacks working to 'correct the balance experimentation had so unpredictably distorted'. He describes these 'feed-backs' as the product of a peculiarly English phenomenon associated with class—'gentility', which he describes as 'a belief that life is always more or less orderly, people always more or less polite, their emotions and habits more or less decent and more or less controllable; that God, in short, is more or less good.'

It is hard to accept this as a true account of what has been happening. The poets I have chosen to exemplify possible false answers to social pressure in this essay have all been American, and this was not by chance. We have to face the idea that our own culture is becoming increasingly like that of the United States in its unwillingness to allow for variations on an uninviting, indeed undistinguished, norm for human achievement. This change is not to be attributed to America's unacknowledged spirit of colonialism, so much as to the increasingly sophisticated technology of our own society which demands a continuing 'rationalization' of social structures that is hostile to individual difference. This 'levelling process', as Kierkegaard named it, is further advanced in America than Europe, but it is, of course, well under way here, as it is in some degree in all the other countries of Europe whether they belong politically in the Western or Eastern camp. That is why our own poetic future can be appropriately discussed in terms of what is to be seen in America now.

The international character of the technological 'revolution' leads one to suppose that Mr Alvarez's 'gentility' is altogether inadequate as an account of the forces at present hostile to the practice of poetry; there is some provincialism in his point of view, nowhere so evident as in his yearning for a new 'experimentalism'. He is not content with the sophistication of poetry itself; he wants a poetry that is not only sophisticated but looks it too. (As a consequence, he seriously underrates the poetry of Philip Larkin.)

In his view, 'gentility' is responsible for the failure to take up 'the experimental techniques' introduced by Eliot and his generation. There is doubtless something in this. But surely the reaction against 'experiment' involved other considerations?

The specialization of poetry and the discussion of its 'techniques', for example, tended to remove poetry from the level of common experience; it is no accident that Dr Leavis in his most recent writing on Eliot's poetry chooses to emphasize its *personal* qualities. These qualities, too, conflict with the symbolist pretensions of Eliot and Pound to some extent; they do not cohere with the avowed intention of *impersonality*. The failure of both Eliot and Pound to remove their poetry from the level of *human* discourse to that of symbolist *poésie pure* is an explanation of their continuing vitality.

The failure to take up 'experimental techniques' may therefore be explained rather as an attempt to overcome the taint of 'specialization' that they entailed and to personalize and individualize the utterances of poetry in the face of that process of civilization described by Dr Leavis in 1932 as 'a process of standardization, mass-production and levelling-down', 'a solidarity achieved by the exploitation of the most readily released responses'. That is still the civilization that we have, and it is one in which the idea of 'minority culture' canvassed by Dr Leavis, because of its isolation and specialization, seems peculiarly vulnerable. Whatever the artist has to do has to be done *in* the world—'I carry them, men and women, I carry them with me wherever I go.' (This is not to say, however, that an equal role in the formation or preservation of the national culture is available to all, or that the poet should act as though that were so. But in proportion as his talent is on a footing with that of the most distinguished poets of the past he will gravitate to themes which will concern the individual throughout society.)

The reaction against experiment is in one sense an illusion, since all poetry involves experiment and risk, and to the extent to which it does not we feel it to fall below the highest achievements of art. Furthermore, the reaction against experimentalism is by no means total, as we can see if we look at the poems of Sylvia Plath or Ted Hughes. It is worth noting, though, that theirs is not the 'experiment' of Eliot and Pound, and that both

owe a good deal more to D. H. Lawrence than to the ack-
knowledged masters of modernism. There is, too, a sense in
which their use of form denotes a point of strain insofar as it
mimes 'formlessness', that is, mimes that condition in which
content is, in Kierkegaard's words again, 'capable of being
extended so as to include everything or touch upon everything'
(whilst a 'true' content is 'clearly and, if one likes, miserably
limited because of its intensity and self-absorption').

The meaning that can be given, then, to this so-called reaction
attaches to the continuing use of conventional forms in poetry.
The Poundian revolution is, after all, associated with the introduction to English poetry of *vers libre*. There seem to me two
reasons for the immovability of conventional forms in poetry.
The first is that they can more easily than *vers libre* suggest a
continuity between the world of the poem and that of our daily
life. Stanza form suggests a pattern of feeling: it does not
demand that its world be self-contained. Because its rhythmical
patterns are irregular, however, *vers libre* tends to distinguish
itself from the discourse of life by the adoption of artificial tones
of voice or a freezing aesthetic preciousness. (Obviously this is
not true of William Carlos Williams, and this perhaps explains
his attraction for a poet like Thom Gunn, who composes in conventional form also.) Berryman and Lowell allude to conventional form as much as they actually employ it: the sort of effect
achieved can be seen from the opening of Lowell's 'Man and
Wife' where the heroic couplets at once contrast with the savage
undertones of the scene described and affirm that an ordered
way of talking of them is conceivable, this order not being
necessarily organic and self-enclosed but more like the reason-
able order of Pope's poetry:

> Tamed by *Miltown*, we lie on Mother's bed;
> the rising sun in war paint dyes us red;
> in broad daylight her gilded bed-posts shine,
> abandoned, almost Dionysian.

(Compare the effect which Eliot gets by enclosing his 'Augustan' couplets *inside* the structure of *The Waste Land*.)

Our second reason for the persistence of rhyme and stanza form lies in the fact that poetry is necessarily concerned in a historical context. There is no adequate definition of poetry because it has been at different times different things, and as time has passed the range of possible and conceivable poetic aims has increased in scope rather than reduced. A poet chooses from the prompting of his own self and of his society and from what his reading in the literature of the past suggests to him. The choice of conventional form, however modified, brings him into a relation with the poetry of the past, and makes clear his refusal to be defined or summed up merely as an inhabitant of the present. To live only in the present is to live without the means of choosing future behaviour, which in order to be exercised requires memory of a past; it is to submit to the 'levelling process' of the present age which is naturally as hostile to historical difference and distinction as it is to difference of any kind.

It does not follow that conventional forms will continue to be used in the future. As the 'levelling process' goes on, it may be that the serious poet in his isolation will seek forms purely expressive of the solitary life, and there would seem to be historical reasons why those forms should be associated with *vers libre*. As things are, even the vestigial rhyme-scheme used by Berryman in *The Dream Songs* serves to establish for the reader that his poetic enterprise is not by intention at odds with the poetry of other times than our own.

The creation of two audiences for poetry, I said earlier on, brings the poet to a new point of crisis in relation to his art. This is not because he has to choose between the two audiences. The 'popular' audience is uncritical and uncertain of its aims. It is in reaction against the society of which it is a part, on which it depends and to which, ultimately, it submits. (Consider, for example, its ambiguous relation to fashions in dress and popular music.) Its admiration for the poet springs from its identification with one who also finds contemporary society repugnant: but it is content, nevertheless, to apply a 'levelling process' to itself that would reduce an Olson to the size of a Ginsberg, and Ezra Pound to the stature of Basil Bunting. It is not Olson's chosen audience; but it has chosen him to a degree, and his work suffers in consequence. The 'academic' audience, on the other hand, suffers also from its willingness to acquiesce in the 'levelling process', as we have seen. It is possible for a man to write well and be read by either audience. But both these audiences threaten the poet's individuality; both exert demands on him that are likely to be intolerable. The crisis for the poet in his art is in the question whether there is actually any one left for whom to write. If it is possible for Larkin to write as he does this is because the historical meaning of poetry, its preservation of certain ways of feeling, is still alive for some of us in this country. But there is no guarantee that this state of affairs will continue.

As for the subject-matter of poetry, now or in the future, it will depend entirely on the individual poet's choice. Mr Alvarez's feeling that a serious poetry should in our present conditions be associated with the experience of violence and cruelty as it has been known to us since the Second World War, and with the new perspectives on human behaviour opened up by psycho-analysis seems, however, to miss the truth of the poet's situation, which requires simply, but above all, not a consciousness of these things, but only (or, if you like, supremely) an *individual* consciousness, and an audience that does not debase it.

Poetry has so far survived the levelling process. But a certain desperation is to be heard in the work of all the poets discussed in this book. It may be that in the next half century or so poets will come increasingly to find the social act of writing poetry burdensome as an expression of their individual judgements on life. They may find that the pressure on them to think and feel as others wish them to think and feel becomes so great as to make the effort of creation fruitless. In that case, a kind of poetry will survive, but it will not be one that can be taken seriously. On the other hand, it may be that the levelling process will only serve to make the obstinately individual gesture of the poem more valuable to those who can still value it, and so more worth the attempting for those who understand it. If this book can offer some insight into the survival of poetry in our own day, then perhaps it contributes its scrap also to poetry's survival in the future. Let us hope so, at any rate.

ANTHONY THWAITE

The Poetry of Philip Larkin

THERE is a certain irony about sitting down to write a critical paper on the poetry of Philip Larkin, when one remembers some remarks of Larkin's about 'poetry as syllabus' and 'the dutiful mob that signs on every September'. Larkin needs no prolegomena, no exegesis: there is no necessary bibliography, no suggested reading, except the poems themselves. In a straightforward Wordsworthian sense, he is a man speaking to men (though his detractors might put it that he is too often simply a chap chatting to chaps). Although few of the poems need any background knowledge beyond that which any reader of English may be supposed to command, when such knowledge is necessary Larkin himself has generally provided it, in his rare but always relevant and commonsensical statements about his work. Beyond that, I can only stand witness to my conviction that he is our finest living poet—and not in any *'Victor Hugo, hélas'* sense—and go on to draw out and underline what seem to me to be his themes, his special voice and his peculiar excellences.

Although Larkin made little impact as a poet until the publication of *The Less Deceived* in 1955, when he was 33, he had started to write and to publish much earlier. In a fugitive essay in the Coventry arts magazine, *Umbrella* (Vol. I, No. 3, Summer 1959), he spoke of writing ceaselessly in his school-days: 'now verse, which I sewed up into little books, now prose, a thousand words a night after homework.' His first publication, apart from the school magazine of King Henry VIII School in Coventry, was a poem in *The Listener* of November 28th 1940, when he was 18. This (titled 'Ultimatum') was one of four poems he had sent in the summer of 1940:

'I was astonished when someone signing himself J.R.A. wrote back saying that he would like to take one (it was the one I had put in to make the others seem better, but never mind).'

Here, as so often, the late J. R. Ackerley showed himself to be a perceptive judge; during his quarter of a century as literary editor of *The Listener*, that periodical probably published more good poetry than any other in England. As it has never been reprinted, it is worth noting this consummately Audenesque piece:

> But we must build our walls, for what we are
> Necessitates it, and we must construct
> The ship to navigate behind them, there.
> Hopeless to ignore, helpless instruct
> For any term of time beyond the years
> That warn us of the need for emigration:
> Exploded the ancient saying: Life is yours.
>
> For on our island is no railway station,
> There are no tickets for the Vale of Peace,
> No docks where trading ships and seagulls pass.
>
> Remember stories you read when a boy
> —The shipwrecked sailor gaining safety by
> His knife, tree trunk, and lianas—for now
> You must escape, or perish saying no.

Later appearances were in the Fortune Press's anthology, *Poetry From Oxford in Wartime*, edited by William Bell in 1944, and in his own first volume of poetry, *The North Ship*, published by the Fortune Press in July 1945. In the republished version of *The North Ship* (Faber, 1966), Larkin wrote a characteristically wry and humorous account of the book's original struggle for birth, assisted by that same L. S. Caton (the owner of the

Fortune Press) who makes fleeting and protean appearances in several of Kingsley Amis's novels, for Amis's own first book of poems, *Bright November*, was published by the same press and no doubt with some of the same attendant difficulties. Later, in 1946, the Fortune Press published Larkin's first novel, *Jill*, a book which had a minor underground reputation at Oxford when I was an undergraduate in the early and mid-1950s: it was difficult to get copies at that time (though I think it has never actually been out of print), and those few there were were passed round and read with great respect and interest, not chiefly for the authentic-feeling atmosphere of 1940 Oxford but for the extraordinary way in which Larkin manages to present the central character's growing and gradually enveloping fantasy about 'Jill' with a clear narrative and realistic dialogue. This is not the place to deal properly with *Jill*, or with its more professional successor, *A Girl in Winter*, published by Faber in 1947; but they mark the brief flowering of Larkin the novelist, and both of them are so memorable that one can imagine him having staked out, if he had continued, an area and a reputation comparable with, say, Forster's up to *Howards End*.

The North Ship is now gently and self-deprecatingly dismissed by Larkin. Indeed, I want to make no great claims for it. It is interesting in the way that any considerable poet's juvenilia are interesting, with a phrase here, a line there, suggesting or prefiguring what was to come. Larkin has written:

'Looking back, I find in the poems not one abandoned self but several—the ex-schoolboy, for whom Auden was the only alternative to 'old-fashioned' poetry; the undergraduate, whose work a friend affably characterized as 'Dylan Thomas, but you've a sentimentality that's all your own'; and the immediately post-Oxford self, isolated in Shropshire with a complete Yeats stolen from the local girls' school.'

I find few traces of Auden; certainly nothing as Audenesque as 'Ultimatum', though 'Conscript' has something of 'In Time of War' about it, particularly the first two stanzas:

The ego's county he inherited
From those who tended it like farmers; had
All knowledge that the study merited,
The requisite contempt of good and bad;

But one Spring day his land was violated;
A bunch of horsemen curtly asked his name,
Their leader in a different dialect stated
A war was on for which he was to blame . . .

I can find nothing at all of Dylan Thomas; perhaps the friend whom Larkin quotes was commenting on poems which did not in fact get selected for *The North Ship*. It is true that a good deal of *Poetry Quarterly* and *Poetry London* in that 1943–53 decade was taken up with Dylanism, and it might be thought surprising that Larkin escaped it; but as he has said:

'The principal poets of the day—Eliot, Auden, Dylan Thomas, Betjeman—were all speaking out loud and clear, and there was no reason to become entangled in the undergrowth . . . except by a failure of judgement.'

Admiration for Dylan Thomas didn't then, and doesn't now, necessarily carry in its wake base imitation.

But of Yeats there is a predominance in *The North Ship*:

'Not because I liked his personality or understood his ideas but out of infatuation with his music . . . In fairness to myself it must be admitted that it is a particularly potent music, pervasive as garlic, and has ruined many a better talent.'

Larkin has said that the edition of Yeats's collected poems he had at the time was the 1933 one, so that he 'never absorbed the harsher last poems'. This might be guessed from such lines as these:

Let the wheel spin out,
Till all created things
With shout and answering shout
Cast off rememberings;

Let it all come about
Till centuries of springs
And all their buried men
Stand on the earth again.
A drum taps: a wintry drum.

For the first time I'm content to see
What poor mortar and bricks
I have to build with, knowing that I can
Never in seventy years be more a man
Than now—a sack of meal upon two sticks.

The beauty dries my throat.
Now they express
All that's content to wear a worn-out coat,
All actions done in patient hopelessness,
All that ignores the silences of death,
Thinking no further than the hand can hold,
All that grows old,
Yet works on uselessly with shortened breath.

Yet though these poems are derivative, their technique is generally quietly assured; their infatuation is self-aware enough to stop short of mere pastiche. And here and there another voice comes through:

This is your last, meticulous hour,
Cut, gummed; pastime of a provincial winter.

Only a name
That chimes occasionally, as a belief
Long since embedded in the static past.

To show you pausing at a picture's edge
To puzzle out the name, or with a hand
Resting a second on a random page.

The cadences are mellifluous, but not in a middle-Yeatsian way; and the sense of time, its preciousness and its passing, is there. °Four lines from 'Songs: 65° N.' directly point forward to 'Next, Please' in *The Less Deceived*, where they are put more sharply in focus:

> I am awakened each dawn
> Increasingly to fear
> Sail-stiffening air,
> The birdless sea.
>
> 　　　　　(*The North Ship*)

> Only one ship is seeking us, a black-
> Sailed unfamiliar, towing at her back
> A huge and birdless silence. In her wake
> No waters breed or break.
>
> 　　　　　(*The Less Deceived*)

In the 1966 re-publication of *The North Ship*, Larkin included an additional poem 'as a coda'. Rather, it is a prelude. In his preface to the Faber edition, he tells how in early 1946 he began to read Hardy's poems, having known him before only as a novelist: 'as regards his verse', Larkin says:

'I shared Lytton Strachey's verdict that "the gloom is not even relieved by a little elegance of diction". This opinion did not last long; if I were asked to date its disappearance, I should guess it was the morning I first read "Thoughts of Phena At News of Her Death".'

Larkin's added poem (XXXII in the re-published *The North Ship*) first appeared in the little pamphlet, *XX Poems*, which Larkin brought out at his own expense in 1951. (There were 100 copies of this pamphlet, most of them—as ruefully described by Larkin—sent to well-known literary persons, the majority of whom failed even to acknowledge it, presumably because he had under-stamped the envelopes at a time when the postal charges had just been increased. It was still possible to order it in early 1954, as I did through Blackwells in Oxford, and to pay 4/6d for it. Its present dealers' value has been quoted at £20.) The first stanza of the new poem immediately establishes not just the new presence of Hardy (it is in fact much less like Hardy than the Yeatsian pieces are like Yeats) but a new way in Larkin of finding and using material. The observation is exact, the framing of mood and incident within description makes a perfect fit:

> Waiting for breakfast, while she brushed her hair,
> I looked down at the empty hotel yard
> Once meant for coaches. Cobblestones were wet,
> But sent no light back to the loaded sky,
> Sunk as it was with mist down to the roofs.
> Drainpipes and fire-escape climbed up
> Past rooms still burning their electric light:
> I thought: Featureless morning, featureless night.

What Hardy taught Larkin was that a man's own life, its suddenly surfacing perceptions, its 'moments of vision', its most seemingly casual epiphanies (in the Joycean sense), could fit whole and without compromise into poems. There did not need to be any large-scale system of belief, any such circum-ambient framework as Yeats constructed within which to fashion his work: Larkin has dismissed all that as the 'myth-kitty'. Like Parolles in *All's Well*, he seems to say: 'Simply the thing I am shall make me live.' As Larkin himself put it in a radio programme on Hardy:

'When I came to Hardy it was with the sense of relief that I didn't have to try and jack myself up to a concept of poetry that lay outside my own life . . . One could simply relapse back into one's own life and write from it.'

Looking again at 'Waiting for breakfast', one sees that what it turns into is an address to the Muse, though in no sense that that habitual Muse-invoker, Robert Graves, would accept. The 'I' of the poem has spent the night with a girl, and his mood is one of almost surprised disbelief that he is so happy:

Turning, I kissed her,
Easily for sheer joy tipping the balance to love.

Yet whatever sparks the poet into writing poems doesn't seem to start from such a mood. 'Perfection of the life, or of the work': one is pushed back to Yeats again, to the sort of conundrum he poses there. Will absorption in the girl and in the happiness she seems to bring stifle his poems?

Are you jealous of her?
Will you refuse to come till I have sent
Her terribly away, importantly live
Part invalid, part baby, and part saint?

This is the first poem of Larkin's maturity, and it links interestingly with the earliest poem in *The Less Deceived*: 'Wedding-Wind', which also dates from 1946. But there is one large difference. The voice of the poem here is in no useful sense that of the poet: a woman on the morning after her wedding night is wonderingly turning over the fact of her happiness, with the force of the high wind 'bodying-forth' not only the irrelevance of such violent elements to the new delight she has found, but also the way in which the whole of creation seems somehow to be in union with her state:

Can it be borne, this bodying-forth by wind
Of joy my actions turn on, like a thread
Carrying beads? Shall I be let to sleep
Now this perpetual morning shares my bed?
Can even death dry up
These new delighted lakes, conclude
Our kneeling as cattle by all-generous waters?

'Wedding-Wind' is the only completely happy poem of Larkin's, the only one in which there is a total acceptance of joy. Perhaps that is why it is liked by some people who otherwise find him too bleak a poet for their taste. Yet it is happy, joyous, without being serene: it implies, in its three closing questions, the impermanence of the very happiness it celebrates, the possibility of its being blown and scattered, made restless as the horses have been and

> All's ravelled under the sun by the wind's blowing.

The poem's three questions remind one of the three questions at the end of 'Waiting for breakfast', suggesting that the balance of 'sheer joy' can as easily be tipped in the other direction.

This emotional wariness, which can too easily—and inaccurately—be labelled as pessimism, is at the roots of Larkin's sensibility. Its fine-drawn expression can be found in most of the poems in *The Less Deceived* and *The Whitsun Weddings*. And it is at this point, when Larkin in 1946 wrote 'Waiting for breakfast' and 'Wedding-Wind', that it seems unprofitable to go on examining his poems in a supposed chronological order of composition; for from now on the personality is an achieved and consistent one, each poem re-stating or adding another facet to what has gone before. Critics who tried to sniff out 'development' when *The Whitsun Weddings* followed nine years after *The Less Deceived*, or who showed disappointment when they found none, were wasting their time or were demonstrating that Larkin was at no time their man. The sixty-one poems in these two books, and the handful that have appeared in periodicals since, make a total unified impact. There have been rich years and lean years (Larkin's remark that he writes about four poems a year shouldn't be taken too literally in any statistical sense), but only quantitatively.

Yet though there has been no radical development in Larkin's poetry during these years, the number of tones and voices he has used has been a great deal more varied than some critics have given him credit for. The 'emotional wariness' can in some of the poems be better defined as an agnostic stoicism, close to the mood (though not to the origin of that mood) of Arnold's

'Dover Beach'. And what he is both agnostic and stoical about is time, the passing of time, and 'the only end of age': death. Indeed, if it had not been used perfectly properly for another literary achievement (and in any case Larkin might reject it as being too presumptuously resonant), 'The Music of Time' could serve as a title for all Larkin's post-1946 poetry.

There are poems in which time, and death as the yardstick of time, are seen in an abstract or generalized context: 'Ignorance', 'Triple Time', 'Next, Please', 'Nothing to be Said', 'Going', 'Wants', 'Age'. They are abstract or generalized in that they don't start from some posited situation, though their language and imagery are concrete enough: the street, sky and landscape of 'Triple Time', the 'armada of promises' of 'Next, Please', the quickly shuffled references ('Small-statured cross-faced tribes/And cobble-close families/In mill-towns on dark mornings') of 'Nothing to be Said'. All our hours, however we spend them,

advance
On death equally slowly.
And saying so to some
Means nothing; others it leaves
Nothing to be said.

This great blankness at the heart of things has to be endured—that is what I meant by stoicism. We bolster up our ignorance, and make ourselves able to bear our long diminution and decay, by being busy with the present and—when we are young—dreaming about the future:

An air lambent with adult enterprise.

So, too, we look at the past, and cling to and preserve those bits of it that belong to us, which we call our memories. It is no accident that of the jazz which Larkin regards with such enthusiasm, it is the blues that he writes about with most feeling (in his prose pieces, that is; for example, in his record reviews in the *Daily Telegraph*. Only one poem, 'For Sidney Bechet', celebrates this 'natural noise of good'). For the blues are thick with the searchings and regrets of memory.

In an often-quoted statement made in 1955, Larkin said:

'I write poems to preserve things I have seen/thought/felt (if I may so indicate a composite and complex experience) both for myself and for others, though I feel that my prime responsibility is to the experience itself, which I am trying to keep from oblivion for its own sake. Why I should do this I have no idea, but I think the impulse to preserve lies at the bottom of all art.'

More recently, commenting on *The Whitsun Weddings* in the Poetry Book Society Bulletin, he wrote:

'Some years ago I came to the conclusion that to write a poem was to construct a verbal device that would preserve an experience indefinitely by reproducing it in whoever read the poem.'

Though he went on to qualify this, the 'verbal pickling' (as he put it) is seen to be the process at work in many of his best and best-known poems: in his two most sustained efforts, 'Church Going' and 'The Whitsun Weddings', and also in 'Mr Bleaney', 'Reference Back', 'I Remember, I Remember', 'Dockery and Son', and elsewhere. All of these start from some quite specifically recalled incident which becomes, through the course of the poem, 'an experience' in the sense intended by Larkin in that prose note. A casual dropping-in to a deserted church; a long train-journey on Whit Saturday; the taking of new lodgings; a visit home to one's widowed mother; another train-journey, which takes one through one's long-abandoned birthplace; a visit in middle age to one's old college at Oxford—these 'human shows' inhabit an area Hardy would have recognized, and each both preserves the experience and allows it to move out into other areas not predicted by the casually 'placing' opening lines. Indeed, in several of them the placing, the observation, is steadily sustained for a great part of the poem, as if the 'impulse to preserve' were determined to fix and set the

moment with every aspect carefully delineated, every shade
faithfully recorded. I remember Larkin writing to tell me, when
I was about to produce the first broadcast reading (in fact the
first public appearance) of 'The Whitsun Weddings', that what
I should aim to get from the actor was a level, even a plodding,
descriptive note, until the mysterious last lines, when the poem
should suddenly 'lift off the ground':

> there swelled
> A sense of falling, like an arrow-shower
> Sent out of sight, somewhere becoming rain.

'Impossible, I know,' he said comfortingly; though I think that
first reader (Gary Watson) made a very fair approximation
to it.

If 'The Whitsun Weddings' is a poem of one carefully held
note until the very end, 'Church Going' is more shifting in its
stance and tone. Both poems are written in long, carefully-
patterned rhyming stanzas (Larkin once said to me that he
would like to write a poem with such elaborate stanzas that one
could wander round in them as in the aisles and side-chapels of
some great cathedral), but whereas each ten-line stanza of 'The
Whitsun Weddings' seems caught on the pivot of the short
four-syllable second line, pushing it forward on to the next
smooth run, the nine-line stanza of 'Church Going' is steady
throughout, the iambic pentameter having to hold together—
as it successfully does—the three unequal sections: the first two
stanzas, easy, colloquial, mockingly casual; then the four stanzas
of reflection and half-serious questioning, becoming weightier
and slower as they move towards the rhetorical solidity of the
final stanza's first line:

> A serious house on serious earth it is. . . .

'Church Going' has become one of the type-poems of the
century, at the very least 'the showpiece of the "New Move-

ment" ', as G. S. Fraser put it; much discussed in every
sixth-form English class and literary extension-course, antholo-
gized and duplicated, so that I sometimes feel it has become too
thoroughly institutionalized and placed. Larkin has quoted
Hardy's supposed remarks (on *Tess*) on the subject: 'If I'd
known it was going to be so popular, I'd have tried to make it
better,' and one senses a wry surprise in that, as one does in
his comment that after it was initially published in the *Spectator*
(after first being lost, and then held in proof, for about a year),
he 'had a letter from one of the paper's subscribers enclosing a
copy of the Gospel of St John':

'In fact it has always been well liked. I think this is because
it is about religion, and has a serious air that conceals the fact
that its tone and argument are entirely secular.'

Here Larkin is perfectly properly fending off the common
misconception that it is a 'religious' poem. It is not so, in any
dogmatic or sectarian sense. It dips not even the most gingerly
of toes into metaphysics, makes not even the most tentative
gestures towards 'belief' ('But superstition, like belief, must
die'). What it does do is to acknowledge the human hunger for
order and ritual (such as go with 'marriage, and birth,/And
death, and thoughts of these'), and to recognize the power of
the past, of inherited tradition, made emblematic in this
abandoned piece of ground,

> Which, he once heard, was proper to grow wise in,
> If only that so many dead lie round.

But 'Church Going' is not a perfect poem, though a fine one,
and it is not Larkin's best. Donald Hall has maintained that it
would be a better one if it were cut by a third, and without
accepting that kind of drastic surgery (American editors have a
reputation for being the 'heaviest' in the world, leaning on their
authors in a way that has more to do with power than with
support) it is fair to say that it has some amusing but distracting
divagations—particularly in the middle section—of a sort which

one doesn't find in the equally circumstantial but more unified 'Whitsun Weddings'. That Irish sixpence, for example— many readers don't know whether they are supposed to laugh here or not (many do in any case); but if the ruined church which started the poem off was in Ireland, as Larkin in a broadcast said it was, wouldn't it make a difference? Does he mean to demonstrate the sort of unthinking piety that agnostics hold to out of habit, or is he chalking up another mild self-revelatory bit of schoolboyish japing, as in the mouthing of 'Here endeth' from the lectern? (What Larkin intends of *that* performance comes out very clearly in his Marvell Press recording.) One doesn't know; and in a poem so specific this is a flaw.

To go on about the Irish sixpence at such length may well seem absurdly trivial, but the uncertainty it suggests is not unique in the poem. One has the feeling that Larkin knows more than he chooses to admit, with the pyx brought in so effortlessly and the rood-lofts sniggeringly made much of: naming them implies knowledge of what they are, and one doesn't need to be a 'ruin-bibber, randy for antique' to recognize such things. They are part of one's general store of unsorted knowledge, like knowing who A. W. Carr or Jimmy Yancey (or, indeed, Sidney Bechet) were. Here, without much relish, I am drawn into mildly deploring what might be called the Yah-Boo side of Larkin's work—a side not often apparent, which he shares sporadically with his admired (and admiring) fellow-undergraduate and old friend from St John's, Kingsley Amis. (Incidentally, *XX Poems* was dedicated to Amis, and Amis dedicated *Lucky Jim* to Larkin.) The 'filthy Mozart' type of jeer is never given the extended outing with Larkin that it is with Amis, and one has to be aware of personae and so forth, but the edgy and gratuitous coarseness of 'Get stewed. Books are a load of crap' and 'What does it mean? Sod all' have always made me wince a bit. This might show a feeble prudishness in me, but rather I feel that Larkin's poems can get by without such manly nudging.

It could be argued that these things are part of Larkin's apt contemporary tone; certainly he has such a tone, more usefully heard in 'Mr Bleaney', 'Toads', 'Toads Revisited', 'Reasons for Attendance', 'Poetry of Departures', and most startlingly in 'Sunny Prestatyn'. In this last poem the calculated violence seems exactly and inevitably matched with the brutalizing of the language: those lunging monosyllables are dead right—and 'dead' is right too. 'A hunk of coast' is drawn into the stabbing words that follow—'slapped up', 'snaggle-toothed and boss-eyed', 'Huge tits and a fissured crotch', 'scrawls', 'tuberous cock and balls', 'a knife/Or something to stab right through'. Like the faded photographs that must lie behind 'MCMXIV', like the medieval figures in 'An Arundel Tomb' that 'Time has transfigured into . . . untruth', the blandishments of the girl on the poster have (with the help of human agency) been reduced to the wrecks of time. As in the lines of the body, in 'Skin', she is the end-product

> Of the continuous coarse
> Sand-laden wind, time.

'Sunny Prestatyn' is the most extreme of Larkin's poems about diminution, decay, death. Elsewhere, he more often brings to them what—in a review of Betjeman's poems—he has called 'an almost moral tactfulness'. 'Faith Healing', 'Ambulances', 'Love Songs in Age', 'At Grass', 'An Arundel Tomb', the more recent and uncollected 'Sad Steps'—all, with perhaps the exception of the last, stand at a reserved but certainly not unfeeling distance from their ostensible subjects. In the broadcast I have already quoted from, Larkin said:

'I sometimes think that the most successful poems are those in which subjects appear to float free from the preoccupations that chose them, and to exist in their own right, reassembled—one hopes—in the eternity of imagination.' And he went on to say, introducing 'Love Songs in Age':

'I can't for the life of me think why I should have wanted to write about Victorian drawing-room ballads: probably I must have heard one on the wireless, and thought how terrible it must be for an old lady to hear one of these songs she had learnt as a girl and reflect how different life had turned out to be.' 'How different life had turned out to be'—here time is shown as the gradual destroyer of illusions. Like the advertisement hoardings in 'Essential Beauty', showing us serenely and purely 'how life should be', the old sheet music summons up and sets blankly before us two things: that lambent air which the future promised, and that present which has hardened 'into all we've got/And how we got it.' ('Dockery and Son'.) Christopher Ricks (who has written particularly well on Larkin) has pointed out how in 'Love Songs in Age' the three sentences of the poem gradually narrow down, from the expansive openness of the first, with its careful proliferation of detail and its almost mimetic lyricism ('Word after sprawling hyphenated word'), through the briefer concentration on 'that much-mentioned brilliance, love', to the blank acknowledgement that love has indeed not solved or satisfied or 'set unchangeably in order':

So
To pile them back, to cry,
Was hard, without lamely admitting how
It had not done so then, and could not now.

That last sentence, so much less serpentine than the others, seems the last brief twist of the knife.

Ricks has also pointed out one of the hallmarks of Larkin's style: those negatives which define the limits and shades of the world, and which coldly confront our flimsy illusions. *Un, in, im, dis*—with such small modifiers Larkin determines the edges of things, which blur into

the solving emptiness
That lies just under all we do.

So we find *unfakable, unspoilt, undiminished, unmolesting, unfinger-marked, unhindered, unchangeably,* set against *unsatisfactory, unlucky, unworkable, unswept, uninformed, unanswerable, unrecommended, untruthful* and *untruth*. *Imprecisions, imperfect, incomplete* and *inexplicable* jostle with *disbelief, disproved, disused* and *dismantled*. They seem to share something—in their modifying, their determination to record an exact shade of response rather than a wilder approximation—with another hallmark: those compounds which one begins to find as early as the poems in *The North Ship*. *Laurel-surrounded, fresh-peeled, branch-arrested, Sunday-full, organ-frowned-on, harsh-named, differently-dressed, luminously-peopled, solemn-sinister*—there are over fifty others in *The Less Deceived* and *The Whitsun Weddings* alone.

Compound-formations bring Hopkins to mind, though his are of course a good deal more strenuous and draw more attention to themselves than Larkin's. Yet Hopkins is, perhaps curiously, a poet Larkin much admires. Indeed, though he has been at some pains to admit how narrow his tastes in poetry are, Larkin's acknowledged enthusiasms show a wider range of appreciation than he seems to give himself credit for. Without at all being a regular pundit in the literary papers, he has written with warmth and depth about not only Hardy but also William Barnes, Christina Rossetti, Wilfred Owen, and among living poets, Auden (pre-1940), Betjeman and Stevie Smith. Not much of a common denominator there, and of them all it is only Hardy who seems to have left any trace on Larkin's own work, and that in no important verbal way. In fact Larkin is very much his own poet. His impressment into the Movement, in such anthologies as Enright's *Poets of the 1950s* and Conquest's *New Lines*, did no harm and may have done some good, in that it drew attention to his work in the way that any seemingly concerted action (cf. The Group) makes a bigger initial impact than a lone voice. But really he shares little with the 'neutral tone' of what have been called the Faceless Fifties: anonymity and impersonality are not at all characteristics of his work, and the voice that comes across is far more individual than those of such properly celebrated poets as Muir, Graves and R. S. Thomas, to pick three who have never (so far as I know) been accused of hunting with any pack or borrowing anyone's colouring.

The case against Larkin, as I have heard it, seems to boil down to 'provincialism' (Charles Tomlinson), 'genteel belly-aching' (Christopher Logue), and a less truculent but rather exasperated demur that any poet so negative can be so good (A. Alvarez). Well, he is provincial in the sense that he doesn't subscribe to the current cant that English poets can profitably learn direct lessons from what poetry is going on in Germany or France or Hungary or up the Black Mountain: poetry is, thank heaven, a long way from falling into an 'international style', such as one finds in painting, sculpture, architecture and music, and such validly 'international' pieces as I *have* seen (e.g. in concrete poetry) are at best peripherally elegant and at worst boring and pointless. 'Genteel bellyaching' and 'negative' are really making the same objection, the first more memorably and amusingly than the second. There is a sense in which Larkin does define by negatives; I have made the point already. He is wary in front of experience, as who should not be: one doesn't put in the same set of scales Auschwitz and the realization that one is getting older, or the thermo-nuclear bomb and the sense that most love is illusory. Yet the fact that Larkin hasn't, in his poems, confronted head-on the death camps or the Bomb (or Vietnam, or Che Guevara) doesn't make him, by definition, minor. His themes—love, change, disenchantment, the mystery and inexplicableness of the past's survival and death's finality— are unshakably major. So too, I think, are the assurance of his cadences and the inevitable rightness of his language at their best. From what even Larkin acknowledges as the almost Symbolist rhetoric of

Such attics cleared of me! Such absences!

to the simple but remorseless

They show us what we have as it once was,

> Blindingly undiminished, just as though
> By acting differently we could have kept it so

is a broad span for any poet to command. And those haunting closing lines to many poems ('Church Going', 'The Whitsun Weddings', 'No Road', 'Next, Please', 'Faith Healing', 'Ambulances', 'Dockery and Son', 'An Arundel Tomb', 'Sad Steps'—the list becomes long, but not absurdly so): they have an authentic gravity, a memorable persistence. I think that Larkin's work will survive; and what may survive is his preservation of 'the true voice of feeling' of a man who was representative of the mid-20th century hardly at all, except in negatives—which is, when you come to think about it, one way in which to survive the mid-20th century.

Lowell's Marble Meanings

————————————

> words
> give marble meaning and a voice to bronze.
> (Robert Lowell, 'The Ruins of Time',
> after Gongora)

To MY mind, *For the Union Dead* remains the nub of the matter,
the sustained moment in which the whole Lowell enterprise
comes into focus. It arrived to the routine chorus of relieved
praise directed to the fact that he was still going and still good.
But one picked up an underswell of private reservation, amount-
ing to the sense that the volume is too low-density—a collection
of jottings, revisions and diary doodlings—to support the
superb title-poem. I shared this view, but have now come to
consider the volume the logical and conscious culmination of
Lowell's effort to regenerate and de-mystify his own literary
career. Much more is involved than just the dismantling of
past structures and roles. *For the Union Dead* stabilizes itself as
the precipitation—as *Near the Ocean* could be the aftermath—of
a total project. This is not to say that there is nowhere else for
Lowell to go, though I capitulate to the glamour of minor
apocalyptics to the degree of not being able to say where that
would be.

Lowell's project amounts to making good the claim that
literature—with poetry as its most refined incarnation—remains
a viable and trustworthy means of shaping and mastering experience. Lowell offers his own literary career (implicitly of course)
as the augury and illustration of some possible ultimate cultural
good health or good management or at least good luck. He re-

affirms the power of literature to order the chaos of society, personality and history, with its own history, its own order, its own virtue. Hence the relief with which each Lowell volume is greeted. The cheers are for fresh news of the survival of literature itself.

Certainly, what must now be counted one main tendency in American poetry—the tradition that stems from Whitman—has turned its back upon literature as an institution or inheritance, or sought to absorb it to its own purposes. Its regeneration comes from the energies it taps from the wilderness (or its destruction), the material growth, the inner turbulence of the American continent which it proposes for its motive and subject. The ocean it is near is not Lowell's Atlantic, whose sea-board he celebrates as the western littoral of an expanded Mediterranean, but the Pacific against whose shore the continental destiny declares itself in the most extravagant terms. It is not a matter of literal, but of imaginative geography, of direction rather than location. The thrust of Olson and Williams—both Easterners—is inwards and westwards, into the continent, while Lowell gazes back towards Europe from the Pilgrim's landfall. The Whitman tradition eschews history and literature in favour of geography and the specificity of speech. Likewise, it replaces the ideal presence (usually actual absence) of a public with the real presence of audience or coterie.

Lowell's career supposes a public and so proposes a public world which almost every other fact of American life declares to be an impossibility. Perhaps it is, in which case Lowell's whole enterprise is doomed, however successful his career as a disburser of cultural amenities, and his poetics, however innovatory and combatative, are ultimately an anachronism. His standing certainly depends on an element of surprise that poetry assuming what his assumes can still get written. Elizabeth Bishop's statement on the cover of the American edition of *Life Studies* aptly summarizes whole volumes of astonishment: 'Somehow or other, by fair means or foul, and in the middle of our worst century so far, we have produced a magnificent poet.' Perhaps this is what the poetry is really about: the astonishing fact of its own existence. Lowell's whole enterprise has a significance far in excess of the aggregated meanings of particular poems or particular volumes.

Does this mean that we can assimilate Lowell to the American tradition, exemplified by Whitman and Crane, which offers the whole life as the burthen of the poetry? I think not. Lowell projects a career, not a life: he is a professional, not, in a complex sense of the word, an amateur. The materials of his own life are there to be made over to art. Interest focuses on that process, not on the life itself as exemplary or holy. I intend only a crude distinction. Lowell does tie his poetry, sporadically, to the line of a biography. But the emphasis is towards self-sufficiency of poetic statement and where this fails it registers as—except in *Life Studies*—a lack, an aspect of cultural deprivation which the poems take as their subject and seek to redress.

Discussion of Lowell's verse as confessional in the manner of Anne Sexton and Sylvia Plath has confused the issue. It seems not to have occurred to those critics who, on the basis of *Life Studies* proclaimed Lowell a confessional poet that, in explicitly treating his life as materials, he was not making his poetry more personal but depersonalizing his own life. True, *Life Studies* gave notice that there would be no embarrassment about where it drew its materials. But confession implies a distinction between private and public, inner and outer, each ruled by known conventions and related in carefully regulated ways, which confession, for its own purposes, violates. Lowell's verse assumes that the distinction has crumbled, that we are all private men and that this is a fact of the utmost public urgency. His verse explores a condition in which public worlds have to be built and sustained out of the rubble of purely personal existence. This may include, for a poet, his own earlier poetry.

This is not to suppress the very real differences between the full-dress formality of treatments of family history in the early poetry and the unbuttoned, informal handling of family figures

in *Life Studies*. The private elements in *Lord Weary's Castle*
come through as pretexts rather than as genuine motives for
poems. A gap opens between ceremonial gesture and the personal
occasion it should envelop which Lowell's rhetoric cannot close.
This gap registers as a kind of mythic boast: names, locations,
family figures, the implied occasions of the poems themselves
are prematurely coerced into significance. Lowell is helped by
being able to evoke historically significant ancestors. Still, the
result is some strikingly grotesque poetry:

> Grandfather Winslow, look, the swanboats coast
> That island in the Public Gardens, where
> The bread-stuffed ducks are brooding, where with tub
> And strainer the mid-Sunday Irish scare
> The sun-struck shallows for the dusky chub
> This Easter, and the ghost
> Of risen Jesus walks the waves to run
> Arthur upon a trumpeting black swan
> Beyond Charles River to the Acheron
> Where the wide waters and their voyager are one.

Lowell's attitudes are not easy to scan. There is a disturbance
due to some failure of the local matter to stretch naturally to the
mythic dimensions required of it. The humour is high-strung
and nervous. It is with a kind of hysterical giggle that Lowell
launches his Jesus upon the waters shoving a now black swan
(boat) bestridden by the shade of grandfather Winslow. The
dissonance between Jesus and these Pagan and Arthurian elements is deliberate. Likewise the 'mid-Sunday Irish' in the
setting of the Public Park (sad travesty and perhaps benefaction
of the public weal that men like Winslow had once swayed)—
the calculated promiscuity of the mix—mimics a state of utter
cultural confusion. The Irish are ambiguously despoilers and
spiritual heirs of Peter. Either way, they debunk Boston's
social, and Puritanism's religious, exclusiveness. The bravura

handling of the elaborately ceremonial stanza adds an element of ironic discrepancy. It is hard to remember that this is a formal commemorative poem about a man whom Lowell reverenced. There seems to be an unacknowledged flight into the omnipotence of manic verbal control which conceals an impotence adequately to mourn.

The early poems displace emotion from the ostensible subject of the poetry on to the existence of the poem itself, the fact of its occurrence as a piece of literature and as a verbal construct. The poem is an image of something other than the poem, of, it appears, the poet's own project of poetry-making. Hence emotion drains away from an Arthur Winslow or a Black Rock or a drowned sailor. It is way-laid, high-jacked, as it were, by the vehicle. Metrical and imagistic violence substitute for the absent emotion. Violence takes the form of near-violations of formal stanzaic, metrical and syntactical equilibrium. Sentences only just achieve their assignations with last lines; images only just do not fail ostentatiously to resolve. It is as though Lowell were dramatizing the recalcitrance of the world to verbal discipline, its wicked will not to accord in rhyme and measure.

The difficulty of these poems does not lie in their meaning but in what Lowell means by them. Poetic acts and occasions are events in some suppressed spiritual monodrama from which they take their true significance. They themselves do not signify, or at least what they signify is simply incredible. What, and to whom, do these modern martyrologies, these *topoi* of the Church year, these spiritual exercises and emblematic and iconic acts of devotion communicate? They have no viable existence as religious statements, because they do not wear or declare their hidden purpose. This poet knows his seventeenth-century devotional and meditative poetry, he knows his Hopkins (he has edited a collection of essays on him) and his election of their kind of emblem-making and poem-building can hardly be innocent.

It is, surely, intended to be outrageous and to express outrage. The world of Black Rock, of war-girt Atlantic America, of the industrial leviathan, of material sordidness, all these threaten the very meaning of the poet's enterprise. The poems retaliate by taking in the modern world—and taking it on—on the most offensively archaic, oppositional and obstructive terms that come to hand. One has the sense of the poems as projectiles, constructed out of the scrap and refuse of history and hurled with a kind of contempt at the huge smugness and indifference of industrial civilization. Also, of the poems as walls, elaborate defensive dispositions, behind which the skulking poet can avoid being overwhelmed. I am suggesting that the poems themselves are in effect political acts, as much so as Lowell's conscientious objection. America offers Lowell no political vision that can accommodate the full range and intensity of his depression, disgust and outrage. Any actual expression of political views is beside the point. The act of making poems, and such conspicuously inappropriate poems as these, is a deed, and the repository of the poet's real emotions. Lowell is close, in this respect, to poets such as Winters and Tate. But Lowell, because younger, more sensitive, for every kind of reason, is much more offended, aggrieved and truculently aggressive than they are. In the end his despair is more bracing and more buoyant, his exposure more eager, his insistence on order and virtue more unremitting.

Lowell presumably derives his tormenting sense of impotent responsibility for the public weal from his Boston and Puritan heritage, though his autobiographical piece '91, Revere Street' makes clear the importance of the hold that martial and naval discipline took on his imagination. The verbal torsions and hardly contained explosiveness of *Lord Weary's Castle* seem to be one way of communicating and dramatizing thwarted ethical imperatives, baffled hunger for righteousness and the ache of the vacuum left by the collapse of civic order. Thus, Lowell can launch his poem 'Concord' on a swell of apparently secure irony:

> Ten thousand Fords are idle here in search
> Of a tradition.

But the irony rapidly evaporates as syntax and image become embroiled with Lowell's violent repudiations. The poem does not go out of control, but as the menace and degradation that occasioned the irony become palpable, the verbal substance of the poem thickens and swells to encounter and overwhelm them:

Crucifix,
How can your whited spindling arms transfix
Mammon's unbridled industry, the lurch
For forms to harness Heraclitus' stream!

The energies seem improperly distributed through the syntax. 'Transfix' is asked not only to act upon 'Mammon's unbridled industry', but the heavy, cluttered apposition it clumsily drags behind it. Clearly, an ironic counterpoint is aimed at between 'unbridled' and 'harness', but the effect is of a contradiction, or at least of a lame explication of what was felt to be too glib a trope: 'Mammon's unbridled industry.' The mythic resonances of Mammon and Heraclitus seem to dampen each other rather than resolve or boldly clash. The poem ends with a confrontation between Thoreau's utopianism—for all its innocence ultimately a derivative of the more sinister forces of Puritan violence—with the fact of the genocide of the natural possessors of the land, the Indians, destroyed in the proto-typical King Philip's War:

This Church is Concord—Concord where Thoreau
Named all the birds without a gun to probe
Through darkness to the painted man and bow:
The death-dance of King Philip and his scream
Whose echo girdled this imperfect globe.

Despite—perhaps because of—its tense rigidities, the poem itself is like an arrested death-dance, a protracted scream. But it is a scream of impotence. Ultimately, the crucifix—or any merely verbal gesture—cannot cope, even within the economy of the poem, with 'Mammon's unbridled industry'. Indeed, its 'whited spindling arms' suggests a complicity with the industrial process itself,* while 'whited' refers us to the phrase 'whited sepulchre'. Lowell's situation is more desperate than Thoreau's who at least could 'name all the birds without a gun . . .' and believe that pacifism and love of nature had some real future. Lowell knows that they have not. All he has is his words, but because his words are his act he cannot get past them or through them. The religious emblems that he substitutes for Thoreau's dream of perfection are not merely futile verbal gestures, but suggest an unacknowledged complicity with what they oppose.

It is not until *Life Studies* and *For the Union Dead* that Lowell comes to terms with the degree to which his earlier poetry, while seemingly constructed out of opposition to the whole acquisitive-Puritan complex, was really an obscure manifestation of it. His implacable verbalism threatened to absorb the natural world and reissue it as an emblematic politics. His own industry, his rapid hunger for significance, was as unbridled as Mammon's. Hence one's sense of something unfulfilled about *Lord Weary's Castle*. Despite the high level of verbal activity, the volume seems dumb and unachieved; the poetry does not square with its manifest intent. It is up to something which it will not acknowledge, a greedy appropriation of the sensuous and natural world, giving rise to a violence that parallels the violence of the world outside it.

Lowell's struggle to escape from this appropriative verbalism takes him through historical poems that proffer the integrity of some event and so resist his insistent re-structuring, through the dramatic monologues of *The Mills of the*

*Lowell must find painfully relevant the fact that it was an ancestor, James Cabot Lowell, who, in 1815 at his Waltham cotton mill, was the driving force behind the establishment of Industrial Revolution factory methods in New England. '. . . The factory at Waltham [was] . . . the first in America, and probably in the world . . . where under one roof, raw cotton could be turned into finished goods. . . . The obvious difference between Waltham and the Rhode Island and the other eastern mills was machinery—specifically the power loom.' 'Mammon's unbridled industry' with a vengeance, and the Lowells were in there at the start! For the quotation and further information see W. J. Cunningham, 'Millionaires in the Making', *History Today*, XIX, No. 6, June 1969.

Kavanaughs, where verbal turbulence is cooled and distanced by being made the property of other (admittedly very Lowell-like) personalities, into *Life Studies,* where history, family, literary friends and mentors and married life are somewhat relinquished to their autonomous and separate existences. The later poetry can be construed as a deliberate discipline of abstention, an effort to recover for his poetry natural limits and lineaments, by touching without violence, greed or repudiation, what is alien in nature. Lowell's mature poetry represents a calculated deflation of afflatus. It abandons itself, in the interest of sane, viable living, to the practice of reduced scales, and, not without reluctance, of diminished pretensions. This does not impair its ethical militancy. On the contrary, it enhances it, by identifying Lowell's earlier moral frenzy as deeply involved with the violence it repudiates.

This, of course, is to be over-schematic. In 'The Quaker Graveyard' for instance Lowell matches his rhetoric against the spiritual pride and commercial greed of the Quaker whalers. Their sin consisted not only in their greedy consumption of the substance of the created world, but in their obsessive and impressive hunger for righteousness. Lowell shares this with them, as he does their attack on 'IS, the whited monster' (we remember the 'whited . . . crucifix' of 'Concord'). We should register in the 'The Quaker Graveyard', how deliberately Lowell seeks to remedy this furious raid on Essence (in which his own manic verse participates) with his blank existential madonna:

> There's no comeliness
> At all or charm in that expressionless
> Face with its heavy eyelids.

Though even here the existential is still apocalyptic.

It is instructive to turn to the unassuming, almost inaudible poem 'Water', which begins *For the Union Dead.* Here, compared with 'The Quaker Graveyard', all linguistic and spiritual grandiloquence has been relinquished in favour of unornamented statement:

> Remember? We sat on a slab of rock.
> From this distance in time,
> it seems the color
> of iris, rotting and turning purpler,
>
> but it was only
> the usual gray rock
> turning the usual green
> when drenched by the sea.

The question 'remember?' calls into question the magic potency of memory which becomes thereby a medium of diminution shot through with further flickers of disenchantment on the repeated word 'usual' and the saliently placed 'only'. The lines pick up the faintest swell of afflatus from the full-bodied 'drenched' which gathers power from the strictly neutral diction and the barely perceptible rhythmic contours of the stanza. The stone itself however has no contours; it is simply 'a slab of rock', which has lost whatever prismatic richness ('iris, rotting') it once had: its vestigial rainbow, diffused back into the sea's flat greens, contrasts interestingly with the last line of 'The Quaker Graveyard'—'The Lord survives the rainbow of his will'—an augury of disenchantment chanted in an inappropriately grand manner. 'Water', while exposing the small-scale destructiveness of time and ocean, diminishes even the psychological glamour of destruction:

> The sea drenched the rock
> at our feet all day,
> and kept tearing away
> flake after flake.

The original faint ripple on 'drenched' is quickly dissipated by this repetition. The rock itself is seen as reduced in the 'distance of time' and is further reduced, visually, by 'at our feet'. The small-scale physical erosion, 'flake after flake' parallels the decompositions of memory. How thinly, thread-barely, 'flake' rhymes uncharmingly with 'rock'.

What happens next is not easy to understand:

> One night you dreamed
> you were a mermaid clinging to a wharf-pile,
> and trying to pull
> off the barnacles with your hands.

Lowell is here concerned with the glamour of madness viewed as a craving to abandon limits and enter the inhuman realm of the undifferentiated and vast. The pulling-off of the barnacles is a kind of sympathetic magic which depicts and so resists the erosions of memory, love, nature. It imitates the will to escape fixed habits and limits. But we are arrested—and the dream disintegrates—on the vulnerability implicit in the phrase 'your hands', those organs of seizure and, in a watery world, of locomotion (to be compared with the very landlocked 'feet' of the stanza above), which seem too delicate and fragile to perform any such unmooring into the oceanic. The dream is an alluring horror for which the diminutions of the poem constitute a therapy.

The last stanza rings out the changes of disenchantment unmistakably:

> We wished our two souls
> might return like gulls
> to the rock. In the end,
> the water was too cold for us.

'Our two souls' sets up a kind of parallel with 'your hands' in the stanza above, but, as plenipotentiaries of wish, they have become, or are rendered, powerless: enfeebled extensions of a subjunctive mood, unlike the gulls of the next line to which they barely adhere through a wistful half-rhyme. The gulls can return effortlessly to the rock because their wish is at one with their natural habitat. The gulls are not in fact 'like' us. The limpness of the simile underlines the dis-similitude. Unlike the gulls, we must abdicate from our wishes, set limits, all of which is to experience—as the phrase 'in the end' implies—a kind of death. But, in the face of this 'end', some kind of human community is achieved: the poem ends upon a fusion of the two souls in 'us'. Shared limitation makes possible human empathy and love.

This mad, 'mermaid' condition resembles that of the bird-girl in 'Thanksgiving's Over' or, I would add, of Lowell himself when, in his own words 'I . . . made my manic statement'. The non-human world in the later poetry is usually evoked as that against which limits must be placed and which then becomes a source of definition of human community. The non-human world is not itself a source of identity. One enters it only as a killer or a suicide. The poem itself is analogously conditioned by the non-human, or non-verbal spaces which envelop and in some sense sustain it, and to whose erosion it is subject. Many of Lowell's later poems are, as it were, frayed, have holes or chunks eaten out. But they remain statues, upright columnar assertions of the human will to survive its own madness and self-destruction. They resist the emptiness around them that yet corrodes them like acid.

The emptiness in the poems of the earlier volumes is both sensed and urgently denied. The poems clamour, bawl, hurl their noise against the silence of the page. The emptiness makes itself felt as the resisted medium in which the poem's energy risks being dissipated. There is then an intense pressure from without and a countervailing pressure from within. The poem assaults its own margins and yet is cowed by them. Formality operates as constriction, inhibiting release into the space beyond the poem's closure. Again and again one finds these tensed, static closures: 'The dove has brought an olive branch to eat'; 'Fear with its fingered stopwatch in mid-air'; 'Till Christ again

67

turn wanderer and child'. True, these formal closures are a feature of the academic neo-metaphysical poetry written in America in the forties. But Lowell's closures are characterized by an unusual degree of rhetorical and rhythmic finality combined with an unusual state of self-cancelling tension.

In his early poetry Lowell is overwhelmed by the ruin of the city and its corruption of the natural world. The poet seems to inhabit a perpetual and squalid winter. Given this overwhelming sense of corruption, of history as nightmare and society as an irredeemable squalor, the poems lack any vision of a normal life from which to derive their ethics. Lowell shores them up with the dogmas and judgements of his Catholic eschatology, turning them into desolate fall-out of the anachronistic cycle of Catholic ritual. Whatever its personal place in Lowell's religious life, his Catholicism has a clear role to play in sustaining the poetry. Besides which, by joining the religion of the despised 'mid-Sunday Irish', Lowell administers shrewd medicine to the ancestral pieties. Moreover, in 'The Quaker Graveyard' and elsewhere, the eschatology achieves some release from ethical impotence by bringing the despoilers of nature before some last tribunal which can judge and, in the most literal sense, sentence them and so bring temporary relief from the nightmare of history. The Last Judgment is always one way to end a poem.

Yet this eschatology can only be a mystique because unmistakably itself a secretion of the historical moment and of Lowell's place within it. The recognition that religion is a historically conditioned product of culture is hard to escape in America. In Europe cultural products often can appear to be facts of nature. But America remains unavoidably, for good and ill, over four centuries, the deposit of explicit human intention.

This is why the American Grainers would so like to extend continental history backwards into a mythic foundation by Eric the Red—and why so many American writers try to recross the Atlantic in the wake of Eliot, and, in imagination, unfound what the Fathers founded. Lowell, to have maintained his mystique, must have turned small, minor and fanatical. Yet the eschatology did serve as a source of imagery whose power matched the turbulence of Lowell's initial reaction to his own times. Besides, it provided the equivalent of a past, a kind of negative substance to be disintegrated into more existential meanings. Lowell constructed *Lord Weary's Castle* as a marvellous and ludicrous edifice and has been living off its demolition ever since. Its stones have gone into the construction of humbler dwellings. The grand eschatology supported grand finished poems, and these haunt the later fragments like giant unavailable norms.

The dismantling is already underway in the monologues of *The Mills of the Kavanaughs*. Eschatology becomes madness or dream, to be viewed as the property of particular persons and so qualified by that particularity. Take the last lines of 'Thanksgiving's Over', one of Lowell's most difficult and most rewarding poems. (The difficulty arises precisely from the, disintegration of Lowell's own religious structures, mirrored, undermined and, in the intolerable glory of her madness assumed by the protagonist's self-slain wife):

> 'O Michael, must we join this deaf and dumb
> Breadline for children? Sit and listen.' So
> I sat. I counted to ten thousand, wound
> My cowhorn beads from Dublin on my thumb,
> And ground them. *Miserere?* Not a sound.

Does Lowell pun upon 'ground'? Probably not. The broken closure, hesitant, sinking, contrasts sharply with most of the poems in the earlier volumes. Michael's whispered interrogation —by the mere fact of being an interrogation—passes a judgement upon the eschatology. Does it not demand the holy madness of St. Francis not to become an abomination in its turn? 'Miserere?' is a hopeless query sighed to the night snows, to the desolations of war and personal disaster, to the attritions of the New York winter. The poem ends in a hush upon the phrase 'not a sound'; if we have listened to the poem's deepest rhythms, we gather how far the poem's end returns it to the first great snows of the American winter, to their oblivion, their blankness, their atoning and annulling purity. The poem's noise is redeemed in the silent indifference of an order ignorant of human purpose and against which human desolations can be sounded:

> Fathoms overhead,
> Snow warred on the El's world in the blank snow.

Lowell's struggle to renew contact with nature and natural feeling entails a struggle with his Puritan antecedents and with their language. The representative dark angel of the struggle is Jonathan Edwards, himself a divided and struggling man. Lowell had once started to write his biography. He made him instead the subject of three poems.

In 'After the Surprising Conversions' Lowell invents, in unemphatic couplets, a letter by Edwards reporting one result of the Northampton Revival, the suicide of Josiah Hawley (Edwards's own uncle). Edwards's language remains plausibly that of the New England divine until the last three lines of the poem:

> September twenty-second, Sir, the bough
> Cracks with the unpicked apples, and at dawn
> The small-mouth bass breaks water, gorged with spawn.

This may be intended as the imagistic equivalent of Edwards's report that 'the temptation now seemed to lie on that hand, to neglect worldly affairs too much, and to spend too much time in the immediate exercise of religion'. Either way, it produces a surprising swerve in the line of the poem which involves a change of key, a modulation from Edwards's normal delivery (as conventionalized by Lowell) to a tone more like Lowell's own, one might think. If so, it merely sponsors a suppressed aspect of Edwards's own personality—that of the boy naturalist who had observed the flying spiders. This suppressed self breaks into the poem with a kind of violence ('cracks', 'breaks') which is not without a note of disgust ('gorged with spawn'). The glut of nature supervenes upon the theological exultations and depressions of the Revival. Punningly, it is itself a literal revival; but we should register the nervous wincing of the verbal man confronted with the happy and inarticulate ('small-mouth'?) *plenum* of the creation. One thinks of Lowell's attitude towards Roethke of whom he remarked in the *Paris Review* interview: 'The things he knows about I feel I know nothing about, flowers and so on.' How felicitously that 'so on' gestures towards the ignorance, the fullness it cannot articulate. In 'For Theodore Roethke' in *Near the Ocean*, Lowell is more explicit:

> You honoured nature,
>
> helpless, elemental creature.
> The black stump of your hand
> just touched the waters under the earth,
> and left them quickened with your name . . .

Lowell could well characterize himself as fallen, with Edwards and his kind, from the Adamic innocence he finds in Roethke.

The better known poem *Mr Edwards and the Spider* addresses itself more explicitly to the conflict between word and world by exploiting the division in Edwards between the naturalist and the preacher of *Sinners in the Hands of an Angry God*, between the young boy who studied the spiders with a natural piety and the sermonizer who made a spider his emblem of the imperilled soul. There is one detail in Edwards's *Of Insects* that does not appear in Lowell's poem but which enforces in one phrase the contrast between the two Edwards's (Lowell refers to this passage in his third poem on Edwards):

'I have seen a vast multitude of little shining webs, and some glistening strings, brightly reflecting the sunbeams, and some of them of great length, and of such a height, that one would think they were tacked to the vault of the heavens, *and would be burned like tow in the sun*, and make a very beautiful, pleasing, as well as surprising appearance.' (My italics.)

It is difficult not to contrast this 'very beautiful, pleasing, as well as surprising appearance' with the ugly reality of hell fire evoked in the sermon as in the poem:

> But who can plumb the sinking of that soul?
> Josiah Hawley, picture yourself cast
> Into a brick-kiln where the blast
> Fans your quick vitals to a coal—
> If measured by a glass,
> How long would it seem burning! Let there pass
> A minute, ten, ten trillion; but the blaze
> Is infinite, eternal: this is death,
> To die and know it. This is the Black Widow, death.

Hell fire is more than torment. It is positive knowledge of death, an eternity of awareness which no nature human or otherwise can abolish or assuage. The innocence of the flying spiders who, unlike men, 'purpose nothing but their ease and die' transmutes into the Black Widow which, far from dying itself, devours its own kind to preserve itself. Edwards's terrible sermon asserts that there is no such thing as natural man and that the burden of consciousness is our own self and can never be lifted. The only story of a man is his salvation or his damnation. The only science is eschatology.

Josiah Hawley is warned that his suicide offers no escape. He cannot shelter in the annihilation of the natural man. The death that awaits him is eternal knowledge of death. The very language witnesses to an inescapable self-consciousness. Yet language can, through the extreme indirection of the poem, articulate a surrender of consciousness. A poem ends and surrenders to the silence that engulfs it. The answer to Edwards is not a suicide but the creation of a poem that dies, and that dies, paradoxically, in uttering the impossibility of death, upon the word 'death'. All emblems breed out of nature, at however many removes. Even the Black Widow, however transmogrified, is a piece of nature. Edwards is answered and, in an unusual sense, redeemed, by being made to utter and end himself in a poem.

The last Edwards poem—'Jonathan Edwards in Western Massachusetts'—though it quotes from him, makes no attempt to assume Edwards's voice. Lowell has opened a cool space between Edwards and himself, which is to say, between Lowell's own natural and verbal man. Edwards himself is allowed an otherness equivalent to the difference between the Edwards of the Revival and the Edwards exiled in his Indian mission, or between the boy naturalist and the hell-fire preacher. Lowell now treats these disjunctions companionably, even compassionately, as though, in the great distance of the historical space he now puts between himself and Edwards, he could at last forgive himself for his inheritance:

> Then God's love shone in sun, moon and stars,
> on earth, in the waters,
> in the air, in the loose winds,
> which used to greatly fix your mind . . .
>
> . . . Yet people were spiders
>
> in your moment of glory,
> at the Great Awakening— . . .

The breath that conditions all utterance is, as it were, turned loose here, in the informal measures of the verse, as after his 'moment of glory' (a temporary state which the holiness of nature lower-cases), Edwards himself loosens and recovers a humanity at the edge of a wilderness. The edge defines a limit to Edwards's eschatological pretensions as indeed to Lowell's:

> . . . In western Massachusetts,
> I could almost feel the frontier

crack and disappear.
Edwards thought the world would end there.

Edwards can now be seen affectionately, humanly, wryly, in the
huge, empty perspective of the death of the Word, which makes
room for human and natural presences:

> Edwards' great millstone and rock
> of hope has crumbled, but the square
> white houses of his flock
> stand in the open air,
>
> out in the cold,
> like sheep outside the fold.
> Hope lives in doubt.
> Faith is trying to do without
>
> faith.

Typography neatly imitates the decline of Faith into faith, yet
suggests a paradox: that 'Faith' comes to 'faith' (the minor,
provisional assumptions that underpin any living), with
difficulty and across (and just barely across) the great distance
that the gap between the stanzas enacts. Further, the un-willing
of faith is still (as indicated by the present continuous tense)
unachieved, though the slackening of tense goes itself—as a
formal operation—a long way towards achieving it. The mill-
stone—the church, the deadly burden, the provisioner—has
itself, in crumbling, produced at least the meal out of which
Lowell can mould his poem. But the poem is so lucidly explicit
as to evade commentary. The poet's pilgrimage is to no state
holier than a salvageable relationship between his empirical
being and his abandoned hunger for salvation. Lowell 'saves'
Edwards by insisting on all that was numb, inexplicit and
unachieved in his life. Edwards's natural self becomes his
destitute fame, his dubious memorials:

> On my pilgrimage to Northampton,
> I found no relic,
> except the round slice of an oak
> you are said to have planted.
>
> It was flesh-coloured, new,
> and a common piece of kindling,
> only fit for burning.
> You must have been green once.

Deliberately flat, unresonant, this verse may be. Yet it is layered
with implication. The word 'common' for example combines
'ordinary', 'vulgar' (in the sense that Hell-fire rhetoric is a
vulgar 'piece of kindling'), 'describing the common lot', 'of one
kind (with me)'. The 'flesh-coloured . . . slice of an oak' is 'fit for
burning' in fires very different from the fires of Hell. That
eschatology, like Lowell's own counter-eschatology, is out-
moded, a product of history rather than its cancellation. Yet
history can be cancelled at any moment, by the Bomb. As this
poem puts it: 'We know how the world will end'. The nuclear
terror described in the poem 'Fall 1961' turns all men into a
community of spiders suspended over a fire:

> A father's no shield
> for his child.
> We are like a lot of wild
> spiders crying together,
> but without tears.

In this poem again, though this time very explicitly, the
poem is redeemed, that is, it ends with, and so becomes
palpable against, a natural image:

> Back and forth!
> Back and forth, back and forth—
> my one point of rest

is the orange and black
oriole's swinging nest!

The natural replaces the merely mechanical measure of time, the
clock. At the same time, the movement of the poem—its 'one
point of rest'—pivots on the word 'nest' which throws into
bitter relief the father's helplessness. Nature is not, in a
traditional way, consolatory. Though the security of cyclic
organic process suggest images of human safety, they are only
images. More to the point are the poems themselves as
images of an order in which human purposes and natural
processes are reconciled. The poet's individual human project
becomes a wake, or trail left by the passage of speech through
the medium of silence, and so can image a consonance, which can
in turn become an image of the good life and the good society.
The poem, or the poet's activity, then becomes a means for
judging history, without having to get outside and so deny it.
Of course, in a situation in which to be a poet or read poetry is at
all remarkable, all poems, and all assumptions of poetic identity
will, irrespective of any content, become images. Poetry is no
longer a natural activity. However, with most poets, the fiction
persists that what they do is natural. Lowell, to an unusual
extent, manages to undermine this fiction, to make each poem
declare its own strangeness; its insistent identity as a piece of
literature calls attention to itself as something alien. Here one
must, at all costs, attend to the full complexity.

Lowell's later poems look informal, easy, natural: poetic
forms really do appear to cleave to, and become one with, their
statement. The breath's utterances and the poem's artifices grow
together in the occasion of the poem's coming into being. It is all
as natural as breathing, a spontaneous order, each poem un-
folding without strain under its own impulse into its proper
shape. But one registers this not simply as an occurrence but an
intention. The poems are not innocent: the informality is part
of an acknowledged design. The contrast ought to be between
closed form and open or projective form, to use Charles Olson's

terminology. Projective poetry, or at least its supporting mystique, assumes an open, never occupied space in front of the poem into which it grows and which it defines in the process. The law of its growth is in no wise given by the existence of literature as an institution. The poem is not a product but a process. It seeks the utmost cultural innocence by insisting upon itself as utterance, by riding off into the wilderness upon the unique breathing of the poet.

Here one must risk being contentious. The fiction of projective verse is the counterpart of an ideology whose central concern is to detach American from its European inheritance, a sticky web in which the destiny of the whole continent seems tramelled. One would wish to add that this attempt is itself part of the destiny, one which has helped construct it. The dream of innocence permits technological man to unknow, positively to unwill and so carry on—in deliberate innocence—performing his deed, freed from traditional sanctities and controls. To return poetry to some base in the physiology of the breath is the equivalent of other forms of sanctioning myth—the myth of the frontier, the myth of economic self-help, the myth of the westward movement of civilization—that underwrote the exploitation and devastation of the continent. It is a form of primitivism, resisting the institutional pressure of literature as a product of history and the repository of human significance. It substitutes a vision of individual initiatives for the containing and sustaining vision of a society. Its insistence upon the atomic valency of the syllable attempts to bypass, by detouring back behind, literary institutions and precedents, returning language to some state of virginity before it became dense with societal and institutional import. Literature, let alone syntax and verse forms, is so much lumber, brought in like the rats with the Mayflower, to be put down as quickly as possible. Clearly this view is absurd: Europe's ghosts groan in the very marrow of the language. But it retains utility as a mystique that has allowed the wildernesses, internal and external, to be dared, penetrated and devastated.

History is canvassed as wholesale myth, to be laid flat and

folded back into the landscapes of a perpetual present, as it is in *The Cantos, Paterson, The Maximus Poems*. The past can always be encountered without guilt, since the present determines the past, never issues from it. And the present can be made perpetually anew, in each poem, in each act. Hence the curious innocent cheerfulness, the ontological optimism, the essential refusal of evil that we find in all these poets, in, most incredibly, the Pound of the *Pisan Cantos*. Figuratively, however horrific the landscape, the poet is always by the side of the road to the infectious hospital. He is never encountered on his way back from it. This is cheering stuff for Europeans, but such poetic versions of the propaganda of good news they breathe all their lives ought to be depressing for Americans.

The myth of Adamic innocence is a deliberate obverse of Puritan eschatology, but, as an obverse must, issues from the same stamp. How it connects with objectivism is too tangled a piece of intellectual history to unravel here. Some parallel gets established between the poem as uncensored utterance and the poem as unauthored object. In Olson's articulation of Whitmanian aesthetic the complex of poet-poem-recipient is to exist innocently, as fact or thing, unprivileged among the objects of the universe. The notion is obviously consolatory. Each object, unique and self-fathered by the law of its own development, cannot be held responsible to anything else. As a project the poem, admittedly lumbered with the common tongue which is as far as possible moulded to local or immediate speech, takes off at right angles from the joint project of human history. It projects outwards into an undetermined field of infinite consciousness. Analogies with journeys, voyages, most pertinently with space exploration are relevant as is indeed the quasi-technological jargon that a theorist like Olson employs. The poem, moving ever outwards, can never really be called to account in terms of any norm. Indeed, it cannot be criticised, since literature ceases to exist.

The urgency of these issues abounds in Lowell's article on Williams in *The Hudson Review* (1961–2). About Williams himself, Lowell is tender and generous. He praises Williams for his vitality, his grip on environment, even 'the shocking scramble of the crass and the august'. Yet a disciple of Williams must feel that despite his human community with him, Lowell is utterly out of sympathy, to the point of not being able to engage with Williams's central project. The substitution of reminiscence for discrimination indicates a wariness, a deep withholding. Lowell finally will not endorse Williams's poetics and myths. He is lucid about the implication of that refusal being, in the end, a refusal of America—as '*the* truth and *the* subject'. Beneath the hesitant, modest surface of his prose ripples a claim to a more comprehensive sophistication which places Williams and could not, conceivably, be placed by him. In this paragraph praise is subtly subverted by Lowell's sense of his own sense of Williams being more complicated than Williams's sense of himself. The evocation of 'Dr Williams . . . rushing from his practice to his typewriter' is faintly patronizing. There is, too, a syntactical cringing produced by the guilt that troubles sophistication in the presence of innocence:

'The difficulties I found in Williams twenty-five years ago are still difficulties for me. Dr Williams enters me, but I cannot enter him. Of course, one cannot catch any good writer's voice or breathe his air. But there's something more. It's as if no good poet except Williams had really seen America or heard its language. Or rather he sees and hears what we all see and hear and what is most obvious, but no one else has found this a help or an inspiration. This may come naturally to Dr Williams from his character, surroundings and occupation. I can see him rushing from his practice to his typewriter, happy that so much of the world has rubbed off on him, maddened by its hurry. Perhaps he has no choice. Anyway, what others have spent lifetimes in building up personal styles to gather what has been snatched up on the run by Dr Williams? When I say that I cannot enter him, I am almost saying that I cannot enter America. This troubles me. I am not satisfied to let it be. Like others I have picked up things here and there from

Williams, but this only makes me marvel the more at his unique and searing journey. It is a Dantesque journey, for he loves America excessively, as if it were *the* truth and *the* subject; his exasperation is also excessive, as if there were no other hell. His flowers rustle by the super-highways and pick up all our voices.'

The notion of a 'Dantesque journey' (Dante being superlatively the exiled questor for spiritual and civil order) places Williams out of reach of any terms he would use for himself. Lowell labels, tickets, tames Williams, assimilating him to an idea of literary tradition whose coercions Williams's poetics is designed to evade. Yet Lowell, ungenerously at this point, grants all too willingly that Williams's poems are not artifices, but unpremeditated, natural occurences. Hence the speculation that his subject matter 'may come naturally to Dr Williams', while, in that curious rhetorical question that looks more like an exclamation, Lowell significantly contrasts 'the building up of personal styles' (the poet as architect) with 'what has been snatched up on the run by Dr Williams', as though Williams were a bank-robber or a swallow. The poems come as easily as roadside, or superhighwayside flowers: they are also—if I pick up the right vibration of 'rustle'—a trifle thin-textured, victimized and undernourished by their industrial environment. And who could determine exactly what elaborate circumspection is danced out in the twice repeated phrase 'pick up'?

Knowing that Lowell has 'picked up things here and there from Williams' we may suspect that his later poetry has been loosened and relaxed by some contamination from the Williams tradition. But the casual address of the poetry should not deceive us. Each poem is in fact braced by a rigorous logic. Even where it does not display, it reaches towards a formal rhetoric that predetermines the poem's shape and destination. Each poem is brought round unmistakably *by* the poet, whose agency the poem declares, to a predestined closure. The poem always exists somewhat after some fact, idea or event; it is not itself a fact, an idea or an event. It affirms some order which is its ground of being.

This order may, operationally, be no more than the conviction that poems should go on being written and that literature is still required. Lowell's poems are always bent on being and making literature. If we remember this, the strategy involved in Lowell's *Imitations* becomes clear. Lowell recreates for his own purposes a corpus of poems belonging to other times and other cultures. He renders them in his own idiom with a freedom and confidence that raises eyebrows. Equally, however, he commits his own idiom to the corpus; he adds, offers, sacrifices it, as it were, in order to bring into existence a usable body of literature, as distinct from an eclectic aggregation, from which to derive sanctions, directives, models. The whole operation involves the exercise of a vast tact. Merely to translate would be to become the avatar of foreign cultures. To transform utterly would be to court the solipsism of all imperialisms. Lowell, in his *Imitations*, has both to honour and render alien visions, to domesticate without destroying them. *Imitations* attempts to create a tradition by an individual effort of will, because a literature without a tradition is unthinkable, and because the tradition that filters down through the academies and organs of cultural diffusion is not a possession but so much booty and plunder. To be possessed it must, in the American way be mastered and retrieved through an individual initiative. Lowell is nowhere more native than in his determination to make Parnassus under his own steam.

For Lowell, literature is a precondition for a human world, defined against the circularities and randomness of natural process—a public space in which specifically human purposes declare themselves. Where this space is threatened or extinguished, literature takes over as the repository of its values. The poet may well find himself, even to his own surprise, mounting guard over dead civic virtue. Each poem becomes a defence of literature and behind that of the public order whose disintegrations the poet now registers but which, in an ideal state, his art exists to celebrate and sustain. Here is the explicit ground of Lowell's career. His poems do not merely perform this function, they reflect and meditate on it as well. Indeed, the defensive action for its effectiveness depends upon the poetry being a conscious assumption of this martial role. Lowell confronts in 'For the Union Dead' a modern urban devastation in which the civic order is being systematically dismantled. To name is in some sense to tame it. Lowell glares at it, eyeball to eyeball, exposing all his nerves, yet constructing, in the poem's own architecture, an alternative order both to that which destroys and that which is destroyed. The poet substitutes his poem for the statue whose commemorative virtue is no longer acknowledged. The statue once preserved the dead, the past, what had been wrested from the flux of history as destiny. Lowell's poem enacts the death of the statue, its final envelopment by unmeaning. The contained chaos of the aquarium has erupted into and drowned out the public domain:

> a savage servility
> slides by on grease.

To name the horror is to encompass it in the name of a possibility that surpasses it. For the poem is not merely, weakly, diagnostic, but militantly braced against the dissolution it utters. The naming is a containment. (Northrop Frye would see it as the myth of the hero's struggle with Leviathan.) Lowell redeems the impotent memorial, by reinvesting it with the immediacy of flesh and blood, while denying none of its commemorative significance:

> Shaw's father wanted no monument
> except the ditch,
> where his son's body was thrown
> and lost with his 'niggers'.

> The ditch is nearer.

In some sense, Lowell's poem unbuilds the statue in favour

of the ditch, the bestial condition of abandonment and loss which the monument traditionally redeems. Characteristically, Lowell's stanza-break enacts the ditch, which now deepens and widens its significance to take in the gouged soil of violated Boston, the uncommemorated wholesale destruction of the last war ('There are no statues of the last war here') and the last-ditch destructions of atomic warfare. With the utmost economy, almost with elegance, Lowell brings into one focus the commercial greed that has devastated Boston and the Puritan Church that has sponsored the same destructive energies. Its contempt for natural limits, its over-weening repudiation of natural death has, paradoxically, leagued it with the turbulence of a demonic nature. Yet the ensuing atrocity is imaged in the mindless medium of an advertisement. For Lowell to be able to contain and relate both the horror and the mass media's numbing of the horror vindicates the poet's role:

> . . . a commercial photograph
> shows Hiroshima boiling

> over a Mosler Safe, the 'Rock of Ages'
> that survived the blast.

Humour plays a liberating part in the effect. It is obscene that a commercial photograph should display the destruction of Hiroshima. But when the sentence carries across the stanza break, 'over' (that wildly active preposition) to a Mosler Safe, we are forced into the release of something like laughter at the solemn, self-important, un-ironic impudence of the commercial imagination. The paradox remains that denials or dishonourings of nature (whether exploitative or theological), give birth not to the super-but the sub-natural:

> the dark downward and vegetating kingdom
> of the fish and reptile.

Hence the ambiguity involved in saying that the Safe has
'*survived* the blast' (a good poet wrests his meanings from the
conceptual sub-stratum of the language itself!). It 'survives'
only at the expense of life. Yet Lowell does not allow himself
easy victories. Obviously, the Mosler Safe is available for every
sort of ironic denigration. Lowell simply states; no more. He
gives the devil his due. And that ability to rest in statement is
in turn an aspect of Lowell's militancy. For it depends upon an
ultimate conviction of the efficacy of language, despite all
debasements, all dishonourings. Lowell's power of statement
points to another use of language, its existence in poems which
unite the world of nature with human intention and meaning. A
poem dies; and human nature can assume nature itself as its
vesture in its submission to and choice of deaths. Lowell's
imagery works incessantly to define, implicitly, the right,
the respectful, the decent order which should govern the
transactions between man and his world. Thus

> Their monument sticks like a fishbone
> in the city's throat

asserts it negatively, aggressively. But of Shaw himself:

> He has an angry wrenlike vigilance,
> a greyhound's gentle tautness . . .

The statuary itself embodies the fusion of nature and artifice:

> William James could almost hear the bronze
> Negroes breathe.

Yet in this very line the afflatus of that fusion is chastened by a
limiting precision, 'almost': artifice and nature are juxtaposed,
not confused through the agents that relate them: '*bronze*
Negroes *breathe*'. The peculiar virtue of Lowell's resistance to
the endemic and literal dehumanizations of American experience,
his refusal to enter America, its vast material growth, slaughter

of Indians, enslavement of Negroes, its spoliation of landscape,
its exportation of massive violence (all themes treated by
Lowell), derives from his realization of complicity in the
glamour of those processes, of which his own dealings with
madness, vastness, oceanic euphoria, verbal affluence, are a part:

> Once my nose crawled like a snail on the glass;
> my hand tingled
> to burst the bubbles
> drifting from the noses of the cowed, compliant fish.

> My hand draws back.

The change of tense from past to present is significant. Merely
to state a past tense represents in so sensitive a structure as this
poem the act of escaping to the past, to childhood, to innocence
and evading the small, drab militant virtues of watching and
warding in the present. Again, the stanza break enacts the
difficulty of the gesture that resists this temptation. The act of
resistance means renunciation of fluency and fluidity, a half-
unwilling assumption of fixity and dryness. The last line of
'Home after Three Months Away' is apposite:

> Cured, I am frizzled, stale and small.

To burst the bubble, as the despoilers of Boston have emptied
the aquarium, promises a return to the *plenum*, to become an
open, undetermined, blessedly irresponsible thing, a sheer
utterance, like the projectivist poem-object, to re-enter the
wilderness that breaks into Edwards's sober couplets:

> the bough
> Cracks with the unpicked apples, and at dawn
> The small-mouth bass breaks water, gorged with spawn.

In 'For the Union Dead', Lowell sees himself simultaneously
on both sides of the glass at once, within and without, feeling

over its surfaces and seeing himself as so feeling from the other side: 'My nose crawled like a snail on the glass.' The aquarium contains, renders visible, yet resists the demonic powers of nature which have returned in parody through the rabid growth of technology: Lowell again 'presses' towards them, but this time with the implication that the medium (and we must consider how far these images of containments are also descriptions of the poem itself) is cruder, improvised out of the violence of desperation and yet less effective:

> One morning last March,
> I pressed against the new barbed and galvanized

> fence on the Boston Common. Behind their cage,
> yellow dinosaur steamshovels were grunting
> as they cropped up tons of mush and grass
> to gouge their underworld garage.

Whether 'underworld' is not too artful, and hence the sign of a nervousness, is a question. Is Lowell again indulging in premature coercion of his material into myth? And if so, is this a defence against the destructive onslaughts of technological and bestial forces? The whole poem is held rigid and yet vibrates between the allure of self-abandonment and the restrictions and tensions of control. Colonel Shaw, Puritan that he was ('he seems to wince at pleasure,/and suffocate for privacy') also 'waits/for the blessed break' into the sinister fullness of creation. The 'Rem Publicam' of the poem's Latin motto—object of the poem's creative act—is built on renunciation ('sparse, sincere rebellion'). The Public Thing is a deliberate artifice, something that stands vertical against all frontal assaults, the lure and corruption of gravity, the erosion of elements. In the very first line, 'The old South Boston Aquarium stands/ . . . now.' The poem too is to stand, like the statue, but more like a piece of architecture. Indeed, architectonic analogies seem in order. The poem appears to be constructed, sustained by a play of tensions, resistances, contained strains. It is a complex arrangement or

investment of spaces. Masses are balanced off against each
other. The reader's attention does not enter the poem, nor does
the poem envelop or absorb it. We register the various
elements of the poem as blocks of discrepant size or weight that
still are locked and held in the grip of a fierce compositional
energy that ultimately distributes and resolves itself through
them. By its last stanza, the poem has achieved the demolition of
the aquarium and named its destroyer. But it has also put
itself in its place. The poem concludes at an intense pitch of
what I can only call compositional irony. All the containments
and restraints of civilization have collapsed. The monsters are
cruising in for the kill. Yet the poem holds, tames them, at the
crux of their unleashed aggression. They become compliant to
Lowell's vast verbal control:

> a savage servility
> slides by on grease.

The destroyers remain 'servile' . . . and one just flirts with the
possibility that this servility may be greasy because proletarian;
the micks and the wops against Colonel Shaw. But this
suggestion merely flickers about the image, and it is one which
Lowell would have no difficulty in confronting.

Lowell knows the dangers of the militant, the statuesque, the
architectural. Other poems in *For the Union Dead* explore the
potential of these for tyranny and petrification. In 'Florence',
Lowell comes out for the monsters ('tubs of guts', 'slop')
against the militant Davids and Judiths, those tyrannicides who
exploit and destroy them. He demonstrates how they can
become agents of the corruption they should resist:

> On the circles, green statues ride like South American
> liberators above the breeding vegetation—
>
> prongs and spearheads of some equatorial
> backland that will inherit the globe.
>
> ('July in Washington')

His own bodily architecture is implicated in that subtle poem
'The Neo-Classical Urn', which, like the Washington poem,
connects with all those Roman allusions, styles, republican
monuments, which sheathe like thinnest bronze the body
politic of America. Lowell, rubbing his skull recalls by association the turtle shells, themselves prison and armour of the
living creatures which he had destroyed by keeping them in a
garden urn overlooked by 'the caste stone statue of a nymph,/
her soaring armpits and her one bare breast,/gray from the
rain and graying in the shade . . . ' whose classicality is rendered
in a faintly Augustan idiom.* Again 'Caligula' explores an
insanity that tries to turn itself into marble:

> yours the lawlessness
> of something simple that has lost its law . . .

Finally, in 'Buenos Aires' Lowell finds a kind of inverted
version of the military virtues, which have turned totally
tyrannical and petrific, the mirror image almost of the devastation of Boston. Lowell now identifies with the natural demonic
forces—'the bulky, beefy breathing of the herds.' Into the stony
solemnity of the southern capital Lowell dances like a bovine
Bacchus:

> Cattle furnished my new clothes:
> my coat of limp, chestnut-colored suede . . .

In 'Buenos Aires/lost in the pampas/and run by the barracks'
with its glum furniture of 'neo-classical catafalques . . . a
hundred marble goddesses', Lowell becomes the therapist of so
much rigour:

> I found rest
> by cupping a soft palm to each hard breast.

*'Caste' is perhaps a misprint for 'chaste' in these lines. If so, it escaped both
Lowell and his printers. M.D.

Throughout his work, Lowell oscillates between oceanic fluxes of euphoria and horror and a corresponding drive to the security of law, logic, stability, structure. The flux is outer and inner; often inner and outer are one and their identification can produce weird puns:

> Now from the train, at dawn
> Leaving Columbus in Ohio, shell
> On shell of our stark culture strikes the sun . . .

which connects, in the same poem, 'In Memory of Arthur Winslow', with water, through another 'striking' image:

> On Boston Basin, shells
> *Hit* water by the Union Boat Club wharf . . .

(My italics. Notice the similar rhyming and syntactical salience of the word 'shells'. Queerer, is the crude and one hopes unconscious pun that connects 'our stark culture' with one of the ancestors, only a few lines on:

> And General Stark's coarse bas-relief in bronze
> Set on your granite shaft
> In rough Dunbarton . . .)

Lowell's extraordinary feel, touch for texture, weight, density, somehow transforms itself into verbal and syntactical equivalents in the poetry itself as well as providing much of the imagery. How much, for example, do these lines

> frayed flags
> quilt the graveyards of the Grand Army of the Republic

owe to the contrasts of texture and weight? The feel of the stuffs somehow becomes the stuff of the lines so that 'Grand Army of the Republic' may look a well stuffed title, but one

which has worn sadly thin. Lowell's poetry returns continually
to some somatic base that is Lowell's real presence in the
poetry, much more important than any grammatical ego. Here,
literally, the poetry is the shadowy but persistent corpus of the
man himself, his volatilized and verbally reconstituted self-
image. The poem, imaged as a shell, itself oceanic, also
represents the tense, elaborate thinness of his own substance,
separating the chaos without from the flux within. The process
is very self-conscious in 'The Neo-Classical Urn':

> Poor head!
> How its skinny shell once hummed . . .

A Lowell poem, however solid its architecture, never looks
other than fragile, friable, only just mastering the pulls and
pressures that threaten to disintegrate it. Freud's view of the
ego as a hard won layer of self that achieves enough stability to
curb—and yet be fed and thickened by—the importunate, blind
drives of the id, and that copes and transacts with external
reality, seems apposite. If Lowell is a post-Freudian poet, this is
not primarily because Freud is an inescapable ingredient of
secular culture, but because Lowell's poetic practice enacts the
Freudian drama and is the therapy of the human condition that
Freud divined.

Freud was concerned, as therapist, with the making of viable
individual existence. He released the fantasies, whose prodigious
allure he knew only too well, not to express but to desensitivize
and reduce them. Lowell's poetic progress could be seen, in
similar terms, as self-therapy. But the terms are too restrictive.
One could put it rather that Lowell's poetic career imitates—in
an Aristotelian sense—the progress of self-therapy, and thereby
proposes itself as a case of an ultimately viable existence. It
becomes exemplary as a measure of the depth and intensity of
the forces that batter the self from within and without, and
describes the forms that resistance to these can assume. Lowell
as poet becomes the implicit hero of his own poetry, but, of

necessity, very much a debunked and debunking hero, diffident, arrogant, self-destructive, perhaps, most of all, despite all, persistent and operative.

It is in some such terms that I would wish to understand the *Life Studies* sequence. Lowell's treatment suggests not an exhibition but a cauterization of private material and emotion. Interest is not in what is revealed but in what is reserved. These nagging, haunting, futile figures, the threadbare deposits of years of private living, are indeed exhibited, not with contempt or love, but only as they can be contained in poetic architectures —like statues in niches—their features cleansed for presentation, but neither exploited nor degraded nor glamourized. The poker-faced numbness of Lowell's handling of these figures—the balance retained between respect for their integrity and refusal of their domination—is more important than the figures themselves. Our fascination is for how much emotional dynamite is off-loaded and safely de-fused. Lowell does not permit himself or us any absorption in the depths of memory, emotion or childhood. We are invited rather to participate in Lowell's craftsmanly concentration on building evanescent emotions and moments and events into solid structures from which they will not evaporate into wistfulness or nostalgia. Lowell hardly permits himself the luxuries of aggression or self-pity or to indulge in Hardy-like pangs at pastness. The poetry is designed to keep the past past and the dead dead. If there is any covert emotion it is the quiet grimness of that determination. The success of this cauterization of the past is summed up by the last line of a poem in *For the Union Dead*:

> Pardon them for existing.
> We have stopped watching them. They have stopped
>   watching.

This is the end-result of the process initiated in *Life Studies*: that phrase that must remind us of the term 'still life' and, just as usefully, of its French equivalent *nature morte*. The deliberate deadening of emotion becomes a kind of spiritual exercise, and even achieves a certain perversity in the poem about bringing the dead mother's corpse home, 'Sailing Home from Rapallo':

> In the grandiloquent lettering on Mother's coffin,
> *Lowell* had been misspelled *LOVEL*.
> The corpse
> was wrapped like *panetone* in Italian tinfoil.

The sequence shows just the thinness of love in the familial scene. But Lowell conspicuously abstains from fastening upon the irony of *'LOVEL'*. He simply hovers, brooding glumly, over it, then relinquishes it in the noun-length line 'The corpse . . . ' Even the grotesquerie of the last couplet is not allowed to lift into any exuberance. The poem rustles to a dry close on the phrase 'Italian tinfoil.'

Lowell is really a very non-intimate poet who holds his readers at arm's length, even though much of his reputation and appeal since *Life Studies* depends on his appearing to offer unmediated, secular experience, almost raw. Pleasure in reading him is partly that of recognition, of being shown the artifacts and objects—many of them dishevelled, casual, almost nameless —of our common environment. Lowell has a superbly developed sense of milieu, of the tacky and gimcrack surfaces, as well as of the bric-à-brac of our civilization of depersonalized intimacy. How characteristic that the beads that Michael clenches at the end of 'Thanksgiving's Over' should be cowhorn and from Dublin. Lowell knows, notices and, with only slightly self-congratulatory hysteria, uses such things. But we should notice how far these objects are re-apprehended and, at it were, redeemed for attention, by being locked and cemented into larger structures. They are never really innocent, autarchic objects like Williams's red wheelbarrow. They are there because they serve a significance or are at least apt for some design. Thus, in 'During Fever' the daughter's 'chicken-coloured sleeping bag' depends for its colour not on the fact that that was the colour that it was but on an association with 'the healthy country' from which the daughter has returned. While within the drab colour scheme of Lowell's recollections in 'Memories of West Street and Lepke', Lowell's daughter's 'flame-flamingo infants' wear' does more than outdo, with that resplendent epithet, the advertiser's euphorics. This is not to deny Lowell's almost uncanny empathy with the furniture of private and mass living, but also to emphasize his simultaneous degree of controlled remoteness from them.

This feel for secular existence finds its counterpart in the casual movement of the poem itself, hardly insisting on its spatial organization, but appearing to unfold without resistance along the line of relaxed reminiscence. For example 'Memories of West Street and Lepke' seems to accrue section by section, without obvious destination and, trailing off into space, to lapse trickling out into a ruminative silence, which may at any moment revive and grow audible again. The poem seems to hold off from judgement and conclusion. 'Ought I to regret my seedtime?', Lowell asks himself, and the poem comes up with no answer, as though it itself were the flower of that seedtime and as such required no confirmation. Anything like a point of view hardly has time to establish itself before it is undercut. Thus, in the first paragraph:

> . . . even the man
> scavenging filth in the back alley trash cans,
> has two children, a beach wagon, a helpmate,
> and is a 'young Republican'.

This looks like pretty main-stream irony, but we are not allowed to indulge it for long: in the very next line Lowell adverts to his own parenthood, the creaturely condition which he shares with the scavenger, and wipes the grin at least off his own face. Likewise, the gusty euphoria of the opening lines rapidly reverses within the perspectives of his reminiscence:

Only teaching on Tuesdays, book-worming
in pajamas fresh from the washer each morning,
I hog a whole house on Boston's
'hardly passionate Marlborough Street . . .'

when we are introduced by way of the laundry to

Czar Lepke,
there piling towels on a rack,
or dawdling off to his little segregated cell full
of things forbidden the common man . . .

which forms a grotesque parallel with Lowell's own situation, hogging a whole house, a thing also forbidden 'the common man'. The Lepke situation throws back a retrospective gloom: the poet's own tranquillity seems a kind of prison, his routines a prison routine. Like Lepke he is a prisoner with privileges beyond the common lot. 'Hog' of course connects with Lepke's flabbiness as it does also with 'the man/scavenging filth'. We become aware of the reek of depression from beneath the rather manic crisp and jaunty production of image and event.

Lowell's right to his mood of euphoria at the beginning of the poem is called into question. It has been bought, apparently, at the expense of a thoroughgoing defensive refusal to make connections. The nine-months-old daughter rising 'like the sun' is not the only—and is perhaps only an irrelevantly posthumous —fruit of his 'seedtime'. There is also the connection, disowned, between Lowell's comparative affluence and 'the man/scavenging filth', between his present tranquil—one might say drug-tranquillized—state and the unprivileged Negro boy with 'curlicues/of marijuana in his hair' with whom he had once awaited sentence. The question arises for the poet whether he had not been in closer connection all round when in the days of his passionate naiveté he had gone to prison than now, and whether the manifest violent horror of the decades that produced *Murder Incorporated* was not somehow more hopeful in its openness than 'the *tranquilized fifties*'. Is not that tranquillity merely a drugged drift towards death, parallel with Lepke's 'concentration on the electric chair'?

> Flabby, bald, lobotomized,
> he drifted in a sheepish calm,
> where no agonizing reappraisal
> jarred his concentration on the electric chair—
> hanging like an oasis in his air
> of lost connections . . .

The poem is a meditation on the edge of middle age. It looks back to a self that is hardly recognizable and—as is to be anticipated on such a theme—forwards to death. But the poem also is about the failure to make the middle of a life span connect with and so unify the beginning and the end. The failure is deep and complex: a failure to make the agonizing reappraisal of a state of mind which refuses agonizing reappraisals. The unformed, drifting, apparently randomly wavering line of the poem is itself an aspect, an expression of this refusal. And yet, despite appearances, this refusal of commitment to a connective structure is turned, against all the odds, itself into a constructive principle. We drift with Lowell's reminiscence as Lepke drifts towards death. And at the moment of the poem's ending, its death, when it runs out upon those eloquent dots, we discover the lost connections that Lepke can never find, the analogies and parallelisms and constructive contrasts that have been holding the poem together. The answer to the question is not the poem itself but the alert, militant and vital chore of unremitting interrogation. The connection in this poem is made through the interrogated fact that everything has come apart and it is made against the defensive grain that would keep it that way. Through this understanding, at the very edge of annihilation, when the poem's sound is about to die away in the air of lost connections, a sense of significance and of coherence is still just able to obtain. So that after all the poem survives as a structure which resists the oceanic drift of death, of which the mechanical operation of reminiscence is an aspect.

The poem remains an architecture that simulates, anticipates and thus prevents its own demolition. It is an artfully designed ruin. It only looks like a piece of nature formed haphazardly out of the forces of erosion and accumulation. Secular experience is never, ever, unmediated in Lowell. Not that in verbal structures it ever really could be, but, despite appearances, in Lowell's case the ultimate tendency of the poem is to insist upon its structure. Even in this poem which comes nearer to unmediated existence than any other, in which the poem—the self-substantive, nominative thing—just manages to crystallize out of the stream of poetry—even here, there is an appeal to a transcending notion of literature through which this poem takes its place with other poems, as part of an order. We are in the presence of a Dejection Ode, of a literary *kind*, and it is that fact that resists the reader's own death-wish, any impulse he might have to drown and be absorbed in the poet's private substance which, until it is owned not as a wholly personal project but as part of a joint human enterprise, must remain part of the chaos out of which order has still to be achieved.

'For the Union Dead' by Robert Lowell

FOR THE UNION DEAD

'Relinquunt Omnia Servare Rem Publicam'

The old South Boston Aquarium stands
in a Sahara of snow now. Its broken windows are
    boarded.
The bronze weathervane cod has lost half its scales.
The airy tanks are dry.

Once my nose crawled like a snail on the glass;
my hand tingled
to burst the bubbles
drifting from the noses of the cowed, compliant fish.

My hand draws back. I often sigh still
for the dark downward and vegetating kingdom
of the fish and reptile. One morning last March,
I pressed against the new barbed and galvanized

fence on the Boston Common. Behind their cage,
yellow dinosaur steamshovels were grunting
as they cropped up tons of mush and grass
to gouge their underworld garage.

Parking spaces luxuriate like civic
sandpiles in the heart of Boston.

A girdle of orange, Puritan-pumpkin colored girders
braces the tingling Statehouse,

shaking over the excavations, as it faces Colonel Shaw
and his bell-cheeked Negro infantry
on St. Gaudens' shaking Civil War relief,
propped by a plank splint against the garage's
    earthquake.

Two months after marching through Boston,
half the regiment was dead;
at the dedication,
William James could almost hear the bronze Negroes
    breathe.

Their monument sticks like a fishbone
in the city's throat.
Its Colonel is as lean
as a compass-needle.

He has an angry wrenlike vigilance,
a greyhound's gentle tautness;
he seems to wince at pleasure,
and suffocate for privacy.

He is out of bounds now. He rejoices in man's lovely,
peculiar power to choose life and die—
when he leads his black soldiers to death,
he cannot bend his back.

On a thousand small town New England greens,
the old white churches hold their air
of sparse, sincere rebellion; frayed flags
quilt the graveyards of the Grand Army of the Republic.

APPENDIX

The stone statues of the abstract Union Soldier
grow slimmer and younger each year—
wasp-waisted, they doze over muskets
and muse through their sideburns . . .

Shaw's father wanted no monument
except the ditch,
where his son's body was thrown
and lost with his 'niggers.'

The ditch is nearer.
There are no statues for the last war here;
on Boyleston Street, a commercial photograph
shows Hiroshima boiling

over a Mosler Safe, the 'Rock of Ages'
that survived the blast. Space is nearer.
When I crouch to my television set,
the drained faces of Negro school-children rise like
    balloons.

Colonel Shaw
is riding on his bubble,
he waits
for the blesséd break.

The Aquarium is gone. Everywhere,
giant finned cars nose forward like fish;
a savage servility
slides by on grease.

Note: At line 47, some texts read 'wasp-wasted' M.D.

John Berryman: An Introduction

I f y o u don't own any of his books, the easiest place to find a few of John Berryman's poems is A. Alvarez's anthology, *The New Poetry*, which first came out in 1962. The book has since been revised, but originally only two American poets were represented—Robert Lowell and John Berryman. It would be hard to miss either of them; they have been given pride of place, right at the beginning. The new view of English poetry which the book aspires to give is offered, no doubt about it, under *their* auspices.

This will not necessarily seem odd to a reader now, seven years or more after *The New Poetry* first appeared, but I think that it really would have at the time. By 1962, of course, there was at least enough interest in Lowell's work to justify the publication of a book about him; three of his books were in print in England, and they had all been well received. Berryman, however, had only one book of poems to his credit in this country. It had been very favourably reviewed by Alvarez, and a climate of respectful interest in his work had probably been established, but his name would have aroused nothing like the feeling stirred by Lowell's. *Homage to Mistress Bradstreet* very much swam in under the protection of Lowell's supposedly 'confessional' *Life Studies*. It too was felt to be an extreme work, Berryman also was felt to be out on a limb. It wasn't so much, then, the pairing of Berryman with Lowell that would have been surprising (for evidently they both expressed an idea of the proper relationship between poet and society as Alvarez saw it, one that was not 'genteel'), as Alvarez's declaration that they were the two best poets of their generation. Did Berryman stand out *that* much over Elizabeth Bishop, Delmore Schwartz or Randall Jarrell?

It was hard to believe it at the time in England, and it must have been equally difficult in America, where Berryman's poems were by no means easy to get hold of. *The Dispossessed* did get some good reviews when it came out in 1948, as did *Homage to Mistress Bradstreet* in 1956, but there was a general refusal to get unduly excited. Nobody ever made the sort of fuss about Berryman that has been made recently in America over James Dickey. I am not arguing that this of itself argues his immense superiority to Dickey and his like, but a reader ought to have some idea of the resonant silence against which one writes in praise of this fine poet.

It is a relief to have Mr Alvarez on one's side, but I find him a slightly worrying companion. It does not seem to me that he puts enough emphasis on Berryman's *art*; he puts his high value on the neurotic element in the poet's work, as though he were content that the subject-matter should be painful, and that the poet should have pushed himself so far as to have discovered *this* variety of pain or *this*. In fact, whilst there is no difficulty in admiring the taste that singled out Berryman as an important poet, it is hard to agree with what Alvarez actually says about him. Of course, since the publication of *The New Poetry* it has become easier to discuss the poet because there has been more of him to discuss; *Berryman's Sonnets*, written in the forties, were published in 1968, and the poet has recently completed the long poem called *The Dream Songs*, the first part of which, 77 *Dream Songs*, appeared in 1964. The second volume, completing the poem, and called *His Toy, His Dream, His Rest*, was published in America at the end of 1968 and in England in May 1969. *The Dream Songs* are an unquestionably major achievement, and accordingly it is with them that this essay is most concerned, although there is also much to admire in *Homage to Mistress Bradstreet* (that is, the long poem of that name—the English edition also contains a generous selection of Berryman's earlier work) and the *Sonnets*.

101

77 Dream Songs was met with near-universal respectful incomprehension when it came out. I don't claim to understand it all myself; the structure of the whole poem seems especially elusive. On the other hand, *The Dream Songs* have a lot more to offer that is immediately attractive than has been suggested—they are, for example, often very funny. Berryman's difficulty can be insisted on too much; it is undoubtedly there, but it is not the only thing, or the most important. If we choose to focus on it before anything else, we risk missing other, larger issues which, when resolved, cast light on the obscurities of his style. One justification for considering Berryman at length is that his work does so directly confront problems facing most poets writing now; the kind of difficulty which he exhibits is itself an answer to the difficulties under which any poet must labour at the present time. Further, Berryman's answer is as successful as it is original.

But is it original? At first sight *The Dream Songs* seem to belong to a familiar movement in modern poetry, that of modernism itself, in the vanguard of which marched T. S. Eliot and Ezra Pound. Looking at such a poem as Dream Song 33, we might well consider it merely a variation on the sort of thing attempted in Eliot's poems in quatrains, or even on a vast scale in Pound's *Cantos*—not genteel exactly, but hardly barbaric, either. Indeed this Song is one of the most literary; it is based on an episode in Plutarch's life of Alexander. It seems that the king had listened with amusement at a banquet to verses made at the expense of some Macedonian officers, recently defeated in battle with the barbarians. Clitus, who was present, grew indignant at this slight on his own people by the king, and a violent quarrel arose between him and Alexander. Berryman's poem begins in the middle of this dispute:

> An apple arc'd toward Kleitos; whose great King
> wroth & of wine did study where his sword,
> sneak'd away, might be . . .

The sword had been hidden in the cause of good order by a member of the bodyguard. The king's rage only increased. He commanded one of his trumpeters to sound, crying out in his native Macedonian, so angry was he, but the man refused the order, which would have panicked the whole camp, and was struck in the face by the king for his refusal:

> An un-Greek word
> blister, to him his guard,
>
> and the trumpeter would not sound, fisted. Ha,
> they hustle Clitus out; by another door,
> loaded, crowds he back in
> who now must, chopped, fall to the spear-ax ah
> grabbed from an extra by the boy-god, sore
> for weapons.

After killing Clitus, Alexander was filled with remorse, and tried to commit suicide. His guards, however, took him back to his own quarters, where he spent the next day and night in lamentation:

> A baby, the guard may
> squire him to his apartments. Weeping & blood
> wound round his one friend.

Now this could reasonably be described as a poetry of allusion, the sort of thing for which the *Cantos* have prepared us; and it would be possible to build an argument impressive in appearance for Berryman's being a writer in the Poundian camp. Even in the trivial discrepancy between *Kleitos* and *Clitus* we are reminded of Pound's principle of diversification in spelling; and the poem's total intention may be seen as a contrast between our own meretricious sophistication, or whatever, and the nobler, if barbaric, age that is gone. The central figure of *The Dream Songs*, about whom we shall have something to say further on, is called Henry; he does appear in this song, though minimally, not unimportantly: 'For the sin:/little it is gross Henry has to say.' If we assume that Henry is *gross* because that is the nature of his civilization, then the poem is a variation on such lines as these in Pound:

> I neither build nor reap.
> That he came with the golden ships, Cadmus,
> That he fought with the wisdom,
> Cadmus, of the gilded prows. Nothing I build
> And I reap
> Nothing . . .

Berryman's past is a good deal more equivocal than that of Cadmus in these lines, though; perhaps a better analogy for Song 33 would be the lines about Elizabeth and Essex in *The Waste Land*. Certainly the transition from Alexander and Clitus to Henry is abrupt, more in the manner of Eliot than of Pound.

As it happens, though, I would not argue the association of Berryman with either of these writers as something of primary importance in his art. This is not, however, because the possible range of association has been already exhausted. Song 33 has, for example, all the subtlety that we would expect to find in modernist poetry: there is almost more than can manageably be demonstrated.

The poem begins with the apple thrown by Alexander not only because it provides an arresting first line, but also because it recalls the apple of discord thrown on Olympus. The verb for the apple's flight, *arc'd*, perhaps compares it to an arrow shot from a bow, and so gives the first hint of the conflict that is to develop; it may also suggest an upward movement followed by a decline—appropriately, since Clitus was at the time of his death about to become King of Bactria. Primarily, I suppose, the word is suggestive of a leisurely movement (it only hints at conflict); this permits *wroth*, at the beginning of the next line, to be nevertheless a surprise. The phrase *of wine* is an elliptical way of saying *on account of having drunk too much wine*; the king was angry, and the reason was that he had drunk too much. The compressed form suggests his excitement, and possibly the poet's, or Henry's, or that of both, as well. The king 'did study where his sword . . . might be': the form of the verb is emphatic, which is unexpected. It is, however, better than the continuous form *was studying* because the king expected to find his sword immediately, but was frustrated; *did* implies his expectation of instantaneous satisfaction, the sword in his hand, and so on, but this instantaneous *did* is converted to a strained continuous *did study* to express his frustration.

It would not be too difficult to carry this kind of exposition right through to the end of the poem. It would only confirm us in the impression that Berryman was writing with authority in the Pound-Eliot tradition. To see in what way this is inappropriate we must look further into the general nature of *The Dream Songs*.

The poem comprises seven Books altogether, and there are seven epigraphs. Each epigraph, I believe, applies generally to the poem but more particularly to one of its Books. The epigraph for Book II would certainly underline Berryman's modernist affinities: Lamentations 3. 63 '. . . I am their musick.'

The phrase is worth quoting in its Biblical context:

> O Lord, thou hast seen my wrong: judge thou my cause.
> Thou hast seen all their vengeance and all their imaginations against me.
> Thou hast heard their reproach, O Lord, and all their imaginations against me;
> The lips of those that rose up against me, and their device against me all the day.
> Behold their sitting down, and their rising up; I am their musick.

This epigraph seems to say: 'I am what society has made of me.' In such an age as this, the poet cannot be expected to produce a poetry of conventional beauty; the enemies of the imagination, the possessors of evil imagination, have with their 'imaginations' come near to ruin the poet, and the music that is his, that springs from his inmost being and may be identical with it, is theirs, and reflects the nature of their hostile, gross civilization.

Yes: there is an element of the reactionary in Berryman: we may find evidence for it elsewhere, in Song 105, for example— 'Let's have a King/maybe, before a few mindless votes'—or the notes for Song 245: 'our contempt for our government is mildly traditional, as represented by the communistic fascists Mark Twain, Stephen Crane, Edmund Wilson, and other mad-dogs.' Of course, he is ironic at the expense of his own reactionary sentiments and those of other 'communistic fascist' 'mad-dogs'. You cannot sum him up in the word; yet it does stand for an important side of his work, one that could link, though not to the extent of common political cause, with Pound, Eliot or Wyndham Lewis.

To believe the sort of thing implied by his Biblical epigraph has in practice involved a belief in a previous golden age, the end of which was marked for Eliot by the dissociation of sensibility and the English Civil War, but which came slightly earlier in history for Pound, who thought in terms of European rather than English consciousness. Poets who share this kind of belief can with difficulty avoid nostalgia for an over-decorated version of the past; they tend to retreat from the actual even as as they seem to be measuring up to it, and in so doing they run the risk of exaggerating the awfulness of the present age as much as the fine qualities of the past.

This is true of the early Berryman at any rate. 'The Ball Poem', for example, which Alvarez included in his anthology, is not a poem concerned with history, but it does draw the kind of sharp dividing line between a tremulously innocent sensibility and the tough indifference of 'maturity' in the world of money and possessions that goes with the way of looking at history implied by the Eliot-Pound view:

> An ultimate shaking grief fixes the boy
> As he stands rigid, trembling, staring down
> All his young days into the harbour where
> His ball went.

In its way it shares a nostalgic sentiment with the Dream Song we have already looked at; and yet, very obviously, it it not 'new' in the sense that the Dream Song is. It is a surprising poem to find in an anthology of 'the new poetry': there is nothing very new, for example, in its debt to Hopkins (who seems to have exercised a large influence on Berryman altogether). The poem is close in feeling to *Spring and Fall:*

> Margaret, are you grieving
> Over Goldengrove unleaving?
> Leaves, like the things of man, you
> With your fresh thoughts care for, can you?

A phrase like 'the epistemology of loss', which comes later in the poem, is, however, more like Auden. I dare say one could trace further influences if one wished. Almost all Berryman's early poems are reminiscent of someone or the other, as he now admits.

Dream Song 33 is superior to 'The Ball Poem' because its excessive feeling is not so obviously there, in the poem, all the way through, though it certainly is there—the poem ends extravagantly with an evocation of some total grief from which no one, you might think, could ever be roused: 'Weeping & blood/would round his one friend.' On the other hand, the poem does not go so far as to *say* that the weeping and blood must stay with the king (or Henry) for ever; the totality of the grief may be qualified by a striving to overcome it which, even if not successful, could still represent a positive value in the life left to be lived. Although the Song ends on an excessive note, that is, because it ends there, the possibility remains that the excessiveness might be tempered in some steadier sequel to the poem.

107

'The Ball Poem' does not allow for this possibility: it is throughout permeated by despair, for despair is its *raison d'être*.

The kind of feeling at work in 'The Ball Poem' is undoubtedly disturbing. 'An ultimate shaking grief' is too strong for what is shown. The boy's grief is supposed to be *ultimate* because the loss of his ball in the harbour marks, by his consciousness of its irredeemable nature, his transition to manhood: 'He is learning . . . how to stand up,' the poem says. But a reader might reasonably doubt whether he has enough evidence to agree that this is so. He is told that the boy is 'staring down/All his young days into the harbour' and the construction has a double meaning; partly it is like *staring down* a corridor: his 'young days' separate him from the harbour, and he realises that they have distanced him from the harbour to which they now lead—he has been apart from the world of loss and possession until this moment, when an understanding of the way things are worked for, paid for and manipulated comes upon him; and partly he is *staring* his days *down*, as though he were forcing his youth and the memory of it into the water with the ball as he gazes at the point where it lies, irretrievable. Can eyes, though, be so expressive? It is hard to believe in this boy's real existence —in which case we feel that something of a fraud is being practised. If Berryman just feels *like* his imaginary and insubstantial boy, why doesn't he say so like a man, and spare us the elaborate and unconvincing window-dressing of boy, ball and harbour? The poet does, after all, want us to trust him, to rely on his sympathy for people, but what in this poem would justify that? It is hardly notable for the qualities of observation that ought to back up such a claim.

In fact, rather than create solidarity with him, Berryman manages to alienate the reader, for example, in his use of the archaic 'merrily' to describe the ball as it bounces:

> I saw it go
> Merrily bouncing, down the street, and then
> Merrily over—there it is in the water!

JOHN BERRYMAN: AN INTRODUCTION

It is difficult to feel that the man who says that is one of us. We are aware of him at a distance from us, cut off, isolated; the dependence on Hopkins and Auden, and the archaic gesture contribute to this impression. Furthermore, our feeling that the author is isolated by literature or the idea of it can be extended to account for the nature of the feelings expressed. *Of course* he sentimentalizes childhood; it represents the only available point of contact with other people for a man who is now out of touch with them. This sentimentalization is a parallel to the circumscribed, less harmful *critical* sentimentalization of Cavalcanti in Pound, or of Donne in Eliot.

There are, then, a number of ways in which Berryman might be linked with the modernist poets. But these do not really go to the heart of the matter. They result in a generally limiting judgement on the poet's quality, and though they point to particular kinds of local excellence, they do not help to locate Berryman's *characteristic* goodness.

The central line of investigation leads straight into the question of style. Both Dream Song 33 and 'The Ball Poem' are in this respect offensive to conventional aesthetic criteria.

In 'The Ball Poem', for example, there is an obtrusive discrepancy between the moralizing tones of the speaker and the rhetorically 'low' object upon which he moralizes: consider the repetition of the word *ball* in these lines:

> He senses first responsibility
> In a world of possessions. People will take balls,
> Balls will be lost always, little boy,
> And no one buys a ball back. Money is external.

It only serves to emphasize the lurch from talk of responsibility to talk of balls and the lurch out of that way of talking back to the high seriousness of the externality of money. The poet's aim appears to be to emphasize the gap between the particular incident and the ineffectual generalizations it provokes. This is disturbing because we expect a successful form of address to be appropriate, ironically or unironically, to its occasion, and this is neither.

There is a similar discrepancy in our Dream Song. What are the extremely artificial exclamations *ha* and *ah* doing there? Why on earth rhyme on them? Surely they are irritating distractions from the account of Clitus's death? Much of the distortion of language is justifiable, but surely not all: for example, 'An un-Greek word/blister, to him his guard.' *Blister* is a puzzle: it could be either a noun ('a word like a blister') or a verb, plural for singular, as often happens in *The Dream Songs* ('a word swells out of him like a blister' or 'a harsh word raises blisters or an effect painful as blisters'). Whatever it means, the problem to which the word gives rise tends to divert attention from the subject of the poem to its style. The style is awkwardly obtrusive, and we should offer an explanation for this if we want to understand Berryman or to rationalize our admiration for him.

Trying to form a view of Berryman's literary personality as a whole, we come across an associated difficulty: in his prose the style is elegantly, yet just as insistently, obtrusive. Take for example, this fragment of a description of the Taj Mahal, published in 1961:

'The tombs blaze, austere. Large, his larger, higher by a little, ascending through their terraced rectangles to the crowning casket-shapes that would hold, each, one of the bodies, they bulk to us in brilliant gloom, their black and reddish floral inlays in the rigid gray-white marble, alive as not before. Half a small cylinder, recumbent, supercrowns his.'

This is literature, brilliant, deliberate, exclusive and *stylish*. Words are chosen with care and delight, then with discrimination placed one against another. The care is important; Berryman *cares* to care. It is his tribute to his subject.

But it is also a way of thinking: this becomes plain when one reads further in his miscellaneous prose. Here, by the way of contrast, is a moment from a story called 'The Lovers' which was published in 1945. It is written throughout in a very

mannered prose, but a piece of dialogue, less remarkable than
the narrative in style, is just as instructive as any more obvious
example. The story contrasts a world of moneyed glamour, to
which the narrator belonged in his adolescence, with a single
unnamed visitor to his parents who does not, or will not, 'fit in'.
He comes to the end-of-season masquerade in everyday dress,
and refuses to dance. The narrator remonstrates with him:

' "I am in danger," he said looking down at me seriously.

I was puzzled or angry: "You keep out of everything, don't
you?"

"Keep out?" he was startled. "Here I am: I came! But the
arrangements are not mine."

His answer, although I did not try to make it out, touched
another bitterness in me. "Is that why you haven't got a
costume on?"

He smiled: "I have. I wear it against danger." '

Quite so: the danger of masquerades and that kind of romantic
folly. The symbolic intent is obvious; the visitor is man become
conscious that 'the arrangements are not mine'. His wisdom
belongs to the alienated; it is what the other people in fancy
dress cannot face up to. Yet what a fancy way of putting it! Not
for a moment would we imagine that this was a really possible
encounter between a boy and a man whose knowledge of the
world was in any way to be admired. Just as much as the Taj
Mahal passage, this is Literature; and it suffers by the fact,
because we feel that the author's attention is divided—what he
has to say needs to be said more urgently: alternatively, his way
of saying it would be better employed on less dramatic con-
frontations, since it has the power of self-consciousness to turn
drama to melodrama.

Berryman's prose style suggests a way of thinking, and also
an aspiration. On the one hand, it says to the semi-literate:
'Keep off! Literature is not for you'; on the other, it says to the
man of culture: 'Would that the world were as stylish as my
prose!' This kind of distinction is made clearly in an essay on
Scott Fitzgerald published in *The Kenyon Review:*

'A division between intellectual and popular culture, between the million semi-literate and the hundred more or less educated, between the standards of *Collier's* and the standards of *The Dial*, is a natural division'. It is certainly one that, in the allusiveness and difficulty of his verse, and in the often superficial sophistication of his prose, Berryman successfully propagates. Writing both, he maintains a complex cultural ideal at least partly by keeping people—'semi-literate' people—out of the part of literature which is in his care—a desperate stratagem. (The weakness of this attitude would seem to lie in the notion that a cultural tradition can be maintained in isolation from the society which nurtured it. Perhaps this accounts for some of the excessive feeling in Berryman: he feels, as well as writes, in a cultural vacuum, and lack of sympathy with the 'semi-literate' leaves him little opportunity to extend his observation of how others actually do feel. Cultural desperation tends to spread into other realms as a consequence. However, it is easy to exaggerate the extent to which this is true.)

The prose style is careful and deliberate, but it does not discriminate much. It is a means of working on the reader and a means of realizing the writer to himself. Its deficiency lies on the side of reason. That is why one feels it to be indicative of a way of thought (of an aspiration for an impossibly pure, dead culture); that is why it is possible to consider it as imprisoning, something unwilled as well as willed.

In his early poems as well as in his prose, Berryman gives the impression of being at the mercy of his style, at once enormously expressive and yet expressive only of other men's ways of looking at the world. 'The Lovers' is a case to the point. Scott Fitzgerald, Henry James and Hawthorne conspire to keep Berryman out; the author exists, like a bankrupt with the bailiffs in, only peripherally, in the margins of the story. The same is true of the poems before *Mistress Bradstreet*: Hopkins, Yeats, Auden and others elbow him out of the way; he is there, but subservient to others, a prisoner in his own poetry, a prisoner, indeed, of Literature.

JOHN BERRYMAN: AN INTRODUCTION

There is irony in this, that literature, which promises a freedom of the imagination at least, should fetter a writer as it does Berryman. Dream Song 364 touches on the point:

> O Henry in his youth read many things:
> he gutted the Columbia & the Cambridge libraries
> & Widener & Princeton
> & the British Museum & the Library of Congress
> but mostly he bought books to have as his own
> cunningly, like extra wings . . .

The wings did not, after all, allow Berryman to fly—at least, not in things like 'The Ball Poem'. Later, he seems to be trying for two things at once—by complicating his verse with Empsonian ambiguities and allusion to give it a meaning complex enough to counterbalance his thin literary personality, and by insulting literary decorum to establish his freedom from it.

That, at least, describes the style of his *Sonnets* accurately. They tell the story of a disastrous love affair, a married man's passion for somebody else's wife; they are frankly, painfully, personal. The sonnet should, for such subject-matter, be the appropriate form; Petrarch, Sidney, Shakespeare have made it so. But Berryman's note is *worry*, a setting of the teeth on edge:

> How can I sing, western & dry & thin,
> You who for celebration should cause flow
> The sensual fanfare of D'Annunzio,
> Mozart's mischievous joy, the amaranthine
> Mild quirks of Marvell, Villon sharp as tin
> Solid as sword-death when the man blinks slow
> And accordions into the form he'll know
> Forever—voices can nearly make me sin
> With envy, so they sound.
>
> (Sonnet 32)

Envy is not the only feeling they can arouse—there is also a sense of superfluity to be evoked, a sense of emptiness before past achievement and present chaos. Berryman's own style hovers between mastery, the mastery of the sentence as it builds up its own 'fanfare' of names in a ripple of syntactic and verbal effects (as in the conjunction of 'when the man blinks slow/*And accordions* . . . ') and oddity, an unhappy, deliberate quirkiness ('so they sound'). Indeed, the style exists to display this unhappiness, to put us face to face with it; it is an un-happiness which literature can neither solace nor express, the trivial and humiliating ugliness or pettiness of misery that the pattern of literature has not accommodated in Petrarch or Sidney or Shakespeare.

Can so much be deduced from a single awkwardness—'so they sound'? I think so, but I am depending, of course, on the repetition of this sort of thing throughout the *Sonnets*. One further example here must serve for many—the sestet of Sonnet 62:

> What makes yóu then this ominous wide blade
> I'd run from O unless I bleat to die?
> Nothing: you are not: woman blonde, called Lise.
> It is I lope to be your sheep, to wade
> Thick in my cordial blood, to howl and sigh
> As I decide . . . if I could credit this.

Berryman, in these lines, sustains an idiom close to Hopkins's, and yet not quite his, a surprising, passionate, interesting use of language, capable of Empsonian analysis, especially where Lise is exonerated from the charge of being an instrument of his suffering by her own wish. 'Nothing: you are not . . .'—not 'this ominous wide blade,' that is; but also *not*: 'You are *not*; you do not exist truly for me, when I feel like this about you.' Yet this idiom is deliberately dropped at the end; 'if I could credit this' with its neat, dull rhythm, does not exactly cancel the baroque and literary grandeur of what precedes it, but does question it, as it declares the poet's own ability to question whether he is or can be the lamb brought willingly to slaughter that he has just, eloquently, declared himself to be.

Berryman's Sonnets are the most accessible of his writings to our present ways of thought about literature. We understand easily that a poet might wish, in the way that I have suggested, to write about the awkward gap between the rich consistency of literature and the quality of life itself, which seems at times intent on denying that complementary richness. Perhaps we can understand too easily; there is something obvious, something monotonous about the device. Our response can quickly become stereotyped, and it is helped to become so by the fact that so much of what Berryman is talking about is insubstantial, born of illusion and obsession, felt as true, but equivocally true.

Nevertheless, the *Sonnets* illustrate perfectly Berryman's special use of style to suggest an imprisoning structure of feeling, and the way in which such structures can be undermined (' . . . if I could credit this'). *Homage to Mistress Bradstreet* and *The Dream Songs* extend the practice of the *Sonnets* by making the precise nature of their attack on 'literary' consistency varied and unpredictable. Reviewing 77 *Dream Songs* in *The London Magazine*, Ian Hamilton found in them 'a silly relish in the dis- ordering of syntax . . . ' He is describing from another point of view the sort of thing in general stylistic terms which has already been discussed—what I would call the *superfluous oddity* of Berryman's style, the source of its offensiveness. This quality is calculated, I think, on the supposition that what is superfluous to the conventional demands of literature may establish a means of personal expression and communication with the reader, something that cannot, as yet, be contaminated by the student's desire to incorporate all literature into some vast and inoffensive system of conventions.

It is no accident that the student and the teacher of literature figure so prominently in Berryman's poems: they are for him the context, metaphorically and literally (because he is himself a teacher), of what he writes. Because that context is to him

115

distasteful, we can take it that the self-description in Sonnet 53 *'Ermite-amateur* among the boobs' is one that he would accept to be generally true of him and any real poet practising now.

The students of literature are boobs for many reasons. A lot of them are only 'semi-literate'—like the class in Song 105:

> we'd time for one long novel: to a vote—
> *Gone with the Wind* they voted: I crunched 'No'
> and we sat down with *War & Peace.*

But even the people capable of 'literacy' sin in their way against literature—for example, the teachers who maintain that 'a poem should not mean but be' and so manage to accommodate a poet's ideas, whether Yeats's faith in reincarnation or Pound's mystic aestheticism, to systems of thought fundamentally unquestioning and undemanding in their view of things.

Especially in America the symbolist ideal of poetry has come to dominate the reader's expectations. (After all, it is what lies behind Yeats, Eliot and Pound.) In symbolist poetry there is an aspiration to remove the poetic experience altogether from the context of human life. The poem is to *have* no message; it is to be its own message. In Mallarmé's words: 'Out of a number of words poetry fashions a single new word which is total in itself and foreign to the language—a kind of incantation'.

It is obvious from what we have seen of Berryman's poetry so far, however, that he does have things to say: his poetry obstinately insists on having its roots in brute reality, and it does so by the excessive nature of its emotions. Like the superfluous oddity of his style (the 'ah' and 'ha' of Song 33, for example) it works to thwart the professional explicators, for whom all is grist to the mill, and to allow a scarifying, immediate contact with the reader. In this, the major sense, Berryman writes far and away from, indeed in reaction to, the modernist tradition of Pound and Eliot.

English poets have tended to react against modernism in a different way from Berryman. It has been possible for them to

revert to pre-modernist forms of writing—one thinks of Larkin
and the conventional form of *New Lines* poets like Donald Davie
and Thom Gunn. The other reaction has been to form a style
that is aggressively personal: this is what Lowell has done, and
also Berryman. But whereas (as Gabriel Pearson brilliantly
shows) Lowell's whole effort has been to *encounter* the public
life, Berryman has occupied himself with the perilous defence of
individuality and idiosyncrasy in the age of democratic semi-
literacy. In Berryman's case, too, the irritating possibility that
after all 'books are a load of crap' has been pushed as far as it can
go: Song 14 is the ultimate affront to the English departments,
the close readers and the systematising theoreticians of art:

> Peoples bore me,
> literature bores me, especially great literature,
> Henry bores me, with his plights & gripes
> as bad as achilles,
> who loves people and valiant art, which bores me.

These things *are* boring, though, as long as we manage to seal
literature off from life—as the world's many departments of
English do for the most part manage. *The Dream Songs* want to
leap out of the world of 'art' into life itself; their own art is an
art that rejects 'art' and the Literature of Berryman's early
poems.

In other words, the sort of poetry that Berryman has been
writing for the last fifteen years or so is of a special kind, one
that he has himself described for us in his book, *Stephen Crane*.
What he says about Crane's poems, in particular that 'they are
not like literary compositions,' has the utmost relevance to our
own discussion:

'The poems have an enigmatic air and yet they are desperately
personal. The absence of the panoply of the Poet is striking. We
remember that their author did not like to be called a poet nor
did he call them poetry himself. How unusual this is, my
readers will recognize: most writers of verse are merely dying

to be called poets, tremblingly hopeful that what they write is real "poetry". There was no pose here in Crane. His reluctance was an inarticulate recognition of something strange in the pieces. They are like things just seen and said, *said for use.*' (pp. 272–73).

That is also what *The Dream Songs*, 'enigmatic,' 'desperately personal' and 'not like literary compositions' are—things *said for use*

> If we sang in the wood (and Death is a German expert)
> while snows flies, chill, after so frequent knew
> so many all of nothing,
> for lead & fire, it's not we would assert
> particulars, but animal; cats mew,
> horses scream, man sing.
>
> (Dream Song 41)

The point about this poem is that it is perfectly comprehensible *despite* the distortions of syntax. One might, perhaps, be able to explain why *snows flies* has a peculiar effectiveness after *we sang*, but any such talk would be irrelevant to what the poem is saying: that poetry is man's natural cry, and a cry of pain; that it has little to do with the Poundian accretion of *particulars*; and that Eliot was totally wrong in saying that 'the only way of expressing emotion in the form of art is by finding an "objective correlative"; in other words, a set of objects, a situation, a chain of events which shall be the formula of that *particular* emotion . . .' None of *The Dream Songs* is a 'formula', or seeks a perfection that Mallarmé would have recognized. These poems are cries of different kinds—not incantations. They are more truly 'song', the more unashamedly they reflect what is *human*. The saving factor in our life, they suggest, is the determination not to give in to circumstance, which leads us to convert our cries to song, as the murdered Jews in the wood did. The poet, traditionally most vulnerable of men, is our sign of hope—he makes songs. All must suffer: some men can wrest suffering to the good purposes of poetry.

> Or: men psalm. Man palms his ears and moans.
> Death is a German expert. Scrambling, sitting,
> spattering, we hurry.
> I try to. Odd & trivial, atones
> somehow for *my* escape a bullet splitting
> my trod-on instep, fiery.

I try to hurry and to psalm; the poet is both in the muck and killing, and out of it, because he can sing. But as a singer he is doomed to perpetual suffering of a different kind—the pain of Philoctetes, wounded in the foot and exiled from the war. His song must always be as 'odd & trivial' as the wound, because it is overshadowed by the forces that have made it. In a discussion of Lowell's poem, 'Skunk Hour', Berryman catalogues the dangers of poetry—madness and suicide—and reminds us that

'Wordsworth once said that if he had written what he most deeply felt no reader could have borne it, Coleridge that he gave up original poetic composition . . . because he was unable to bear it.'

The Dream Songs owe their disquieting force to the extent to which the poet exposes his suffering and to the extent to which our own capacity to bear is tested.

In other words, and despite all appearances, these poems are not hermetic in intention; they seek to *expose* the poet's most remote level of consciousness, to present the reader with the kind of experiences Berryman believes and feels to be behind the superficies of life, but which we are ordinarily content to ignore. This partly involves a descent into the world of dreams, since these represent the furthest extensions of consciousness, the point where unconscious mental processes make themselves tentatively available to our understanding. It also entails the formulation of an attitude to life which can be illuminated by further reference to Berryman's critical writing, this time his essay on Scott Fitzgerald. He speaks there of an attitude in Fitzgerald's work not far removed from what we found in Dream Song 41:

'a view of life in which the creature's supreme admiration is commanded by that which the artist knows to be *wrong*, in which the supreme allegiance is forced to be felt—producing "creative passion"—toward a hopeless error.'

The poet's song is the sign of 'creative passion', product of his wrong-headed faith in life (Death always wins against Life). In similar fashion, the obstinate desire for Lise in the *Sonnets* produced poetry; the poetry springs from a desire to cry out, which in turn derives from an obstinate refusal to accept the inevitable supremacy of circumstance.

It has been suggested that there is something wrong with the *Sonnets*, a want of variety in the poems, of a kind very easy to fall into for someone writing out of an extreme situation. The coherent narrative structure of *Homage to Mistress Bradstreet* shows his determination to avoid that kind of monotony. Indeed, whilst the central cry of despairing isolation comes over as clearly as ever—

> I cannot feel myself God waits. He flies
> nearer a kindly world; or he is flown.
> One Saturday's rescue
> won't show. Man is entirely alone
> maybe.

—whilst that note is just as audible, it is made more moving because it contrasts sharply with the crowded life of Anne Bradstreet who is, nevertheless, just as lonely herself. Because it includes much more of the world of children and neighbours than the *Sonnets*, and because Anne's loneliness is seen and felt to coexist with that world, year in, year out, the delirious feeling associated with it cannot be dismissed as *merely* delirium, as it can in the *Sonnets*.

The poet's involvement with literature, too, here seems more solid, because the poem is evolved from the contemplation of it, and a proper attitude to it is clearly implied. Anne's poems are important not because they are critically or historically valuable (her verse is 'all this bald/abstract didactic rime I read appalled' and when Berryman loses sight of *her* he is 'drowning in this *past*') but because they record an aspiration, a cry to which the reader can respond, like Berryman. Poetry is the sign of *caring:*

> We are on each other's hands
> who care. Both of our worlds unhanded us.

The pun on *unhanded* ('cast us off' and 'deprived us of the means of living contact') and its counterpoint with *on each other's hands* emphasizes the difficulty of such a response as the poem imagines and yet declares possible. A critic trained in the academies and shackled by them might think that *care* refers to the poet's craft, the love which is dedicated to the poem's shaping; but this is only the sign of another, transcendent *care*, the desire to live fully, that finds its expression in Anne's anguished admission to the twentieth-century poet's ghostly presence: 'I *want* to take you for my lover.'

We find also a greater appropriateness in the odd style of the narrative poem. Berryman no longer relies on the single device of changes in style that we have glanced at in the *Sonnets*; he now employs a style that is homogeneous in its oddity, expressive both of the things described and of the distance stretching between Berryman the poet who records them and Anne the poet who experiences them, as here, where Anne is imagined talking about her children:

> And they tower, whom the pear-tree lured
> to let them fall, fierce mornings they reclined
> down the brook-bank to the east
> fishing for shiners with a crookt pin,
> wading, dams massing, well, and Sam's to be
> a doctor in Boston.

The children *tower* and grow tall; they escape the perils of infancy. The word is careful, deliberate, *not* self-explanatory. It suggests a contrast with *let them fall*—that is the sign of Berryman's 'care'. It suggests that Anne feels in some way threatened by her enormous brood—that is the sign of *her* 'care'. The sentence permits the reader no dwelling on the word —that is the sign we are not to prostrate ourselves merely before the poet's art.

The Dream Songs substitute Berryman's own life for that of Anne Bradstreet as a means of anchoring the poems to the world of reality. This is not to say that they are primarily 'about' his life. Berryman categorically denies this in the note to *His Toy, His Dream, His Rest*; he says there that

'The poem, then, whatever its wide cast of characters, is essentially about an imaginary character (not the poet, not me) named Henry, a white American in early middle age sometimes in the first person, sometimes in the third, sometimes even in the second . . . '

Essentially, the poems are about Henry; but it is hard not to feel that they are also, and less importantly, about the poet. The poems about poets—Randall Jarrell and Delmore Schwartz among them—are poems about dear and close friends of the poet. *His Toy, His Dream, His Rest* is dedicated to Mark Van Doren and 'to the sacred memory of Delmore Schwartz'. Henry's trip to Ireland in the seventh book parallels a visit paid there by Berryman at about the time (one guesses) the poems were being written.

It is obvious that Berryman wants to dissociate himself from *The Dream Songs* in the way he does because they are not for him in any important sense autobiographical. I would not want to suggest that that is so any more than he does. The poem *is* essentially about Henry. But he, I think, is an imaginary self of the poet—not the 'real' Berryman, but one of the persons he is used to seeing when he looks at himself, one of the many Berrymans who could, for example, appear and act in his dreams. *The Dream Songs* are more like the *Sonnets* than *Homage to Mistress Bradstreet* in that their world is one of frequent delusion. In the *Sonnets* it is often hard to judge the *substantiality* of the feelings expressed (their intensity is obvious); in *The Dream Songs* it is often impossible even to tell who is speaking. Yet more of the 'real' world comes through in *The Dream Songs*; the doubt is continually present that after all the speaker may not be Berryman's *persona*, Henry, but Berryman himself.

The doubt is necessary; it exposes us to a force of feeling in the poems from which conventional responses would protect us, if, that is, the poems used conventional forms in a thoroughgoing manner. Paradoxically, our uncertainty about what precisely is happening makes it possible for us to feel whatever it is:

> These Songs are not meant to be understood, you
>   understand.
> They are only meant to terrify and comfort.
>
> (Dream Song 366)

It is plain in what way the form of *The Dream Songs* aptly reflects terror, the causes of which are well summed up in the job-hunting conferences of the Modern Languages Association, the waste land of appreciation of *The Waste Land*, where 'only deals go screwing/some of you out, some up—the chairmen too/are nervous, little friends.' Contemporary American civilization spells death to poets; and the death of poets (Robert Frost, Delmore Schwartz, Randall Jarrell, T. S. Eliot, among many) recurringly evokes the most anguished cries. 'The poet can be made helpless by what is part of his strength: his strangeness, mental and emotional,' Berryman has said; the poet is, in any case predisposed to neurosis by his intense sympathy for those who suffer. This predisposition conspires with his environment to hasten the poet's death, or to make his life a living death. *The Dream Songs* are about the point where popular culture has become an intolerable pressure on the already hard-pressed culture of the intellectual—one who has, personally, suffered 'an irreversible loss'.

It has been suggested that Henry is an 'imaginary self' of the poet. It might be truer to call him the poet's *better* self. Henry represents a vulnerable, innocent and childish self which must be saved from the attacks of an impertinent and hostile world outside—

> For the rats
> have moved in, mostly, and this is for real.
> (Dream Song 7)

He must also be saved from the hallucinations of his own guilt in relation to other people. The dreams which are the subject-matter of *The Dream Songs* are Henry's—they are also Berryman's dreams about Henry. The ambiguity is calculated and masterly.

Some further light on the dream element in these poems is cast by another passage from the book on Stephen Crane; for in discussing Crane's poetry Berryman establishes a polarity of dream on the one hand and style, our cardinal term, on the other. He does so in developing an account of the origin of poetry found in Robert Graves:

'A savage dreams, is frightened by the dream, and goes to the medicine man to have it explained. The medicine man can make up anything, anything will reassure the savage, so long as the manner of its delivery is impressive . . . Poetry begins—as a practical matter, for *use*. It reassures the savage. Perhaps he only/hears back again, chanted, the dream he has just told the medicine man, but he is reassured; it is like a spell . . . Now Crane's poetry is like a series of primitive anti-spells. Sometimes he chants, but for the most part on principle he refuses to . . . Crane just says, like a medicine man *before* chanting or poetry began. Man's vanity and cruelty, hypocrisy and cowardice, stupidity and pretension, hopelessness and fear, glitter through the early poems.' (p. 273).

Berryman explains the delay in recognition of Crane's merits as a poet in this way:

'I take the steady drift of our period toward greater and

greater self-consciousness, an increasing absorption in *style*, to be what has obscured the nature of his work and delayed its appreciation.' (p. 275: my italics).

Finally, what he has to say about Crane becomes entirely applicable to his own latest work:

'The poetry, then, *has* the character of a "dream", something seen naively, in a new relation. It *is* barbaric, and so primitively blunt that one sees without difficulty how it can be thought a trick. But tricks are not this simple. And tricks can be learned; [Crane's cannot] . . . Crane was not only a man with truths to tell, but an interested listener to this man. His poetry has the inimitable sincerity of a frightened savage anxious to learn what his dream means.' (p. 277).

One of the most intense moments in *Homage to Mistress Bradstreet* must also be associated with the idea of dream in *The Dream Songs*; it is the poet's most desperate cry across the centuries to Anne:

> I suffered living like a stain:
> I trundle the bodies, on the iron bars,
> over that fire backward & forth; they burn;
> bits fall. I wonder if
> *I* killed them. Women serve my turn.
> —Dreams! You are good.—No.

The poet insists that these are not dreams, at least not 'mere' dreams; he asserts his complicity in murder, maintains that Hell is not so much other people as ourselves. By not resisting to the full the ways of the world that made, for example, Hitler's murder of the Jews possible, we become in part responsible for those deaths. The price of compromise with society is the toleration of wrong on a more or less obvious scale, and the visitation of guilt in our dreams. Dreams tell the truth, and it is unpalatable, about the extent of our love, our hatred, and our guilt:

But never did Henry, as he thought he did,
end any one and hacks her body up
and hides the pieces, where they may be found.
He knows: he went over everyone, & nobody's missing.
Often he reckons, in the dawn, them up.
Nobody is ever missing.

(Dream Song 29)

It is not much consolation that dreams are not the product of consciousness, if one is driven *often* to reckon up the living, *often* to find that, after all, 'nobody is missing.' 'A dream is a panorama/of the whole mental life' (Song 327); it is not lightly to be shrugged off.

Yet living is living with one's guilt; there are still things to be done. Henry's father committed suicide: he was not right. The last two songs of all are poised one against another, as final attempt to present life as worth the living. Song 384 gives us Henry's enduring rage at the father who deserted him:

I'd like to scrabble till I got right down
away down under the grass

and ax the casket open ha to see
just how he's taking it, which he sought so hard
        . . . & then Henry
will heft the ax once more, his final card,
and fell it on the start.

'Better never to have been born': but, being alive, one must answer, after all, one's responsibilities:

My daughter's heavier. Light leaves are flying.
Everywhere in enormous numbers turkeys will be dying
and other birds, all their wings.
They never greatly flew. Did they wish to?
I should know. Off away somewhere once I knew
such things.

Growing up, the little girl gets heavier, less able to fly, feels a little more the weight that life is placng on her. She is like the turkeys: fattening for death; perhaps they never wanted to fly much, to exercise their freedom.

> Fall is grievy, brisk. Tears behind the eyes
> almost fall. Fall comes to us as a prize
> to rouse us toward our fate.

Fall is the autumn setting of the poem, but also the latter part of life, as well as man's share of guilt, by allusion to Genesis. It does not, however, compel our every action: tears can be held back. Approaching death, the autumn season of life comes 'as a prize', the pressure reduces; we are roused to action as we are roused to come to terms with death, and with our sense of guilt.

> If there were a middle   ground between things and the soul
> or if the sky resembled more the sea,
> I wouldn't have to scold
>
>   my heavy daughter.

It is because we are torn squarely between our fate ('things'— death, guilt, sorrow, 'the sea') and our belief in our freedom to choose ('the soul'—whatever finds death abhorrent, whatever understands guilt *as* guilt, 'the sky') that we see a need to 'scold' and to show our feelings responsibly, believingly. There is no *middle* ground: eventually one has to choose, and choose that *ambiguous* ground where scolding is the sign of our love.

The Dream Songs record the painful process of an acceptance of the way the world is. The conclusion is muted, and properly so; we understand why. But the poems are nevertheless in Whitman's vein: they seek to embrace all there is:

> These were enough for him
> implying commands from upstairs & from down,

Walt's 'orbic flex', triads of Hegel would
incorporate, if you please,

into the know-how of the American bard
embarrassed Henry heard himself a-being . . .
                                                    (Dream Song 78)

The *triads of Hegel* identify the process by which *The Dream
Songs* attempt the impossible synthesis of 'things and the soul';
the process is made possible by a Whitmaniac submission to the
totality of experience, as in the twenty-sixth section of *Song of
Myself*, where the poet is filled by the world's music ('I am
their musick . . . '):

I hear the chorus, it is a grand opera,
Ah this indeed is music—this suits me.

A tenor large and fresh as the creation fills me,
The orbic flex of his mouth is pouring and filling me full.

I hear the train'd soprano (what work with hers is this?)
The orchestra whirls me wider than Uranus flies,
It wrenches such ardors from me I did not know I
                                    possess'd them.
It sails me, I dab with bare feet, they are lick'd by the
                                                    indolent waves,
I am cut by bitter and angry hail, I lose my breath,
Steep'd amid honey'd morphine, my windpipe throttled in
                                                    fakes of death,
At length let up again to feel the puzzle of puzzles,
And that we call Being.

Berryman's wild music, springing from and colliding with his
own life, is Whitman's 'barbaric yawp', but imbued with a more
intense consciousness of the 'fakes of death' as *his* America is
indeed closer to death:

JOHN BERRYMAN: AN INTRODUCTION

> I am the enemy of the mind.
> I am the auto salesman and I lóve you.
> I am a teenage cancer, with a plan.
> I am the blackt-out man.

As much as Lowell, Berryman is concerned with the health of America today, but where Lowell fights to keep poetry in the arena of public debate, Berryman withdraws into contemplation of the universal human, of each man's apprehension of death, for example; his subject is the individual at those moments in his life when he experiences what all must feel sooner or later.

The value of the poet's neurosis lies in its power to dissolve the compound of a sick situation back to its pure elements. As his hold on his own personality becomes less secure, the poet is increasingly able to identify with the perilous lives of others. Berryman has said: 'I am less impressed than I used to be by the universal notion of a continuity of individual personality . . .' Both *Homage to Mistress Bradstreet* and *The Dream Songs* are built around the notion that individual identities can merge. When the poet and Anne Bradstreet meet in the 'concord of our thought,' it is in a spiritual act of love, for 'Love has no body and presides the sun,' and in this form of love, one can solace the other. (Our 'heavy bodies' do not prevent us from flying, though it is a condition of flying that we should have bodies.) Similarly *The Dream Songs* are an expression of love for people, for the variety of the world, that does not overlook what is rotten in that world. The many different voices of *The Dream Songs* are to be contrasted with the unconscious mimicry of literary voices in the early poems: they represent the conclusive answer to the apparently overwhelming professorial force of Literature. It is an answer long meditated, however; the point about 'The Ball Poem' is that you cannot tell at the end of it whether it is Berryman's voice or the boy's that is speaking. (In *The Dream Songs* there are two forms of identification with people—the first is at the level of dream, where all men must suffer the enactment of the same psychic processes, the second is at the level of intention, and is made actual in the constant confusion of tense and person in the verbs used.)

The result of this identification with others is often humour, a humour achieved by suddenly switching from one kind of voice to another. The effect is simple:

> That isna Henry limping. That's a hobble
> clapped on mere Henry by the most high GOD
> for the freedom of Henry's soul.
>
> (Dream Song 113)

But it is devastating: the contrast between the two orders of speech (between *isna*, *hobble*, and *mere Henry*, and *the most high GOD*) is such that we feel they connect only fortuitously, and that linking a limp with the affairs of God is the sort of absurd thing only a man could do: but it is also the mark of how hard-pressed the creature is. Christopher Ricks, reviewing 77 *Dream Songs*, objected to the infantile nature of many of Berryman's jokes. This quality, though, is dramatically appropriate to the primitive level at which dreams are supposed to be enacted. And it is emotionally appropriate too, because it is expressive of a subdued hysteria. Finally, it is far from all infantile:

> —I can't read any more of this Rich Critical Prose,
> he growled, broke wind, and scratched himself & left
> that fragrant area.
>
> (Dream Song 170)

Perhaps it is rash to quote this. But then, one feels there is a certain kindliness available even to critics:

> Now back on down boys; don't expressed yourself,
> begged for their own sake sympathetic Henry.

Why should Berryman be severe? He has, after all, his

company of friends; he has his *Songs* completed; he has put his
faith, not in some literary perfection to be endlessly haggled
over, but in a life which he induces us to feel is worth the living.
He has his fateful solidarity with the poets who suffer; he has
also his solidarity with America, with its present and its past.
He has, too, his sense of place, his sense of identity with that
place:

> My house is made of wood and it's made well,
> unlike us. My house is older than Henry;
> that's fairly old.
>
> (Dream Song 385)

His *house* is his family (Henry is Henry House): it is made to
last, it is sounder than Henry. His 'heavy daughter' is well-
built like the house; she will survive, and survive better than he,
perhaps. It is appropriate that *The Dream Songs* should come to
rest on relationship within the family, source of our first guilt,
and yet, in a barbaric age, preserver of life. Berryman writes
for a barbaric age.

Evidently, it is not desirable that a reader should be guided
through *The Dream Songs* painlessly as thousands of students
are now shown through *The Waste Land* each year. Just as
evidently, the poem will be subjected to a process of analysis
and sifting more thorough than anything here. The directness
of its attack on a stultifying notion of Literature and its
embarrassing truth to feeling will nevertheless withstand the
assaults of the system-makers. So also will the mystery remain
of what can link grief with a calmer sight of things, though it is a
familiar one. We do leave behind, we can leave behind, one
mood, one self, for another:

> Henry's mind grew blacker the more he thought.
> He looked onto the world like the act of an aged whore.
> Delmore, Delmore.
> He flung to pieces and they hit the floor.

Nothing was true but what Marcus Aurelius taught,
'All that is foul smell & blood in a bag.'
(Dream Song 147)

We can pass from that to this:

> I see now all these deaths are to one end—
> whereby I lost a foe, friend upon friend—
> room.
(Dream Song 196)

Most consolingly, *The Dream Songs* are about continuity: about passing on, about death and the survival of death, about the continuity not of persons, but of things and ideas that enable us to survive our selves, our own lives. They help, too, to redeem an idea of literature consonant with our lives, and, like them, impure.

Ted Hughes

THE MOST confident English poetry of the late 1950s was about a lack of confidence. In fact much of it set out, with considerable skill, precisely to undermine confidence: unsettling the reader and leaving him with the uncertainties that the poet had experienced. Something of this purpose runs almost everywhere, for example, in the poetry of D. J. Enright at that time. Enright constantly tempts the reader into assent to some high-minded denunciation or renunciation; then deftly brings up an aspect of the matter that has been overlooked, leaving the reader gently exposed as having reacted in a silly and superficial—and, above all, an over-confident—way. (Kingsley Amis, another characteristic poet of the period, uses the same device in the opening of his novel *One Fat Englishman*, where he lures the reader into sympathy with the witty anti-Americanism of his hero, before going on to show up the vulgarity and pettiness of that attitude.) The exposures are made in the name of humanity, tolerance, commonsense—all of which virtues they do admirably foster. But there is also in these writers an unmistakable sense of powerlessness when faced with the more intense feelings and desires of men. It is a powerlessness they hardly acknowledge themselves, however, since another strong suggestion present in their teaching is that intense feelings and desires must—and generally can—be indiscriminately given up and healthily forgotten. Here is a major difference between, say, Enright and Amis on the one hand, and Philip Larkin on the other. Larkin's poetry is often equally concerned with doubt, or at any rate with the moment of faltering confidence. But Larkin is not interested in teaching the desirability of strict self-criticism and control. His poetry of doubt is an openly poignant affair, a full rendering of situations in which the protagonist's history of inner conflicts and failures has left him grievously bewildered or resigned. These poems, while often portraying a state of 'powerlessness', nonetheless offer the compensating strength of a full and steady imaginative understanding of that state and all the feeling it entails, both for the protagonist and for the observer in the form of the reader.

Larkin stands out, in this way, as the most considerable poet of the time. But it can be judged how, even in its distinctive superiority, his poetry seemed to partake of the period's prevailingly sceptical character. It is against that background that the appearance of Ted Hughes's first book *The Hawk in the Rain*, has to be seen. The book came out in 1957. At once it was evident that there was a gifted new poet on the scene who was prepared to make strong, confident assertions about the importance of strong—even confused or blind—feeling. And not only assertions; for the poems were often simply like assaults, designed to provoke the reader into vigorous—and in this poet's view, it seemed, perfectly healthy—responses of scarcely rational dismay or anger. *Lupercal* was the title of Hughes's second book, but what it suggests about the character of that volume could equally well be applied to *The Hawk in the Rain:* Lupercalia was a Roman festival at which the priests struck women to make them fertile.

One of the most tactically assured of these assaults is the poem in *The Hawk and the Rain*, 'October Dawn'.

> October is marigold, and yet
> A glass half full of wine left out
>
> To the dark heaven all night, by dawn
> Has dreamed a premonition

Of ice across its eye as if
The ice-age had begun its heave . . .

'Marigold'—the adjective is brilliantly judged to conjure up the
richly beautiful and benign character of the late autumn,
pervasive inasmuch as one colour can stand for that whole
character, yet as delicate and as unchallenging to human
mastery as the single flower that the word could also stand for.
And the second line of the same couplet, letting drop its defining
references to the glass in the course of its steady progress
towards the verb, throws out casually yet with perfect sureness
a perspective in which human figures, intimate but unnamed,
enjoy warmth, languor, carelessness, abundance. The 'dark
heaven' of the next line is the bridge to the threatening evocation
that the poem is, by contrast, going to be mainly concerned with.
The dark heaven might, in the glow from the marigold, also be
benign. But this suggestion is dispelled almost as soon as
raised: in fact the darkness prefigures the assault to come. The
ice is in fact the 'spearhead' of the returning ice-age.

The lawn overtrodden and strewn
From the night before

now suggests a scene not of careless pleasure but of panic-
stricken flight. As the couplets spell out the increasing grip of
ice on the land their half-rhymes mount a crescendo of creakings
and crackings; until finally we read

a fist of cold . . .

Squeezes the fire at the core of the heart,
And now it is about to start.

The rapping full rhyme of the last couplet brings the pre-
liminaries—the prophesying—sharply to an end, and simultaneously announces the beginning—left to the imagination— of
a new, more terrible monotony.

These effects are achieved with a masterly instinct. Yet, although the emotions and sensations created in one by the poem are sharp and memorable, to scrutinize them is, after all, to find doubts coming in. On a banal factual level, to begin with, a frosty night in October would certainly be a clear night with stars, not a night with a 'dark heaven': a small point, but, I think, quite proper to notice, for the reflecting mind cannot help noticing it. Then the fantasy itself, powerfully evoked though it is, is on an instant's consideration just a tale to frighten us, without giving us any genuine grounds for fear. The return of the Mammoth and the Sabre-tooth, and *their* party (without wine-glasses)—

> . . . Mammoth and Sabre-tooth celebrate
>
> Reunion . . . —

begin on reflection to take on a comic, nursery-rhyme aspect. In fact in the end one may begin to enjoy the poem again in a further way: as a witty example of the mock-sinister. But this appreciation continues to accord ill with the genuine feeling found at the beginning of the poem and the unmistakably seriously-intended—if unrewardingly vague—reference to 'the core of the heart' at the end.

Many of the assaults and arguments in *The Hawk in the Rain* are marked by this aggressive exaggeration that it is difficult after the first impact to take seriously, though one respects often in the same poems the justice—as it were, the sound theatrical imagination—with which the effects are managed: the impression the book made on its first appearance is wholly understandable. In 'The Dove Breeder' a full-rhyming four-stressed couplet again concludes the poem, this time with a statement that invites the reader to take up its crisp challenge. The earlier part of the poem describes, in unrhymed lines hovering between two and three stresses, how a hawk struck into a dovecote, and the effect it had on the dove-breeder. It is a sustained

metaphor for the way in which love has struck into a man's
life. The man's fate is elaborated with mock-sympathy:

> He will win no more prizes
> With fantails or pouters . . .

The metaphor—if by this point it has a strong enough connection with its subject to be called that—seems to allude to the
finicky, self-conscious relationships that have characterized
the man's life before the catastrophe, and perhaps also to
the conceited, coy women he has known. But there is a reversal
of fate for the better:

> Now he rides the morning mist
> With a big-eyed hawk on his fist.

The last couplet thrusts the man's final condition cockily,
almost insultingly, at the reader. It has a 'Go and do thou likewise *if thou canst!*' note about it. But if one should humbly ask
what this evidently far superior condition that is being flaunted
before one actually is, one has to put up with the fact that it is
very ill-elaborated: it is some strong, steady, confident—but
quite imprecisely rendered—emotional state. In the end the
picture of the now tamed hawk—big-eyed, as opposed presumably to the small-eyed pigeons—sitting on the fist of the smug
ex-breeder starts to take on a rather ludicrous air: who is the
fantail or pouter now? In fact, of the poems in *The Hawk in the
Rain* that aim to challenge or shock the reader, some which
deliberately practise a comic exaggeration are the most wholly
successful: like 'Soliloquy of a Misanthrope', which is hostile
precisely to complacent smirks, and rejoices in the way that
death forces its victims to recognize the undignified necessities
of the flesh:

> Whenever I am got under my gravestone . . .

. . . I shall thank God thrice heartily
To be lying beside women who grimace
Under the commitments of their flesh
And not out of spite or vanity.

Some poems in *The Hawk in the Rain* engage more specifically
in assertion and argument concerning the desirability of a
certain kind of emotional and moral life. Two that seem to be
presented as a pair, one following the other, are 'Egg-Head' and
'The Man Seeking Experience Enquires His Way of a Drop of
Water'. They are about two contrasting kinds of self-assertion,
that may remind us respectively of the way of life of the dove-
breeder before and after the hawk struck. 'Egg-Head' represents,
with explicit scorn, a man who establishes his individual
existence in the world (his 'I am') by resisting all those
experiences that might upset his settled and complacent ways.
The poem begins with a list of objects, from the sea-bottom and
the mountain peaks to a leaf, that might cause a man to be
'struck dead' at a glance. With a passing word of praise for
those who dare to undergo such an experience, it then turns to
describing the strategies of the resister, the egg-head—

circumventing sleights
Of stupefaction, juggleries of benumbing—

culminating in the need of the man's complacency to

. . . stop the looming mouth of the earth with a pin-
Point cipher . . .

. . . and, opposing his eye's flea-red
Fly-catching fervency to the whelm of the sun,
Trumpet his own ear dead.

The second poem is about a man who is supposed to be learning
a lesson from a water droplet—a lesson that the man in the

previous poem would obviously not listen to. To this man the
water-drop seems to show how it is possible to go through
extremes of experience and take full cognition of that experience
—at the same time, casting benefits about one—and survive
with unimpaired capacity to go on doing the same thing. The
droplet has been in the Pacific depths of the Tuscarora and in a
cup of tea, in the bodies of the sweating victor and the dead
bird, in

> The abattoir of the tiger's artery,
> The slum of the dog's bowel.

It has 'travelled far and studied hard' and

> there is no place
> His bright look has not bettered.

But when the man asks the droplet to 'read us a lesson', an
ironic note enters the poem. The man 'knows' his own nature is
'all droplet-kin'. But he has misjudged, at least in one respect.
There is no response from the water-drop, which is, rather, like
the new-born baby

> . . . who lies long, long and frowningly
> Unconscious under the shock of its own quick.

Here too, then, we find a comic aspect to what might be taken
for a wholly solemn poem. The conclusion does not seem to
repudiate the man's dreams and ideals: the baby's—and one
supposes by implication the droplet's—'I' is described in the
last line as 'world-shouldering'. But the poet suggests that the
shocks of experience of the kind the man wants do not issue in a
reaction that can encompass reason or language. And that the
man supposes they do is turned comically, if sympathetically, to
his disadvantage. His words are like 'coy baby-talk'; he has a
long way still to go.

In a good essay on Ted Hughes in *Essays in Criticism*, C. J. Rawson takes up argument with the poet over the scheme of values that these two poems seem to be advocating, and tries to show its limitations and inconsistencies. But I think that to do this is to put down an opponent of one's own devising. It is neither possible nor relevant to treat the 'arguments' in these poems as forms of sustained rational disquisition. There is neither evidence nor ratiocination offered here; nor, what is more, is there really any appeal *by demonstration* to our feelings. The first of the two poems is just a brilliant—and, taken in this way, also rather funny—display of abuse and verbal bullying from a wholly unargued viewpoint; the second might be described as a sort of awed comedy about fascinating but tantalisingly obscure ideas that the poet does not get down to scrutinising at all seriously in the end. At most we are left with hints at possibilities that we may be inspired to follow up.

More of Ted Hughes's work is marked by an extravagant but sardonic humour than has, I think, been stressed before (though, as we have seen, it sometimes shows lurches into portentousness that suggests he has not always been quite sure where the humour begins and ends). But *The Hawk in the Rain* also has some poems of a different kind that point forward to his finest work so far. (And here it must be said that his own work—particularly his most recent work—largely provides the criteria for the judgements made in this essay, just as, more widely, all literary judgements must finally proceed from a sense of what literature in fact has offered, an experience of the realisable achievements of literature being the only grounds for criticism at all.)

Any poem in some degree establishes simultaneously for the reader the presence of a speaker, and the independent presence of a situation external to the speaker to which he is responding. What characterizes Hughes's most remarkable poetry to date is the large part played in that 'external situation' by objects from nature—mountains, plants, birds—and the intricacy and force of the speaker's response to them. It is in these poems, rather than those more concerned with shock and assertion, that he most successfully conveys his sense of the importance of strong feelings and desires: important in some cases as being rewarding, in others simply as being present in human existence and necessary to recognize and cope with, and perhaps most often, in a tangled way, for both these reasons together.

The art of establishing those simultaneous presences is, all the same, only very intermittently present in Hughes's first two volumes. A good example is the title-poem of the first book. What such a poem calls for is a voice that in speaking of the objects it is concerned with conveys the speaker's reaction to them implicitly. The meaning-associations of the words, and their delivery under the thrust of the conventional rhythm and the supporting or contrary pull of the stresses normal to speech tax: these must offer as a composed whole a sense of the scene and its responsive occupant.

The poem 'The Hawk in the Rain' is the work of a poet prodigal with effects that are in this particular case over-employed: an undercommitted armoury, as it were. At the beginning the speaker energetically describes his own state as he crosses a ploughed field in the rain. But the rhythm crashes down with self-conscious heaviness on the key verbs and nouns, the alliteration echoes thunderously; the hyperboles come thick and fast, the double meanings ('habit', 'dogged grave') come to the surface and hesitate ineffectually there:

I drown in the drumming ploughland, I drag up
Heel after heel from the swallowing of the earth's mouth,
From clay that clutches my each step to the ankle
With the habit of the dogged grave . . .

I think one could extract a title and four lines from this poem that on their own would make a 'composed whole' saying almost as much as the whole poem as it stands is straining to say:

The Hawk

Effortlessly at height hangs his still eye . . .
That maybe in his own time meets the weather
Coming the wrong way, suffers the air, hurled upside down,
Fall from his eye, the ponderous shires crash on him.

These lines, though at first sight they might be thought almost pure imaginative description of the hawk's activity and experience, are in fact quite as much concerned with the responding presence of the speaker. In the very act of describing the effortless hovering of the hawk, the stillness of its eye bent to look down on the farmland below, the speaker (and the reader as he 'becomes' the speaker) is gasping both with awe and with effort to mime the hawk hanging in the sky. 'Effortlessly': the first stress of the line demands, precisely, a sudden un-expected effort from one, the more to be sustained as there is not just the expected single unstressed syllable but three more unstressed syllables before the second stressed syllable comes, 'height'. This is followed immediately by a third stressed syllable, 'hangs', so that these last two syllables themselves hang, as it were, at the crest of the line, each with its initial 'h' demanding the lifting of the breath to the roof of the mouth so that both body and spirit are felt to rise with it. And after another unstressed syllable (which nevertheless begins again with the breath-lifting 'h') come two further isolated stressed syllables 'still eye'—a pair, again, that together would not normally both take a stress on them if the formal metre of the line did not, as here, compel it: so once more the effort is forced on the reader of, so to speak, holding the words in the air there, sharing with the imaginary speaker *his* experience of sharing, with a kind of thrilled joy, the hawk's experience. Later in the poem we read:

. . . I
. . . strain towards the master-
Fulcrum of violence where the hawk hangs still . . .

But this fact has already been wholly conveyed in the line I have been discussing.

In the other three lines I have extracted from 'The Hawk in the Rain' there is the same remarkable richness both of description and of response to what is described. The effect of the beginning of these does owe something to a contrast with what has gone directly before, so picking out the lines in this way diminishes them slightly. After the lines about the speaker 'straining towards the master-fulcrum of violence where the hawk hangs still' (these last three stressed words again seeming to reiterate the presence of the hawk poised in the air), the tone suddenly modulates into something quieter:

> That maybe in his own time meets the weather . . .

There is a sudden easing of the strain—of the envy and emulation—here. The line lacks urgent stresses; the words are all either tentative or at any rate not bearing their full possible weight of meaning yet. 'In his own time' might suggest an act of choice on the hawk's part, rather than the comparison that is about to be made between the man's present experience and the hawk's in the future; 'meets', in 'meets the weather', again stands ambiguous for a moment—it too might suggest some act of choice, some agreeable encounter. So the sharp beginning of the next line puts the current of feeling in this poem at this moment dramatically in reverse:

> Coming the wrong way . . .

There follows the brilliant impression of the hawk falling: the sky seeming to fall away under it, the ground below seeming to crash down on it. These two lines, far from either lacking strong stresses or placing them on words with no unstressed syllables either side, is filled with stresses and half-stresses whirling one after the other with no consonantal impediment. And just as the reader has lived with speaker and hawk through a sense of aspiring desire and mastery, so now he lives through a sense of terror and disaster.

143

Here, then, is that 'appeal by demonstration to our feelings' that I described as lacking in 'Egg-Head' and 'The Man Seeking Experience Enquires His Way of a Drop of Water'. It would obviously be quite wrong to suggest that the hawk in this poem, and the stones, animals, other birds and so on in other poems by Hughes, are simply there as vehicles for reflecting human situations in which they ultimately have no place. This poem would not have been possible without the existence of hawks—more specifically, of kestrels: the human sensations and emotions that the poem is about could only have been evoked by observation of the bird itself, and indeed to some extent by sympathetic feeling for it. Yet the poem, opening up as it does a shareable experience of a man living intensely through a certain situation, manages to establish a set of human possibilities for the feelings and the will, and of dangers and failures, that it might be possible to apply more largely, by making our own analogies, in our lives. Other poems in *The Hawk in the Rain* that recreate a response to natural phenomena —envy, in some cases, at unmatchable simplicity or ease, or in other cases fascination and fear at the fierce spectacle—are 'The Jaguar', 'The Horses', 'September', 'A Modest Proposal' and, perhaps best of all, 'Wind', where the constant flicker of humour at his own exaggeration lends, this time, a greater air of authority to the speaker's description of the wind's violence.

Lupercal, Ted Hughes's second book, published in 1960, probably won greater acclaim than his first. To my mind, though, it does not show any great advance in the poet's powers of development or in his themes. There are force-fully-phrased pieces of thin argument or specious exhortation, dazzling curses and outbursts of hero-worship, but only a few poems in what I think is his most satisfying vein. The more aggressive poems assert points of view already familiar from *The Hawk in the Rain*. 'Strawberry Hill' is a zestful scarer: a symbolic 'stoat with the sun in its belly' who 'danced on the lawns' of Horace Walpole's Gothic castle but also 'bit through grammar and corset' was nailed to a door—

> But its red unmanageable life
> Has licked the stylist out of their skulls,
> Has sucked that age like an egg and gone off . . .

Any number of vague threats are shaken at us in those two lines—all the forces of life and death at once, it seems. However, this poem, with its challenge to the playful macabre of Walpole's, does not lack its own lightness of touch—no stoat has licked the stylist out of Hughes's skull here; and the end of the poem, announcing the re-emergence of the stoat, takes quite an insouciant pleasure in the witty combination of rightness and arbitrariness in the word that provides its final half-rhyme:

> . . . Has sucked that age like an egg and gone off
>
> Along ditches where flies and leaves
> Overpower our tongues, got into some grave—
> Not a dog to follow it down—
> Emerges, thirsting, in far Asia, in Brixton.

'Fourth of July' mocks contemporary America, where

> . . . the mind's wandering elementals . . .
>
> Wait dully at the traffic crossing,
> Or lean over headlines, taking nothing in.

'The Good Life' sympathizes sardonically with a hermit who found that in his 'poor-bare' life his spirit was too occupied in patching his boot, and returned to the world again thinking

> Only a plump, cuffed citizen
> Gets enough quiet to hear God speak.

But he was disappointed there, too:

Loud he prayed then; but late or early
Never a murmur came to his need
Save 'I'd be delighted.' and 'Yours sincerely',
And 'Thank you very much indeed!'

These are impatient dismissals. But the alternatives to such
lives that are offered in *Lupercal* are more deeply considered, if
only in a handful of poems like—most impressively—'Thrushes'
and 'November'. 'Thrushes' begins with a fine description of
thrushes feeding on the lawn:

More coiled steel than living—a poised
Dark deadly eye, those delicate legs
Triggered to stirrings beyond sense—with a start,
    a bounce, a stab
Overtake the instant and drag out some writhing thing.

In this poem the contrast is made explicitly with men's usual
inability to act with such speed, decisiveness and success: the
birds display

No indolent procrastinations and no yawning stares,
No sighs or head-scratchings . . .

The thought widens out in the second stanza, to compare
Mozart's brain-mechanism with that of the thrushes, and to
register awe at the similar efficiency of the shark

That hungers down the blood-smell even to a leak of
    its own
Side and devouring of itself.

But on the whole these further reflections after the first stanza
weaken the poem. There seems to be a confusion between
different concepts of cause when Hughes asks:

Is it their single-mind-sized skulls, or a trained
Body, or genius, or a nestful of brats
Gives their days this bullet and automatic
Purpose?

These are not equivalent alternatives. (There are also heavy,
rather unsatisfactory Shakespearean echoes here—the 'bullet
and automatic' purpose reminds one inescapably of Lady
Macbeth's 'self and violent' hand.) And the last stanza again
seems rather loosely to lump cerebration, doubt and emotional
complexity together as enemies in man of his desire 'to be
blent in the prayer'—itself a rather rough parallel to the
thrush's and shark's unselfconsciousness.

In 'November', as in the title-poem of Hughes's first book,
the speaker is describing an experience when out walking in the
rain. This time it is another human being who provides the poet
with an intimation of desirable life: a tramp seen sleeping in a
ditch. But this is a classic case of a distinction without much
difference. What the speaker sees of the tramp's behaviour is
about as near to the instinctive life of animals as man can
perhaps get. The sodden land, the mist on the thorn-bushes,
the renewed fall of the rain's 'dragging grey columns'—these
are superbly evoked in the poem. All that the speaker sees the
tramp do, though, is described in five lines:

> A wind chilled,
> And a fresh comfort tightened through him,
> Each hand stuffed deeper into the other sleeve.
>
> His ankles, bound with sacking and hairy band,
> Rubbed each other, resettling . . .

But it means this to the speaker:

> I thought what strong trust
> Slept in him—as the trickling furrows slept,
> And the thorn-roots in their grip on darkness.

The speaker runs on into a wood to get out of the rain, and there sees a gamekeeper's gibbet with owls, hawks, weasels, cats, crows on it. And in a fine conclusion he describes them.

> Some, stiff, weightless, twirled like dry bark bits
>
> In the drilling rain. Some still had their shape,
> Had their pride with it; hung, chins on chests,
> Patient to outwait these worst days that beat
> Their crowns bare and dripped from their feet.

This time no comparison or contrast is pressed: we are left—perfectly successfully—to feel for ourselves the fancifulness of the thought that the dead creatures are patient, and so feel also with a fresh shock the force of life in the man who might have seemed to be existing about as minimally as it is possibly for a man to do. The movement of these last lines is especially beautiful, with the corpses' 'patience' already prefigured in the repetitions of structures and sounds—

> Some still had their shape,
> Had their pride with it; hung, chins on chests—

and the sense of the merciless beat of the rain in the last line and a half.

Ted Hughes did not bring out another volume of poems for adults for general distribution until *Wodwo* in 1967, seven years after *Lupercal*. But in those intervening years he did publish a book of poems, supposedly for children, that seemed really to be something more than that, *The Earth-Owl and Other Moon-People*, in 1963; and another volume of poems in limited edition, *Recklings*, in 1966.

The Earth Owl* describes some of the creatures Hughes has chosen to imagine living on the moon. They are mostly

---

*I have incorporated here one or two of the remarks I made on this book in a review originally published anonymously in *The Times* in 1963.

sinister or tragic creatures, though they often possess fascinating powers. The success of the book lies not only in this rich inventiveness, but also in the tone Hughes has devised to talk about the creatures in. The speaker has a grave, worried air, with many a head-shaking or bit of homely advice for anyone confronted with the moon-people. The kind of mimicry that makes both situation and speaker come simultaneously alive for the reader is lavishly on show here:

Tree Disease

On the moon with great ease
You can catch tree-disease.
The symptoms are birds
Seeming interested in your words
And examining your ears.
Then a root peers
From under the nail
Of your big toe, then
You'd better get cured quick
Or you'll be really sick.

Many similarities could no doubt be found between the threats and sicknesses in *The Earth-Owl* and those spoken of in Hughes's other books, but I think it would be solemn to suppose that this book is really another covert assault on certain ways of the world, rather than a piece of enjoyable play both in ingenious imagining and in tone-finding. However the concluding poem is about a 'moon man-hunt', and in spite of its deliberately exaggerated trembling—

It is terrible, it is terrible, O it is terrible!—

the poet clearly does take a certain earnest delight in thrusting on its readers a reversal of the normal relation between animal and man:

149

'Ha! Ha' go all the foxes in unison.
'That menace, that noble rural vermin, the gentry,
    there's one!'
The dirt flies from their paws and the squire begins
    hopelessly to run.

Recklings has a self-deprecatory title, 'recklings' being the
weakest members of a litter or brood (this is also the first
time Hughes has expressed in a title an identification of his
poems with animals or birds, though in the poem 'The Thought-
Fox' in *The Hawk in the Rain* he describes the writing of a poem
in terms of a fox entering 'the dark hole of the head'). *Recklings*
fairly evidently consists of poems that Hughes had rejected the
idea of using in his next book for general distribution, which
was to appear the following year in the shape of *Wodwo*.
(Actually one poem, 'Logos', is to be found in both books, as is
one other title, 'Public Bar TV', though in this case the poem is
completely changed in the later book.) *Recklings* is a strange
book, full of magnificent fumblings. There is an account of
'Stealing Trout on a May Morning', at some moments extremely
vivid and delicate, at others crude and clumsy, as though a
wealth of impressions and ideas had not been fully sorted out.
In a poem called 'Trees', pictures blending into imaginative
personifications of a holly tree and a birch tree lead on to a
response to the personalities thus conjured up that seems
strained and wilful. One very enjoyable description of a
'Heatwave' ends with a sundown when

> the walker's bones
> Melt in the coughing of great cats.

The most interesting thing about *Recklings*, though, is that in
some poems it shows Hughes reaching out more fully for a vein
only hinted at in earlier books: a mythical or visionary presentation of his experience, that tries to show it as part of a larger,
sometimes cyclical, history, or as if seen by the eye of a

variously-rendered God. In 'Fishing at Dawn', the speaker is conscious of the buried blood of centuries being exhaled again in the night-fog—a vision which leads on to a still more grandly desolate one:

God yawns onto the black water.

In 'Dully Gumption's Addendum' there is a brief, savage history of England: out of

the head of the dead god king
Cromwell cut from the country body but could not bury
or silence

came maggots.

These maggots multiplied, spilling into the shires . . .
And the bumpkin English took them for the words of
god-sent law.
So these maggots bit deep into the brains of the
bumpkin English.

Englishman after Englishman fell eaten to a mummy
skin
Around a man-weight maggot and stiffened
To a chrysalis from which a black fly in no time
Flew up into the rotten face of the kingdom.

It is the old Hughes story of the interfering mind destroying the natural, spontaneous life:

At grammar school this remorseless strain of maggot
Behind greying disciplinarian masks
Of Addison of Gladstone and of Arnold
Ate into his brain, ate into his brain.

Here the story has a Celtic anti-English note that adds to the spice of it—but does not exactly make its diagnosis more convincing.

At any rate, the best poems in Hughes's most recent book, *Wodwo*, are the ones that follow on from those I have already argued most strongly in favour of, the poems of direct—though complex and imaginative—response to nature. And some of these in *Wodwo* are magnificent. Poems like 'Skylarks', 'Thistles', 'Still Life', 'Fern', or 'Sugar Loaf' wholly fulfil the promise of the earlier books. These poems, together with a number of marked successes in other modes, easily make *Wodwo* Hughes's best book yet.

In 'Skylarks' the speaker tells of being out on a spring Sunday morning watching the larks climb into the sky and sing. The casual reference to its being a Sunday morning roots the experience in the realities of an ordinary life—Sunday being the most likely day for a man to be out standing in the fields with nothing else on his mind. Also, as it is described as a 'dreary Sunday morning', when 'heaven' is by contrast 'a madhouse with the voices and frenzies of the larks', there is a hint of the speaker's experience being the most satisfactory replacement for Christian religious experiences that are no longer accessible— even if they ever were desirable. As with 'The Hawk in the Rain', the poem depends wholly on the existence of the particular species of bird it is about: its six parts all describe exactly-observed stages in the lark's flight. But as the poem proceeds, a wonderful range of human aspiration, struggle and joy is also revealed.

The poem opens briskly and factually enough:

> The lark begins to go up . . .

But at once the speaker senses implications:

> Like a warning
> As if the globe were uneasy.

Not only does the bird rise into the sky like a Verey light. There is indeed something threatening, for the watcher at least: but the bird itself is, ironically, the threat, with the disturbance it is going to cause in his imagination. Yet at the same time the bird is going to provide the necessary healing power: the disturbance is itself going to be not merely salutary but richly rewarding. And the watcher's thoughts turn next to the contrasting strengths in the small bird: its lightness, its capacity for filling its 'barrel-chested' body with air, and at the same time its 'leaden' qualities:

> But leaden
> With muscle
> For the struggle
> Against
> Earth's centre.
>
> And leaden
> For ballast
> In the rocketing storms of the breath.

The movement of the poem here mimes that struggle with very apparent force. This first part ends with the thought of a further 'leaden' quality in the bird:

> Leaden
> Like a bullet
> To supplant
> Life from its centre.

With perfect ease, the threat that the bird poses comes clearly to the fore.

The second part opens up a new set of paradoxes. The bird has this ambivalently destructive force—but it is itself a victim too. It is

. . . shot through the crested head
With the command, Not die

But climb

Climb

Sing

Obedient as to death a dead thing.

And again the three short lines—two syllables, then just one—
followed by the sweeping forward movement of the fourth, with
its run of unstressed syllables and its final, hammering 'death'
and 'dead', embody perfectly the watcher's simultaneous sense
of the bird's extraordinary effort and of its utter passivity.

The third part of the poem expands the idea of the lark as
sheer instrument for the song:

> I suppose you just gape and let your gaspings
> Rip in and out through your voicebox
> O lark

The effect of the long lines in this section is precisely caught in
the simile one of them gives for the lark's experience of the
'gaspings' ripping in and out through its voicebox:

> Like a breaker of ocean milling the shingle.

(It is hard to think of a line of verse that *is* so completely what it
means as that one.) And the apostrophe 'O lark' at the end of
each pair of lines in this section suggests the at any rate
momentary flooding through the watcher of waves of un-
controllable awe and delight, inspired by the experience of the
bird but also similar to what the bird is experiencing.

By contrast, the fourth part dwells on the bird's efforts.

My idleness curdles
Seeing the lark labour near its cloud.

The watcher's eye follows the climbing bird till it passes out of sight; then the watcher—whose solid physical presence is no more forgotten than the bird's is—moves for a moment into the centre of the picture:

> Till my eye's gossamer snaps
> and my hearing floats back widely to earth

> After which the sky lies blank open
> Without wings, and the earth is a folded clod.

A moment of peace and harmonious unity has been attained for man, bird and world; and the last line of this part swells out with the music of this moment—which is, as a final paradox, apparently 'endless':

> Only the sun goes silently and endlessly on with the
> lark's song.

Then in Part Five the agitated multiplicity of the universe suddenly breaks back into the writer's consciousness. The sky is not 'blank', in fact: it is full of skylarks. All the paradoxes of the lark's song-flight that the watcher has been registering return with renewed force:

> Heads flung back, as I see them,
> Wings almost torn off backwards—far up

> Like sacrifices floating
> The cruel earth's offerings

> The mad earth's missionaries.

And the sixth and final part begins with a fresh comparison—but a more material, visual one again, the last impression we are to get of the violence of the birds' efforts—

> Like those flailing flames
> That lift from the fling of a bonfire
> Claws dangling full of what they feed on—

before the beautiful conclusion of the poem. This conclusion follows very closely the actual behaviour of larks as they descend. 'When . . . when . . . and . . . and . . . ': the fullness and finality of their soaring flight is pressed on us before the superb moment when their flight and song alter:

> So it's a relief, a cool breeze
> When they've had enough, when they're burned out
> And the sun's sucked them empty
> And the earth gives them the O.K.
>
> And they relax, drifting with changed notes . . .

The next two lines catch both a physical movement in the birds, and the associated, slightly tense lightness in the speaker's feelings, with perfect phrasing:

> Dip and float, not quite sure if they may
> Then they are sure and they stoop.

Lastly we witness their 'plummeting dead drop' to the earth—'and maybe the whole agony was for this' reflects the watcher, with a deep sense of satisfaction in the release. But it is still not the end of the experience. We experience a final perfect unity of exact attention to the birds and distinctly human feelings evoked by that attention:

But just before they plunge into the earth

They flare and glide off low over grass, then up
To land on a wall-top, crest up,

Weightless,
Paid-up,
Alert,

Conscience perfect.

It is possible to take the account of the skylark's experience offered in this poem as in some way analogous to the artist's, or to satisfying sexual experience, or to heights of heroism, or perhaps to mystical experience. But to make such comparisons explicitly is, I think, both to broaden the meaning of the poem too much and at the same time to limit it unduly: it is to lose sight of the birds that the poem is on any account primarily about, and to diminish the pleasure to be had from the sheer observation of them. Hughes might say (though I don't *know* that he would) that there is in fact a biological analogy between the bird's behaviour (and what we may imagine to be its experience) and the kind of human activities I have just mentioned. That seems too tricky a question both in fact and definition to be fruitfully followed up here. What we can say is that the poem leaves us with both a real sense of effort and joy experienced, through the observation of a specific natural phenomenon, and some kind of residual psychological pattern that might, it seems, in some way stimulate and guide in other situations.

In a short essay like this, one such discussion must suffice to illustrate the accomplishment of *Wodwo* in this poetry of nature. But a few more examples might be briefly given. In 'Thistles' there is the way in which the bursting open of the thistles becomes a full burgeoning from one to the next of the three line-ends of the second stanza:

Every one a revengeful bur*st*
Of resurrection, a grasped fi*st*ful
Of splintered weapons and Icelandic fro*st* thru*st* up . . .

In 'Fern', the grave dance of the earth and the fern is presented beautifully to our senses in the pause after the noun at the end of these lines:

And, among them, the fern
Dances gravely, like the plume
Of a warrior returning . . .

This is also perhaps the point at which to mention the title-poem of *Wodwo*. The 'wodwo' is a wild, but possibly half-human, creature encountered in lonely places by Sir Gawain in the 14th-century poem *Sir Gawain and the Green Knight*. Hughes's portrait of it is of a gentle, puzzled beast, looking carefully at nature around it to try to get some clue to its own nature:

Why do I find
this frog so interesting as I inspect its most secret
interior and make it my own? Do these weeds
know me and name me to each other have they
seen me before, do I fit in their world? . . .
again very queer but I'll go on looking

It is a mild-voiced, fanciful poem, but these lines could certainly provide an epigraph for poems like 'Skylarks'.

Wodwo also contains some excellent poems in Hughes's fierce, critical style, offering as little argument as usual but powerful in the intensity of their scorn. The earlier version of 'Public Bar TV' in *Recklings* was explicit in its contempt for both the viewers and the programmes:

They swallow all its drizzling nothings, like the mild earth.

But the version in *Wodwo* is more effective in its indirectness, and with its final hint of pity tempering the scorn. The viewers in the pub are this time portrayed as outriders in the desert who have 'found foul water' and

> Crouch numbed by a wind howling all
> Visible horizons equally empty.

The slender link of the physical posture of the numbed searchers and the TV viewers is quite enough to bind together the subject and the disparaging metaphor for it. And of course the indignation at this passive watching of manufactured entertainment in a bar is understandable in a poet who has praised heroic drinkers —if with grim asides—in all his books: 'Roarers in a Ring' in *The Hawk in the Rain*, 'Singers' in *Lupercal*, 'Guinness' in *Recklings*, and 'Wino' in *Wodwo*.

The sense of outrage is greater in one or two poems about a subject that has also appeared in his earlier books, the indignity of suffering and the horror of death in war. 'Out', in *Wodwo*, while full of bitterness at the mutilations of body and spirit that men suffered in the First World War, ends with a violent resolution by the speaker not to let memories of it go on 'gripping' him: he repudiates the whole of that history, the grief as well as the misplaced heroism.

The 'visionary' poems in *Wodwo* have a tone somewhat in common with 'Out': most of them try to express a sense of prevailing failure and misery in human life. 'Logos' presents God as the force that presses for life and strength and order in the universe, but is always failing because

> God is a good fellow, but His mother's against Him.

'Reveille' is about the unhappy waking of Adam and Eve to find that the serpent's coils

> Had crushed all Eden's orchards.
> And out beyond Eden

The black, thickening river of his body
Glittered in giant loops
Around desert mountains and away
Over the ashes of the future.

But 'Theology' presents the serpent a shade more sympathetically. After

Adam ate the apple.
Eve ate Adam.
The serpent ate Eve.

we find the serpent sleeping off his meal in Paradise and—with
an air of complicity on the poet's part—

Smiling to hear
God's querulous calling.

Since *Wodwo* appeared, Hughes has published in magazines a
number of new poems to which the last three poems mentioned
—especially 'Theology'—can be seen as pointing the way.
These new poems are his most successful attempts so far at
finding a 'mythical' situation and characters to dramatize both
his sense—apparently growing—of the cruelty and arbitrariness
of life, and some form of acceptable human riposte to it. What is
especially interesting is that it is a bird, once again, that has
provided him with the necessary inspiration. The poems belong
to a sequence called, provisionally, 'Crow Lore', and the chief
figure in them is Crow. Crow seems to represent, at the same
time, various forces in the universe and various human attitudes;
but he is always a bird, and in fact always easy to visualize
immediately as none other than a crow. He is destructive and
has a small, callous sense of humour; but he is heroically
stubborn and indeed apparently indestructible. God, who in
these poems is well-intentioned but not very bright, is usually
worsted by him. In 'A Childish Prank', for instance, God is

pondering what to do about the fact that man and woman have
no souls, and are 'dully gaping, foolishly staring'.

> Crow laughed.
> He bit the Worm, God's only son,
> Into two writhing halves.

> He stuffed into man the tail half
> With the wounded end hanging out.

> He stuffed the head half head first into woman
> And it crept in deeper, and up
> To peer out through her eyes
> Calling its tail half to join up quickly, quickly
> Because O it was painful.

> Man awoke being dragged across the grass.
> Woman awoke to see him coming.
> Neither knew what had happened.

In 'The Battle of Osfrontis' Crow is attacked by words—they
carry the offer or threat of all the pleasures and pains in the
world—but Crow's joky indifference defeats them all:

> Words retreated, suddenly afraid . . .

In 'Crow's Last Stand' the heat of the sun has reduced the whole
world to ashes; but there is a 'final obstacle'

> Limpid among the glaring furnace clinkers
> The pulsing blue tongues and the red and the yellow
> The green lickings of the conflagration

> Limpid and black—

> Crow's eye-pupil, in the tower of its scorched fort.

Many of Hughes's themes and arts come together in these poems. It is as though in his earlier work birds, animals and plants gave him a sense of certain possibilities of instinctual life or of simple moral life with a certain similarity to the life of natural phenomena; while human life mainly offered a spectacle of failure that he could only hold up to contempt. In the Crow poems he has found a way of drawing these intuitions into a unity. We follow the acts of Crow with the same closeness, and the same sense of ambivalent human possibilities being delineated, as we do with the earlier non-mythological birds (though the possibilities are rather different now). But these acts take place now in a different sort of setting, still always vividly physical but reflecting—through its scenery and characters—a wider range of human emotions and decisions, and impersonal forces, that enter powerfully into our lives. The fable-form both gives scope for a multiplicity of mirrorings of human experience, and fixes them in a single dramatic narrative of a kind that does not allow us to say—as we so often feel obliged to say of Hughes's more direct poems about human life—that he is over-simplifying. And all his powers of mimicry are splendidly and relevantly on display.

Looking back at his work as a whole, so far, it is as a *mime* that it is perhaps most useful to consider Ted Hughes. Though he is a traditional poet of the written word, and the normal action of the meanings of words is essential to his effects on us, he has an exceptional gift for making words act out the processes they are describing. This is a particularly important gift for a writer with Hughes's themes. (One must suppose, in fact, that this is not entirely fortunate coincidence, but that his preoccupations and his gifts have some common origin in his own nature: however that is a matter about which one can only surmise, if one is dependent simply on the evidence of his poems.) At any rate, the kind of instinctual, physically responsive life that Hughes has a particularly strong feeling for is displayed in action in the best of his work rather than simply argued for. He argues for it, too: but as I have tried to show, though he does

162

this with wit and aplomb, he never really makes a case until he goes back to the poems in which he 'imitates' and embodies it.

The best of his poems till lately are, in my judgment, the ones that in this way reveal clues to possible joys and satisfactions for man in the life of nature. It is only in his most recent work of all that another sort of largely instinctual life is insistently put on show for its attractions: Crow's refusal to be beaten in any circumstances, his determination to pounce and disarray first whenever there is any danger of his suffering that fate. Hughes has never gone far in trying to offer solutions to the more intricate moral and emotional perplexities of modern life, and his comments on the social scene have been pungent but perfunctory. But it seems no more proper to reproach him with this when he writes of Crow than when he writes of the skylarks. What he can offer is a confidently presented and beautifully judged demonstration of certain needs that are known to him being fulfilled. This, in a sceptical age, seems a starting point worth having.

BARBARA HARDY

The Poetry of Sylvia Plath:

Enlargement or Derangement?

PASSIONS OF hate and horror prevail in the poetry of Sylvia Plath, running strongly counter to the affirmative and life-enhancing quality of most great English poetry, even in this century. We cannot reconcile her despairing and painful protest with the usual ideological demands of Christian, Marxist, and humanist writers, whether nobly and sympathetically eloquent, like Wordsworth, breezily simplified, like Dylan Thomas, or cunning in ethical and psychological argument, like W. H. Auden or F. R. Leavis. Her poetry rejects instead of accepting, despairs instead of glorying, turns its face with steady consistency towards death, not life. But these hating and horrified passions are rooted in love, are rational as well as irrational, lucid as well as bewildered, so humane and honourable that they are constantly enlarged and expanded. We are never enclosed in a private sickness here, and if derangement is a feature of the poetry, it works to enlarge and generalize, not to create an enclosure. Moreover, its enlargement works through passionate reasoning, argument and wit. Its judgement is equal to its genius.

The personal presence in the poetry, though dynamic and shifting, makes itself felt in a full and large sense, in feeling, thinking and language. In view of certain tendencies to admire or reject her so-called derangement as a revelatory or an enclosed self-exploration, I want to stress this breadth and completeness. The poetry constantly breaks beyond its own personal cries of pain and horror, in ways more sane than mad,

164

enlarging and generalising the particulars, attaching its maladies to a profoundly moved and moving sense of human ills. Working through a number of individual poems, I should like to describe this poetry as a poetry of enlargement, not derangement. In much of the poetry the derangement is scarcely present, but where it is, it is out-turned, working though reason and love.

I want to disagree with David Holbrook's view that hers is a schizophrenic poetry which 'involves us in false solutions and even the *huis clos* circuits of death', while indeed agreeing with much that he has to say about the cult of schizophrenia in his essay 'The 200-inch distorting mirror':

'Sylvia Plath's poetry demands a selfless mirror-role from us; we feel that it would be worse than inhuman of us not to give it. If this involves us in entering into her own distorted view of existence, never mind. We will bravely become the schizoid's 200-inch astronomical reflector'.

An excessive love for the cult of pain and dying, in such tributes as those of Anne Sexton and Robert Lowell, seems to divert our attention from the breadth and rationality of Sylvia Plath's art. Lowell is strongly drawn to that very quality which David Holbrook finds repulsive or pathetic, the invitation to a deadly closure:

'There is a peculiar, haunting challenge to these poems. Probably many, after reading *Ariel*, will recoil from their first over-awed shock, and painfully wonder why so much of it leaves them feeling empty, evasive and inarticulate. In her lines, I often hear the serpent whisper, "Come, if only you had the courage, you too could have my rightness, audacity and ease of inspiration." But most of us will turn back. These poems are playing Russian roulette with six cartridges in the cylinder, a game of "chicken", the wheels of both cars locked and unable to swerve.'

It seems worth recording a different reaction.

I want to begin by looking at a poem from *Ariel* which shows how dangerous it is to talk, as Holbrook clearly does, and as Lowell seems to, about the 'typical' Sylvia Plath poem, or even the 'typical' late poem. I must make it clear that I do not want to rest my case on the occasional presence of life-enhancing poems, but to use one to explain what I mean by imaginative enlargement. 'Nick and the Candlestick' (from *Ariel*, 1965; written October/November 1962)* is not only a remarkable poem of love, but that much rarer thing—are there any others?—a fine poem of maternal love. It is a poem which moves towards two high points of feeling, strongly personal and particular, deeply eloquent of maternal feeling, and lucidly open to a Christian mythical enlargement. The first peak comes in the tenth stanza, and can perhaps be identified at its highest point in one word, the endearment 'ruby', which is novel, surprising, resonant, and beautiful:

> Remembering, even in sleep,
> Your crossed position.
> The blood blooms clean
>
> In you, ruby.
> The pain
> You wake to is not yours.

The second peak comes at the end, in a strongly transforming conclusion, a climax in the very last line. It comes right out of all that has been happening in the poem but transforms what has gone before, carrying a great weight and responsibility, powerfully charged and completing a process, like an explosion or a blossoming:

> You are the one
> Solid the spaces lean on, envious.
> You are the baby in the barn.

The final enlargement is daring, both in the shock of expansion and in the actual claim it makes. She dares to call her

*Reproduced at the end of this essay.

baby Christ and in doing so makes the utmost claim of her personal love, but so that the enlargement does not take us away from this mother, this child, this feeling. This most personally present mother-love moves from the customary hyperbole of endearment in 'ruby' to the vast claim. When we look back, when we read again, the whole poem is pushing towards that last line, 'You are the baby in the barn'. The symbol holds good, though at first invisibly, for the cold, the exposure, the dark, the child, the mother, the protection, and the redemption from a share of pain. Each sensuous and emotional step holds for the mother in the poem and for Mary: this is the warmth of the mother nursing her child in the cold night; this is a proud claim for the child's beauty and the mother's tenderness; this is love and praise qualified by pain. Any mother loving her child in a full awareness of the world's horror—especially seeing it and feeling it vulnerable and momentarily safe in sleep—is re-enacting the feeling in the Nativity, has a right to call the child the baby in the barn.

'Ruby' is a flash of strong feeling. It treasures, values, praises, admires, measures, contemplates, compares, rewards. Its full stretch of passion is only apparent when the whole poem is read, but even on first encounter it makes a powerful moment, and strikes us as thoroughly formed and justified at that stage. Like every part of the poem, even the less urgent-sounding ones, it refers back and forwards, and has also continuity not only within the poem but with larger traditions of amorous and religious language, in medieval poetry (especially *The Pearl*), in the Bible, in Hopkins. The fusion of the new and the old is moving. This baby has to be newly named, like every baby, and has its christening in a poem, which bestows a unique name, in creative energy, as ordinary christenings cannot, but with something too of the ritual sense of an old and common feeling. Sylvia Plath is a master of timing and placing, and the naming endearment comes after the physically live sense of the sleeping child, in the cold air, in the candlelight, in its healthy colour. The mildly touched Christian reference in 'crossed position' prepares for the poem's future. Its gentleness contrasts strongly, by the way, with the violence of very similar puns in Dylan Thomas, and confirms my general feeling that Sylvia Plath is one of the very few poets to assimilate Thomas without injury, in an entirely benign influence. Her sensuous precision is miles away from Thomas: 'ruby' is established by the observation, 'The blood blooms clean/In you', and the comparison works absolutely, within the poem, though it has an especially poignant interest when we think of the usual agressiveness and disturbance of redness in her other poems, where the blooming red of tulips or poppies are exhausting life-demands, associated with the pain of red wounds, or the heavy urgency of a surviving beating heart. Here it is a beloved colour, because it is the child's, so in fact there is a constancy of symbolism, if we are interested. 'Clean', like 'crossed' and 'ruby' has the same perfectly balanced attachment to the particularity of the situation—this mother, this baby—and to the Christian extension. 'The pain/You wake to is not yours' works in the same way, pointing out and in, though the words 'out' and 'in' do less than justice to the fusion here.

The perfected fusion is the more remarkable for being worked out in a various tone, which includes joking. Like the medieval church, or the Nativity play, it can be irreverent, can make jokes about what it holds sacred, is sufficiently inclusive and sufficiently certain. So we are carried from the fanciful rueful joke about 'A piranha/Religion, drinking/Its first communion out of my live toes' to the final awe. Or from the casual profane protest, 'Christ! they are panes of ice' to the crossed position, the pain not his, the baby in the barn. An ancient and audacious range.

If this is a love-poem, it is one which exists in the context of the other *Ariel* poems, keeping a sense of terrors as well as glories, in imagery which is vast and vague: the stars 'plummet to their dark address'; and topically precise and scientific: 'the mercuric/Atoms that cripple drip/Into the terrible well'. It is a poisoned world that nourishes and threatens that clean blood.

Perhaps only a child can present an image of the uncontaminated body, as well as soul, and there is also present the sense of a mother's fear of physical contamination. The mercuric atoms are presumably a reference to the organo-mercury compounds used in agriculture, and the well seems to be a real well. There may also, I suppose, be a reference to radioactive fall-out. Ted Hughes has a note about the poet's horror of 'the chemical poisonings of nature, the pile-up of atomic waste', in his article in *Tri-Quarterly*.

The poet loves and praises, but in no innocent or ideal glorying. This is a cold air in which the candle burns blue before yellow, nearly goes out, reminds us of the radiance in so many paintings of Mother and Child, but also of a real cold night, and of the miner's cold, his dark, his cave, his nightwork, his poisoned breathing. The intimacies and protections and colours are particular too: 'roses', 'the last of Victoriana', 'soft rugs'. The expansion moves firmly into and out of a twentieth-century world, a medieval poetry, ritual, and painting, and the earliest Christ-story, and this holds for its pains and its loving. It moves from light to dark, from love to fear. It moves beyond the images of mother-love, indeed begins outside in the first line's serious wit, 'I am a miner'. It uses—or, better, feels for—the myth of Redemption not in order to idealize the particulars but rather to revise and qualify the myth, to transplant it again cheerfully, to praise only after a long hard look at the worst. The love and faith and praise are there, wrung out and achieved against the grain, against the odds. David Holbrook is sorry that Sylvia Plath, judged from *The Bell Jar*, shows no experience of togetherness. This poem seems to embarrass his case, and it strikes me as being far beyond the reach of diagnosis or compassion. She said of the poem, in a B.B.C. broadcast quoted by Lois Ames: 'a mother nurses her baby son by candlelight and finds in him a beauty which, while it may not ward off the world's ill, does redeem her share of it'.

True, it is not typical. There are two other very loving poems of maternal feeling, 'Riddle' and 'You're', happy peals of conceits, but nothing else moves so, between these two extremities of love and pain, striking spark from such poles. 'Nick and the Candlestick' is not proffered as an instance of togetherness, but as a lucid model of the enlargement I want to discuss.

At the heart of her poetry lies the comment that she herself made about this enlargement:

'I think my poems come immediately out of the sensuous and emotional experiences I have, but I must say I cannot sympathize with these cries from the heart that are informed by nothing except a needle or a knife or whatever it is. I believe that one should be able to control and manipulate experiences, even the most terrifying—like madness, being tortured, this kind of experience—and one should be able to manipulate these experiences with an informed and intelligent mind. I think that personal experience shouldn't be a kind of shut box and mirror-looking narcissistic experience. I believe it should be generally relevant, to such things as Hiroshima and Dachau, and so on'. (*Tri-Quarterly* 7, p. 71.)

It is interesting that Sylvia Plath uses the image of the mirror which David Holbrook also uses in that *New Society* article, called 'The 200-inch distorting mirror', in order to reject the kind of poetry he also rejects (to my mind, rightly) and which he finds (to my mind, wrongly) in Sylvia Plath.

A mere explicit statement that the poet believes personal experience of pain should not be a mirror or a shut box but should be relevant to Hiroshima and Dachau, is plainly not an answer to Holbrook. Nor would a mere listing of such references do much: the intelligent poet can after all attempt but fail to break open the shut box, may impose intellectually schematic associations with the larger world. Resnais in *Hiroshima Mon Amour* seems to be open to the charge of using the larger pain of atomic war to illuminate his personal centre, so that the movement is not that of enlargement but of diminution. Something similar seems to happen in a good many Victorian attempts to enlarge the personal problem, to combine the personal and social pain, and we may well object that the endings of *Bleak House* and *Crime and Punishment* are unsuccessful attempts to solve the large pain by the smaller reconciliation. I have spent what may seem an excessive time on 'Nick and the Candlestick' in order to establish not so much a typical feeling, but a form: the particularity and the generalization run together in equal balance, asking questions of each other, eroding each other, unifying in true imaginative modification. I want to suggest that this is the mode of Sylvia Plath's major poetry, and that it succeeds exactly where Resnais failed. But it should be said, perhaps, that this problem of combination or enlargement works in a special way, involving artists working from experience of personal pain, depression, despair. The optimist, like Dickens and Dostoevsky, may well find it easy to join his larger pain and his smaller triumph. For the tragic artist like Sylvia Plath it is more the problem of competitive pains: how to dwell in and on the knives and needles of the personal life without shutting off the knives and needles in Biafra, Vietnam, Dachau, and Hiroshima. It is almost a problem of competing sensibilities, and the tragic artist's temptation in our time is probably to combine indecorously, like Resnais, to make the Hiroshima a metaphor for an adultery, to move from outer to inner and confirm an especially terrible shut box.

Before I move from 'Nick and the Candlestick' to the more terrible fusions elsewhere in *Ariel*, I want to look at some of the earlier attempts in *The Colossus* (1960). Many of the poems here show a fairly familiar and conventional tension and control. In some poems there is a narrow sensuous or social image of something painful, something dying: the dryness, unpleasant fruition, hard and yellow starlight, and difficult 'borning' of 'The Manor Garden' have nothing to say for nature; the inhuman boom and monotony of 'Night Shift' show men reduced to tend the machine; 'Hardcastle Crags' defeat the walker's energy by massive indifference and hard labour. Such poems accumulate the sense of unreward, ugliness, labour, repulsion, hostility, but each makes only its individual assertion, proffering no generalization.

In another group of poems in this volume, there is an attempt to break up such hardness, though scarcely to redeem or transform. Such poems as 'Two Views of a Cadaver Room,' 'Watercolour of Grantchester Meadows', 'The Eye-Mote' or 'Black Rook in Rainy Weather' show a darkening, rather than a darkened, vision. Affirmation is there, is valued, but is unstable. The destructive eye-mote is there for good, enlarged and confirmed as more than temporary by the move towards Oedipus, so we know that the sight cannot return, that the 'Horses fluent in the wind' are gone. In 'Black Rook in Rainy Weather' the poem sets out a belief in meaningful experience, but the belief rocks unsteadily, the experience is erratic and unguaranteed, can only bring 'A brief respite from fear/Of total neutrality'. The vigour of the meaningful moment is certainly there, 'hauling up eyelids', but in most of these poems that weigh gain against loss, there is less vigour, or a final movement towards the loss. 'Black Rook' ends with the naming of the spasmodic trick, the random rare descent, but 'The Eye-Mote' moves more characteristically away from the balance between easy fluid harmony, and the pained, blurred distorted vision, to tip the scales. We move over into blindness, guilt, loss of more than a small beauty. 'Watercolour of Grantchester Meadows' has a dark landscape, uses the spring idyll ambiguously and sharpens one point to drive it hard against our senses and sense. It creates a swimmy swoony dream of spring, water, love, in the impressionist blurring and the little nursery plate brightness, to build a bridge from the world of (superficial) sweetness to destructiveness. In 'Two Views of a Cadaver Room' the movement from death to love is deceptive: the poem allows only a tiny ambiguous space for 'the little country' where the lovers can be 'blind to the carrion army'. No redeeming corner, this, because 'foolish, Delicate' and 'not for long', stalled only 'in paint', and responding in true Brueghel disproportionateness to the earlier apparent redemption, in the first half of the poem, where after the dissection, 'He hands her the cut-out heart like a cracked heirloom'. All these poems, with the possible exception of 'Black Rook', fall out of love with the world of love, yearn for it but know what they are up against. They share a certain static quality: the pastoral term, for instance, in the Grantchester poem, is decorously but very carefully planning its own erosion, right from the start, and the poet's stance seems to be well outside the poem. Even in 'The Eye-Mote', where there is an expansion into the Oedipus myth, it is told rather than enacted: 'I dream that I am Oedipus'. Though 'the brooch-pin and the salve' effectively revise the splinter and the eye-bath, they do so by a movement of literary reference, very different from the total resonance in 'Nick' where the poem is plainly gathering its strengths and meanings, like all the best art, from conscious and unconscious assembling. The brilliant stroke of wit in 'Before the brooch-pin and the salve/Fixed me in this parenthesis' is perhaps a limited one: the pun is dazzling in the light of the Oedipal situation, and plainly relates to all those other poems about parent-relation-ships. But after a little reflection one begins to wonder if *parenthesis* is quite the best word, after all, for either the Oedipal blindness or a loss of innocence. A spurt of wit remains on the superficial level. As a pun, it is not quite up to Mercutio's or Lady Macbeth's.

Ted Hughes tells us, in his *Tri-Quarterly* piece, that the personality of Oedipus and others were important *personæ* in her life, but he is right to say that in this poem, and elsewhere, they may seem literary. It is not a matter of artificiality but of a certain thinness of feeling: the enlargement does not quite come off. Similarly, in the Grantchester poem, which strikes me perhaps as a subdued answer to Dylan Thomas's 'Sir John's Hill' (just as 'Nick' seems like a subdued answer to Hopkins's 'The Starlight Night') the movement from the human situation to the animal world seems relaxed, cool, insufficiently felt—or rather, felt to be felt in the poem. Her feelings for Greek tragedy and animal life were evidently far from thinly literary, but in some of these poems they were not yet getting sufficiently incorporated and expressed.

There are a number of poems in *Colossus*, however, where a different stance and structure achieves something much more imaginatively substantial: 'Lorelei', 'All the Dead Dears', 'Suicide Off Egg Rock', 'Full Fathom Five', 'Medallion', 'The Burnt-Out Spa' and 'Mussel Hunter at Rock Harbor' are most impressive poems of a dying fall. Each moves slowly and lucidly into a death or a longing for a death or a blessing of death. They are, if you like, perverse love-poems. Instead of working by the usual kind of enlargement, from the personal to the larger world, they attempt an empathetic drama, where a kind of death is explored, imagined, justified. If I list the last lines, a common quality in the conclusions can be my starting-point:

> Stone, stone, ferry me down there. ('Lorelei')
> Deadlocked with them, taking root as cradles rock.
> ('All the Dead Dears')
> The forgetful surf creaming on those ledges. ('Suicide
> Off Egg Rock')
> I would breathe water. ('Full Fathom Five')
> The yardman's/Flung brick perfected his laugh.
> ('Medallion')
> The stream that hustles us
>
> Neither nourishes nor heals. ('The Burnt-Out Spa')
>
> . . . this relic saved/Face, to face the bald-faced sun.
> ('Mussel Hunter at Rock Harbor').

Each poem is dramatized, individualized. Each constructs a different feeling for death. These conclusions, which all settle for death, are earned in separate and solidly substantial ways, emotionally intense and rationally argued, each working through a distinct human experience which ends by wanting death.

In 'Lorelei' it is the peace of death that lures, which is why the sirens' song and their silence are both maddening. The sense of 'maddening' is both superficial and profound, for the listener knows that what the sirens offer is illusion, cannot be a solicitation except in nightmare or when 'deranged by harmony'. The images are fully responsive: 'descant from borders/Of hebetude, from the ledge/Also of high windows' and 'Drunkenness of the great depths' and 'your ice-hearted calling'. It is the earlier 'Sisters, your song/Bears a burden too weighty/For the whorled ear's listening' that earns the sense of inevitability in the final weight of 'Stone, stone'.

The same can be said of all the other poems in this group. Each makes its individual movement to death, each is a dying. In 'All the Dead Dears' death is repulsive, but none the less urgent for that. The dead pull us, willy-nilly, into our graves and the three skeletons in the Archaeological Museum are suitably and grotesquely 'unmasked' and 'dry' witnesses to life's (death's?) eating-game. The poem moves step by step from the first instance, from the stranger-in-blood to the sense of ancestral pull, to the father's death, through the family feasts, into a coffin as inevitable as a cradle. The whole poem takes colour from the first grotesque image, so that her father's death (of course a recurring image) is seen in the right bizarre fashion: 'Where the daft father went down/With orange duckfeet winnowing his hair', and the right, though typically very mild (it strengthens terribly once we see through it, though, this mildness) sense of the animal and human, and the live and dead, overlapping. The final Gulliver image completes the grotesque line and the imagery of a trap.

The image of clarity and cleanness at the end of 'Suicide Off Egg Rock' finishes off the man who walks away from the débris of the beach and the muck of living—'that landscape/Of imperfections his bowels were part of'. Each poem is a separate dying, thoroughly imagined. The apparently stoical image of the crab's face at the end of that very fine poem 'Mussel Hunter at Rock Harbor' may look like an emblem proffered to the human world by the animals, but must take on the colour of all that goes before. It is only a crab face saved, a crab death, a scrupulous rejection of symbol made at the end of a poem that has slowly forced the human being to feel itself reduced in and by the seabeast world. The terrible 'Full Fathom Five' creates an oceanic image with human features, and the real drowned father colours the terror and makes possible a childlike plea for water rather than thick and murderous air. 'The Burnt-Out Spa' establishes, rather like 'Suicide Off Egg Rock', a rubbishy land in contrast to a pure water, and this is reinforced in the final yearning for the purified human reflection: 'It is not I, it is not I, it is not I', whose sad wail is explained by all that has gone before.

These are individuated dramas of dying. The obsession is evident: the poetic flexibility, the inventive enlargements, and the self-explanatory structures show the control and the unenclosed sensibility. The actual mythological or literary symbols are part of such enlargement: the Lorelei, the drowned father in Ariel's song, the museum skeletons, Gulliver, the oriental crabface are all part of a dense formation of feeling, not tenuous-seeming annexes, like the Oedipus of 'The Eye-Mote'. It is such density that may take them to the verge of allegory, but keeps them substantially on its right side. Like much good poetry, it is tempted to be allegory, but refuses.

Moving to *Ariel*, the later volume, it is to recognize that such inventiveness has become more powerful, and sometimes less lucid. In a poem of pain and delirium, 'Fever 103°', the wildness and fast movement of the conceits are excused by the feverishness they dramatize. They cover a wide range. They jerk from Isadora's scarves to Hiroshima ash to lemon water and chicken water; from the bizarre conceit to the simple groping, 'whatever these pink things are'; glimpses of horrors to lucidity, self-description, affectionateness, childishness: the range and the confusion establish the state of sickness. There are the other well-known poems of sickness, 'Tulips' 'In Plaster' and

'Paralytic' which dramatize individual, and different, sick states, all of them appropriately formed, in process and style. Each of these four poems is personal (which is not to say that the *persona* is not imaginary: in 'In Plaster' and 'Paralytic' it seems to be so, judging from external and internal evidence) but each is a complete and controlled drama of sick mind and body. Because it is sickness that is overtly dramatized there is no sense of an improperly won competition with the world's ills. They are brought in, by a species of decorous hallucinations. But the plainness of the act of hallucination, the lucid proffering of a febrile, convalescent, enclosed or paralysed state, allows the larger world to make its presence properly felt. The burning in 'Fever 103°' reminds us of atomic ash, while keeping the separation clear. The plaster cast in 'In Plaster' reminds us of the other imprisonments and near-successful relationships: 'I used to think we might make a go of it together/After all, it was a kind of marriage, being so close'. I think Alun Jones is wrong to see this as an allegory about marriage: these poems of sickness allow her to suggest a whole number of identifications which move towards and back from allegory. David Holbrook seems to make a different though related error in his discussion of 'Tulips': this is not a sick poem but a poem about being sick. Quite different. Of course it is a sick person who is drawn to poems about sickness, but the physical sickness makes up actual chunks of her existence, and sometimes the poems are about chilblains, cuts, influenza and appendicitis. She is drawn to sickness, mutilation, attacks, and dying, but each poem is a controlled and dynamic image with windows, not a lining of mirrors. In 'Fever' and 'In Plaster' the dramatized act of hallucination holds the personal and the social in stable and substantial mutual relationships, neither absorbing the other.

In 'Tulips' there is a slow, reluctant acceptance of the tulips, which means a slow, reluctant acceptance of a return to life. The poem dramatizes a sick state, making it clear that it is sickness. The flowers are hateful, as emblems of cruel spring, as presents from the healthy world that wants her back, as suspect, like all presents. They are also emblems of irrational fear: science is brilliantly misused (as indeed in feeble and deranged states of many kinds) and phototropism and photosynthesis are used to argue the fear: the flowers really do move towards the light, do open out, do take up oxygen. The tulips are also inhabitants of the bizarre world of private irrational fantasy, even beyond the bridge of distorted science: they contrast with the whiteness of nullity and death, are like a baby, an African cat, are like her wound (a real red physical wound, stitched so as to heal, not to gape like opened tulips) and, finally, like her heart. David Holbrook's analysis of this poem seems to stop short of the transforming end, which opens up the poem. The poem, like the tulips, has really been opening from the beginning, but all is not plain until the end, as in 'Nick'. Holbrook says, 'The tulips, as emissaries of love, seem to threaten her with emptying of the identity: "the vivid tulips eat my oxygen",' but the tulips win, and that is the point. It is a painful victory for life. We move from the verge of hallucination, which can hear them as noisy, or see them as like dangerous animals, to a proper rationality, which accepts recovery. The poem hinges on this paradox: while most scientific, it is most deranged; while most surreal, it is most healthy:

> And I am aware of my heart: it opens and closes
> Its bowl of red blooms out of sheer love of me.
> The water I taste is warm and salt, like the sea,
> And comes from a country far away as health.

It is the country she has to return to, reluctant though she is: the identification of the breathing, opened, red, springlike tulips with her heart makes this plain. She wanted death, certainly, as one may want it in illness or, moving back from the poem to the other poems and to her real death, as she wanted it in life. But the poem enacts the movement from the peace and purity of anæsthesia and feebleness to the calls of life. Once more, the controlled conceits; and the movement from one state to another creates expansion. The poem opens out to our experience of sickness and health, to the overwhelming demands of love, which we sometimes have to meet. The symbolism of present-giving and spring-flowers makes a bridge from a personal death-longing to common experience: something very similar can be found in the short poem 'Poppies in October' which uses a similar symbolism and situation for a different conclusion and feeling; and in the magnificent Bee poems, where the solid facts and documentations of beekeeping act as a symbolic base for irrational and frightening fantasy *and* as a bridge into the everyday and ordinary explanations and existences.

The concept of explicit hallucination seems useful. In the Bee poems we move away from the poetry of sickness to another kind of rejected allegory. These poems stress technical mysteries. The craft and ritual of bee-keeping are described with a Kafkaesque suggestiveness, and can take off into a larger terror and come back after all into the common and solid world. In 'The Bee Meeting', her lack of protective clothing, her feeling of being an outsider, then an initiate, the account of the disguised villagers and the final removal of disguise, the queenbee, the spiky gorse, the box—all are literal facts which suggest paranoiac images but remain literal facts. The poem constantly moves between the two poles of actuality and symbolic dimension, right up to and including the end. A related poem, 'The Arrival of the Bee Box', works in the same way, but instead of suggesting paranoiac fear and victimization, puts the beekeeper into an unstable allegorical God-position. The casual slangy 'but my god' unobtrusively works towards the religious enlargement:

> I am no source of honey
> So why should they turn on me?
> Tomorrow I will be sweet God, I will set them free.
>
> The box is only temporary.

After the suggestiveness comes the last line, belonging more to the literal beekeeping facts, but pulled at least briefly into the symbolic orbit. These are poems of fear, a fear which seems mysterious, too large for its occasion. They allow for a sinister question to raise itself, between the interpretation and the substance. The enlargement which is inseparable from this derangement is morally vital and viable: these poems are about power and fear, killing and living, and the ordinariness and the factual detail work both to reassure us and to establish that most sinister of fears, the fear of the familiar world. Perhaps the most powerful Bee poem comes in the New York edition of *Ariel*, 'The Swarm'*. Here the enlargement is total and constant, for the poem equates the destruction of the swarm with a Napoleonic attack, and presents a familiar argument for offensive action: 'They would have killed *me*'. It presents two objective correlatives, the bees and Napoleon, in an unfailing grim humour

> Stings big as drawing pins!
> It seems bees have a notion of honour,
> A black, intractable mind.
> Napoleon is pleased, he is pleased with everything.
> O Europe! O ton of honey!

The humour comes out of the very act of derangement: imagine comparing this with that, just imagine. It depends on the same kind of rationally alert intelligence that controls 'Fever 103°'.

It is present in the great *Ariel* poems: 'Lady Lazarus', 'Daddy',† 'Death & Co.', 'A Birthday Present' and 'The Applicant', which are very outgoing, very deranged, very enlarged. In 'Lady Lazarus' the *persona* is split, and deranged. The split allows the poem to peel off the personal, to impersonate suicidal feeling and generalize it. It is a skill, it is a show, something to look at. The poem seems to be admitting the exhibitionism of suicide (and death-poetry?) as well as the voyeurism of spectators (and

---

*Reproduced at the end of this essay; also in *Encounter*, xxi 4, October 1963.
†A. Alvarez is particularly good on this poem.

readers?). It is also a foul resurrection, stinking of death. This image allows her to horrify us, to complain of being revived, to attack God and confuse him with a doctor, any doctor (bringing round a suicide) and a Doktor in a concentration camp, experimenting in life and death. It moves from Herr Doktor to Herr Enemy and to miraclemakers, scientists, the torturer who may be a scientist, to Christ, Herr God, and Herr Lucifer (the last two after all collaborated in experiments on Adam, Eve, and Job). They poke and nose around in the ashes, and this is the last indignity, forcing the final threat: 'I eat men like air'. It is a threat that can intelligibly be made by martyred victims (she has red hair, is Jewish), by phoenixes, by fire, by women. The fusion and dispersal, once more rational and irrational, makes the pattern of controlled derangement, creating not one mirror but a hall of mirrors, all differently distorting, and revealing many horrors. Such complexity of reference, such enactment of desperation, hysteria and hate, permits at times the utterly bare cry, like the endearment in 'Nick': 'I turn and burn'. Again, the range of tone is considerable. There is the dry irony, only capable of life in such surroundings of hysteria: 'Do not think I underestimate your great concern', and the slangy humour, 'I guess you could say I've a call', which, like the communion tablet in 'Tulips' is an anti-religious joke, not a solemn allusion, though you do not see the joke unless you feel the solemnity. There is the sensuous particularity, extremely unpleasant. It is tactual, visual and olfactory: 'Pick the worms off me like sticky pearls', 'full set of teeth' and 'sour breath'. The sheer active hostility of the poem works through the constant shift from one mode to another, one tone to another, one *persona* to another. It races violently and spasmodically towards the climax.

This kind of structural derangement of structure, which allows for collision, a complex expansion, and a turn in several directions, sometimes becomes very surrealist in dislocation. It fragments into opaque parts, as in that most baffling poem, 'The Couriers', and in 'The Applicant'. We might be tempted to see the enlargement in 'The Applicant' as an allegory of marriage,

relationship, dependence, were it not for the violent twist with
which the poem shuffles off such suggestions:

> First, are you our sort of a person?
> Do you wear
> A glass eye, false teeth or a crutch,
> A brace or a hook,
> Rubber breasts or a rubber crotch,
>
> Stitches to show something's missing? No, no? Then
> How can we give you a thing?
> Stop crying.
> Open your hand.
> Empty? Empty. Here is a hand
>
> To fill it and willing
> To bring teacups and roll away headaches
> And do whatever you tell it.
> Will you marry it?
> It is guaranteed
>
> To thumb shut your eyes at the end
> And dissolve of sorrow.
> We make new stock from the salt.
> I notice you are stark naked.
> How about this suit—
>
> Black and stiff, but not a bad fit.
> Will you marry it?
> It is waterproof, shatterproof, proof
> Against fire and bombs through the roof.
> Believe me, they'll bury you in it.

The hand to fill the empty hand and shut the eyes, or (later) the
naked doll that can sew, cook, talk, move towards this allegory,
but the black stiff suit 'waterproof, shatterproof' in which 'they'll
bury you' moves away towards any kind of panacea or protection.

What holds the poem together, controlling such opacities of derangement, is the violent statement of deficiency hurled out in the first stanza, and the whole violent imitation of the language of salesmanship, the brisk patter of question, observation, suggestion and recommendation. The enlargement works not just through the ill-assembled fragments—hand, suit, and in the later stanzas, doll—but through the satirized speech, which relates needs, deficiencies, dependence and stupid panaceas to the larger world. Life (or love) speaks in the cheap-jack voice, as well it may, considering what it may seem to have to offer. This is an applicant not just for relationship, for marriage, for love, for healing, but for life and death.

This brilliant linguistic impersonation works more generally in these poems, as a source of black humour, as satiric enlargement, as a link with ordinariness, as unselfpitying speech. It is present in small doses but with large effect in the massive, rushing, terrible poem, 'Getting There'. Here the death train is also the painful dying, the dragging life, also wars, machines, labour. The poem questions, and the questions stagger: 'How far is it? How far is it now?' It dwells painfully and slowly in the present tense: 'I am dragging my body . . . And now detonations . . . The train is dragging itself'. Its derangements present animals and machines in a mangling confusion: the interior of the wheels is 'a gorilla interior', the wheels eat, the machines are brains and muzzles, the train breathes, has teeth, drags and screams like an animal. There is a painful sense of the body's involvement in the machine, the body made to be a wheel. The image creates an entanglement, involves what Sartre calls the 'dilapidation' of surrealism. There is the horror of a hybrid monster, a surrealist crossing of animal with machine. The rational arguments and logical connections are frightening in their precision. The wheel and the gorilla's face can be confused into one image, big, round, dark, powerful. Krupp's 'brains' is almost literally correct. The train noise can sound like a human scream, the front of a train can look like a face.

The method of combination as well as the content, as in all

good poetry, generates the passions. The sense of strain, of hallucination, of doing violence to the human imagery is a consequence of the derangements. The rational excuses simply play into the hands of such sense of strain, by making it work visually, bringing it close, giving it substance and connection with the real European world. The movement is a double one, it creates a trope and a form for unbearable pain, and intolerable need for release. It enlarges the personal horror and suggests a social context and interpretation, in Krupp, in the train, in Russia, in the marvellously true and fatigued 'some war or other', in the nurses, men, hospital, in Adam's side and the woman's body 'Mourned by religious figures, by garlanded children'. And finally, in Lethe. Its end and climax is as good as that in 'Nick':

> And I, stepping from this skin
> Of old bandages, boredoms, old faces

> Step to you from the black car of Lethe,
> Pure as a baby.

There is the naked appearance of the myth new-made, the feeling that Lethe has had to wait till now to be truly explained, as the Nativity had to wait for 'Nick'. After such pain of living and dying, after so many bewildered identifications, after such pressure and grotesque confusion, we must step right out of the skin. And when we do, the action reflects back, and the body seems to have been the train. This adds another extension of the derangement of human, animal, and mechanical. After this, only Lethe. The poem then begins to look like a nightmare of dying, the beginning of forgetting, the lurching derangements working as they do in dreams.

Once more, the expansion permits the naked cry. This happens more quietly and sadly in 'The Moon and the Yew Tree' where the movement outward is against the Christian myth, but works so as to generalize, to show the active seeking

mind in the exercise of knowledge and comparison. This movement explains, permits, and holds up the bare dreadful admission, 'I simply cannot see where there is to get to'. The feeling
throughout is one of deep and tried depression. The moon is no
light, no door:

> It is a face in its own right,
> White as a knuckle and terribly upset.

The oddity and childishness of the funny little analogy, and
the simple bare statement, 'terribly upset' all contribute to the
tiredness. So does the science of 'drags the sea after it like a dark
crime' and the conceit 'the O-gape of complete despair', which
have a slight archness and flickering humour, like someone
very tired and wretched who tries a smile. Nature is all too
simply interpreted, coloured by 'the light of the mind', is cold,
planetary, black, blue. The moon is quite separate from the
consolations of religion, though there are echoes of other myths
which emphasize this, of Hecate and witchcraft, as in 'The
Disquieting Muses'. Such sinister suggestions, like the remote
and decorative images of the saints, 'all blue,/Floating on
their delicate feet over the cold pews,/Their hands and faces
stiff with holiness' are made in a matter-of-fact, slightly arch
way. These are Stanley Spencer-like visions, made in a childish,
tired voice: 'The moon is my mother. She is not sweet like
Mary./Her blue garments unloose small bats and owls'. The
very quietness, compared with her more violent poems of fear,
has its own stamp of acceptance. The several bald statements in
the poem belong to the quiet tired prevailing tone: 'How I
would like to believe in tenderness' and 'the message of the yew
tree is blackness—blackness and silence'.

This poem of deep depression still enlarges, still knows about
the larger world, still tries a tired but personal humour:

> Eight great tongues affirming the Resurrection.
> At the end, they soberly bong out their names.

The poem's empathy is powerful, but it is perhaps most powerful when it is dropped. The end returns to the explicit act of interpretation—what do the moon and the yew tree mean?—of the beginning. The poem moves heavily into the meditation, then out of it. There has been an attempt at enlargement, but the colours here are the colours of the mind, and the attempts at mythical explanation or extension all fail. It seems like a poem about making the effort to write out of depression, where the act of enlargement is difficult, the distance that can be covered is short.

In 'A Birthday Present' the same process shapes a different passion. The enlargement in this poem is again a movement towards Christian myth, this time a perverted annunciation. The poem longs for release, like so many others, but in its individual mood. This time she pleads and reasons carefully, patiently, with humility, is willing to take a long time over it. The pace of her poems varies tremendously, and while 'Daddy', 'Lady Lazarus' and 'Getting There' move with sickening speed, 'A Birthday Present' is appallingly slow. Its slowness is right for its patience and its feeling of painful burden. It is created by the pleas, 'Let it not . . . Let it not', and the repetitions which here put the brakes on, though in other poems they can act as accelerators. Its questioning slows up, and so does its vagueness, and its unwillingness to argue endlessly—or almost endlessly. The humilities are piteously dramatized: 'I would not mind . . . I do not want much of a present . . . Can you not . . . If you only knew . . . only you can give it to me . . . Let it not'. There is the childishness, horrifying in the solemn pleasure of 'there would be a birthday'. From time to time there is the full, adult, knowing, reasoning voice, that can diagnose, 'I know why you will not'; reassure, 'Do not be afraid'; and be ironic, 'O adding machine/Is it impossible for you to let something go and have it whole?/Must you stamp each piece in purple . . . '

It is not surprising that Sylvia Plath felt constrained to speak these late poems: they are dramatized, voiced, often opaque but always personalized. Their enlargements are made within the personal voice: groping for the resemblance to some war, some annunciation, some relationship, some institution, some Gothic shape, some prayer, some faith. Even where there is a movement towards the larger world, as in 'The Moon and the Yew Tree' or 'A Birthday Present', it has a self-consciousness, a deployment of knowledge, a reasoning, a sense of human justice, that keeps it from being sick or private. The woman who measures the flour and cuts off the surplus, adhering 'to rules, to rules, to rules', and the mind that sees the shortcomings of adding-machines is a *persona* resisting narcissism and closure, right to the death.

Ronald Laing is involved in that cult of schizophrenia which has encouraged both an excessive admiration and an excessive rejection of a clinically limited poetry of derangement. I believe that Sylvia Plath's poetry is not so limited, but I should nevertheless like to remember Laing's comment that few books in our time are forgiveable, and to suggest that *The Colossus* and *Ariel* are amongst those few.

Nick and the Candlestick

I am a miner. The light burns blue.
Waxy stalactites
Drip and thicken, tears

The earthen womb
Exudes from its dead boredom.
Black bat airs

Wrap me, raggy shawls,
Cold homicides.
They weld to me like plums.

Old cave of calcium
Icicles, old echoer.
Even the newts are white,

Those holy Joes.
And the fish, the fish—
Christ! they are panes of ice,

A vice of knives,
A piranha
Religion, drinking

Its first communion out of my live toes.
The candle
Gulps and recovers its small altitude,

Its yellows hearten.
O love, how did you get here?
O embryo

Remembering, even in sleep,
Your crossed position.
The blood blooms clean

In you, ruby.
The pain
You wake to is not yours.

Love, love,
I have hung our cave with roses,
With soft rugs—

The last of Victoriana.
Let the stars
Plummet to their dark address,

Let the mercuric
Atoms that cripple drip
Into the terrible well,

You are the one
Solid the spaces lean on, envious.
You are the baby in the barn.

The Swarm

Somebody is shooting at something in our town—
A dull pom, pom in the Sunday street.
Jealousy can open the blood,
It can make black roses.
Who are they shooting at?

It is you the knives are out for
At Waterloo, Waterloo, Napoleon,
The hump of Elba on your short back,
And the snow, marshalling its brilliant cutlery
Mass after mass, saying Shh!

Shh! These are chess people you play with,
Still figures of ivory.
The mud squirms with throats,
Stepping stones for French bootsoles.
The gilt and pink domes of Russia melt and float off

In the furnace of greed. Clouds, clouds.
So the swarm balls and deserts
Seventy feet up, in a black pine tree.
It must be shot down. Pom! Pom!
So dumb it thinks bullets are thunder.

It thinks they are the voice of God
Condoning the beak, the claw, the grin of the dog
Yellow-haunched, a pack-dog,
Grinning over its bone of ivory
Like the pack, the pack, like everybody.

APPENDIX

The bees have got so far. Seventy feet high!
Russia, Poland and Germany!
The mild hills, the same old magenta
Fields shrunk to a penny
Spun into a river, the river crossed.

The bees argue in their black ball,
A flying hedgehog, all prickles.
The man with grey hands stands under the honeycomb
Of their dream, the hived station
Where trains, faithful to their steel arcs,

Leave and arrive, and there is no end to the country.
Pom, pom! They fall
Dismembered, to a tod of ivy.
So much for the charioteers, the outriders, the Grand Army!
A red tatter, Napoleon!

The last badge of victory.
The swarm is knocked into a cocked straw hat.
Elba, Elba, bleb on the sea!
The white busts of marshals, admirals, generals
Worming themselves into niches.

How instructive this is!
The dumb, banded bodies
Walking the plank draped with Mother France's upholstery
Into a new mausoleum,
An ivory palace, a crotch pine.

The man with grey hands smiles—
The smile of a man of business, intensely practical.
They are not hands at all
But asbestos receptacles.
Pom, pom! 'They would have killed *me*.'

Stings big as drawing pins!
It seems bees have a notion of honour,
A black, intractable mind.
Napoleon is pleased, he is pleased with everything.
O Europe! O ton of honey!

MARTIN DODSWORTH

Thom Gunn: Poetry as Action and Submission

PERHAPS IT is not very flattering to compare a poet with Lord Byron these days. But I think that it is there that one has to begin to describe Thom Gunn's work. He is the same kind of poet, with many of the same faults, though with a good many more poetic virtues too, it should be said. Like Byron, Gunn thinks of the poet as *one who acts*; he does not think like a philosopher, because his thoughts take the form of action, of a doing something—they are immediately expressed as deeds. To be sure, these deeds are of a special kind; they are poems. They differ from the poems of other men in this way: the reader feels that in writing them the poet has committed himself to what he has to say in such a manner that he is irrevocably changed by it. The poem is an action, because it represents an attempt to form or to transform the poet's identity.

'He writes as habitually as others talk or think—and whether we have the inspiration of the Muse or not, we always find the spirit of the man of genius breathing from his verse.' Hazlitt's description of Byron is useful to us not in its emphasis on the *habitual* nature of his writing verse, but in the suggestion that it was a natural activity, like talking or thinking, only secondarily self-expressive. It is for this reason, one supposes, that the author's spirit is displayed whether his poem succeeds or not—something that is certainly true of Gunn too, although, like Byron again, he is often shamelessly imitative in style. Both poets exercise over us a command of personality, a force which Hazlitt describes as 'genius'. We would not; we have misgivings about that word which are surely justified. Yet Gunn's poetry, by contrast with Byron's, reminds us that poetry can usefully serve to realise for us the idea of a character made strong by the candour with which its conditions of life are regarded. Byron's adversities are largely self-willed, and strike us as though he had in the first place brought them into being, yet is now only half-conscious of the fact; Gunn's really do exist, not only for him, but for all of us, though we are not necessarily continuously aware of them. This marks a very large difference between the two poets. What we feel to be a fine phrase when applied to Byron—'he grapples with his subject, moves, penetrates and animates it with the electric force of his own feelings'—is seen simply to be true when applied to Gunn. In the one case, the active imagination drove Byron further and further into a world of animated fantasy; on the other, it has brought Gunn further and further into the world of all of us, where there really are substantial powers to be grappled with.

Like Byron and unlike: of course. Any account of Gunn's work must deal with the movement away from fantasy in his verse which distinguishes him so clearly from the author of *Childe Harold* or *Don Juan*. Nevertheless, it seems good to begin with an account of the personality felt to underlie all the poems, that is, with the part of Gunn which we may imagine to have set his poetry in one direction rather than another, and to have made of his poems more than receptacles of thought—to have made them that kind of poetic act of which a description has already been attempted. The conviction is strong that the valuable quality in Gunn's work lies in the *whole* of it rather than in those moments of success that we often believe it is a critic's first duty to sort out. A good deal of Gunn's excellence, that is, has to do with his general aim in writing poetry, and this quality, whilst not blinding us to his defects, can lead us to see merit in those very defects.

There certainly are some embarrassingly bad things in his poetry—one is reminded of another Byronic attribute, *notoriety*. One of Gunn's most obvious vices in the early books is their derivativeness, and this is still to be seen to some extent in his latest book, *Touch*. In the early work of any poet, of course, one expects an element of imitation, but not, I think, to the extent to which it is present in *Fighting Terms* and *The Sense of Movement*. The dominant influence is that of Yeats, though other voices—Donne, Eliot and Auden, for example—cut in from time to time. That awful bombastic frankness of Yeats is heard all too clearly in the last poem of *Fighting Terms*, especially in the refrain:

> My lust runs yet and is unsatisfied,
> My hate throbs yet but I am feeble-limbed;
> If as an animal I could have died
> My death had scattered instinct to the wind,
> *Regrets as nothing.*
>
> ('Incident on a Journey')

The same influence is at work in the sudden and rather surprising introduction of a Yeatsian saint into the world of Gunn's leather-kitted motor-cyclists:

> The towns they travel through
> Are home for neither bird nor holiness,
> For birds and saints complete their purposes.
>
> ('On the Move')

And the saint reappears, by the way, in 'Jesus and his Mother', another attempt at the Yeatsian refrain: 'I am my own and not my own.' This is truer of no one more than Yeats's man in quest of reality, who bends all his nature to becoming what he is not, that is, to donning the mask of his anti-self:

'Saint and hero cannot be content to pass at moments to that hollow image [of their opposite] and after become their heterogeneous selves, but would always, if they could, resemble the antithetical self.'

Gunn uses a Yeatsian form to treat this Yeatsian theme.

The derivative element hardly bulks so large in Gunn's later work, though it is there, most obviously in *Positives*. It is worth dwelling on, however—not in order to suggest that Gunn 'has no style of his own', or anything like that, but rather the opposite, that he has, not a style, but *styles*. *Touch*, for example, is a book quite without a consistent manner of speaking, and this fact distinguishes it pretty sharply from books by other poets discussed in this volume. *The Whitsun Weddings* and *Ariel* have each of them a unity of style quite absent from Gunn's book.

There is one thing further to be said about this diversity of styles, and that is that they are patently modifications of styles belonging to other men. This must make a difference to the way in which we read Gunn's poems; along with all the other impressions that we register in reading them, we have to interpret the significance of this fact also.

One effect must be a lack of immediacy in our response to whatever the poet is saying; generally, we are very conscious that what he has to say is being mediated *through* a style, whether it be the Yeatsian mode of 'Incident on a Journey', the Williams-esque free verse of 'Taylor Street', or the more idiosyncratic version of Williams and Marianne Moore offered in poems like 'Considering the Snail'.

A second effect depends on how far we are inclined to generalize about a poet's work in terms of personality. I have already hinted broadly at my own feelings on this point. If Wordsworth is marked by egotistical sublimity, as Keats thought, then what marks Gunn? That does not seem such a very unreasonable or unnatural question, though Gunn's rank in relation to Wordsworth is obviously open to dispute, and one wouldn't certainly want to suggest that he be compared with a poet of quite that stature. One answer to our question might be the following: Gunn's derivativeness suggests a willingness to be influenced, a susceptibility or even submissiveness before other people, and indeed before the world of things.

This hardly tells us the whole truth about Gunn's poetic character; if it did, where would the 'command of personality' be of which I have already spoken? Yet, difficult though the idea is to handle, it does seem to hold a valuable truth for us. For one thing, the idea of submissiveness fits in interestingly with the popular charge against Gunn's poetry that it involves a corrupting admiration for power without responsibility, embodied, for example, in the motor-cyclists of 'On the Move'. This was a charge more easily brought against *The Sense of Movement* than later volumes: I don't know, for example, that Alan Brownjohn would still be tempted to see 'a somewhat displeasing cult of romantic toughness showing a preference at heart for the brutal, the irrational and the wilful instead of accepted humane standards' in any critical enthusiasm for Gunn's work. His attitude is still represented, however, in the headnote on the poet in Kenneth Allott's *Penguin Book of Contemporary Verse*, and continues to crop up here and there. Idolisation of 'the brutal, the irrational and the wilful' could well be the compensatory other side of a submissive nature.

'Lines for a Book' is the prize exhibit when Gunn's supposed uncritical adulation of power is to be arraigned. Allott quotes with distaste the lines where it is said we do better

> To be insensitive, to steel the will,
> Than sit irresolute all day at stool
> Inside the heart . . .

Gunn himself has since said that he thinks the poem is rather bad, 'but I almost invariably like the reactions of people against it. They react against it in such a way as to make me feel that maybe it is a good poem after all.' He says this whilst admitting that the attitude behind the poem could ultimately lead to Fascism. It seems to me that he is right to treat the matter with some calm. The poem is very unlikely to make a Fascist where there was none before, and he himself has moved on to poems that do qualify his admiration for strength of will and so on in a way that we should find morally acceptable. Generally the fulminations about the poem are wrong-headed because they attribute to the poem more power to harm than it actually possesses. When this happens, Gunn can rightly feel tender towards it, because, bad though it is, it does serve to show up a real intellectual absurdity in its critics. Perhaps, too, they protest too much at what is after all an inescapable part of our nature, its hankering to have everything its own way.

It might help, of course, to know what book the lines were written for: but then again, it might not. For the important thing about the poem, insofar as its badness characterizes Gunn's poetry good and bad, is that it is written *in the void*. This is reflected in the very form of the poem, which begins and ends with the same two lines:

> I think of all the toughs through history
> And thank heaven they lived continually.

Despite its concern with action, despite its bravado, the poem is essentially static. By this means it reflects expressively the situation of the author himself who (in a very Byronic mode— and there is certainly a pejorative implication in using the word 'Byronic' at this point) is projecting his own fantasies into a void. These make no contact with the human; nothing in the poem works to relate these heroes, the toughs, to the world we share in common with the speaker. That world, in which we can find the mind 'marvelling at its mirrored face/And evident sensibility', exists imaginatively in the poem only to be rejected. The positive quality is noticeably missing from this poem about the positive of action. We are told that

> Their pride exalted some, some overthrew,
> But was not vanity at last . . .

and the *negative* conclusion epitomises the poem's oddly contrary spirit, whereby action can only be conceived within the bounds of stasis.

Now all this is surely very obvious; a negative judgement of the poem based on this sort of view is unsatisfactory because it supposes that the author doesn't see the kind of criticism to which he lays himself open. Yet all the evidence goes to show that he is intelligent enough to do so. What then are the virtues which he sees in the poem notwithstanding its faults?

One might be, paradoxically, the fact that it is so bad. It is *irredeemably* bad, not the sort of poem that can be patched up with a fresh adjective here, a new phrase there, and a revised conclusion. However unsatisfactory the ideal set up in the poem, the author is felt to be fully committed to it; that is for Gunn a virtue, since the poem is really addressed to those who will not choose to commit themselves to anything. It has the irritant power of Blake's Proverbs of Hell, and is as extreme as some of them: 'Sooner murder an infant in its cradle than nurse unacted desires.' One suspects that some readers resent the poem's act of aggression on the sensibility as much as the shortcomings of its moral position.

'Lines for a Book' is uncharacteristic of Gunn because it circles about a point of imaginative stasis. Nothing is changed or changing in the poem's world. On the other hand, its starting off in the void does seem something held in common with much of the rest of his work, although where this poem remains in the empty realm of fantasy, others, especially later ones, set off for our own, populated country. Finally, even this static and negative poem has its positive side; it does at least *act upon* the reader, who must himself submit, or stand up and fight.

Yet in and through most of Gunn's poems a change of some kind takes place, and we do not find this in 'Lines for a Book'; we will find it rather in a poem like 'Touch', one of Gunn's more recent poems. It is about getting into bed in the dark, where a lover is already lying in the warm, about the thawing-out of body and consciousness in the embrace of the sleeping lover, and, finally, about the commitment of our own natures that seems to be inextricably involved in our experience of love. Here are the last lines of the poem:

What I, now loosened,
sink into is an old
big place, it is
there already, for
you are already
there, and the cat
got there before you, yet
it is hard to locate.
What is more, the place is
not found but seeps
from our touch in
continuous creation, dark
enclosing cocoon round
ourselves alone, dark
wide realm where we
walk with everyone.

This is very hard kind of verse for someone to grasp who has been brought up to think largely in terms of fixed metrical feet. Here there is nothing fixed; on the contrary, everything flows. The lines are irregular, but they may have one thing in common, that each one leads into the next, either from a verb to its complement, or from a subject to its predicate, from an adjective to its noun or from a conjunction to the clause it introduces. The full stop in the middle of the passage is only a pause, and is immediately seen to be so, since the next line begins by emphasising its own continuity: 'What is more . . .' The shortness of the lines plays its part in working on us, too; it makes it difficult for a rhythmical norm to be set up, so that the reader's efforts to discern or to impose an order of some conventional kind are defeated. He is compelled to read the lines in a groping way, uncertain where the emphasis may fall as each sentence develops, and given no hints by the arrangement of the lines themselves. Their continuity is hesitant, the continuity of exploration and discovery.

Gunn takes advantage of this at the very end of the poem,

where he allows new meanings to explode on us in a process of 'continuous creation'. The 'dark/enclosing cocoon' changes to a 'dark/*wide* realm', from the exclusiveness of 'ourselves alone' to the inclusiveness of walking 'with everyone'. The change is a change in consciousness, from one way of looking at 'the place' to another; there is a suggestion that what we have in common with each other is our very aloneness. But that is represented not as an 'enclosing', imprisoning condition, but as one in which we may walk—that is, one which permits us continuing free action.

It is consistent with this poet's emphasis on *doing* that there is a subdued and unostentatious quality about the language of 'Touch'. This may at first seem surprising; we might expect the verbal equivalent of action to lie in the field of the extraordinary, to constitute a verbal assault on the sensibility. There is no such attack in 'Touch'; instead, the minimum of artifice required to make a complete and expressive statement is used. One cannot say that the poem uses entirely the speech of common life, but when it deviates from that language it is to make emphases that are at least not in conflict with the view that poetry should be subservient to the common life. In language and syntax, the poem seeks to persuade us that life can be lived as a process of 'continuous creation', and that the process can be as simple and natural as walking. Its persuasiveness is not that of logic but that of experience; the poem is persuasive if at all by its own nature, and not by the cogency of what is said. It wants to work on us directly and immediately, by contact—to induce in us the sense of being 'in touch' in the metaphorical sense underlying the whole poem.

'Touch, is a poem that acts on us, but it does not do so by means of verbal aggression, as 'Lines for a Book' does. The poem's own movement is a seeping from line to line, which we must follow in a careful, groping movement of the mind. In a sense we are *seduced* by the poem, which acts by refusing us a point of rest until we have reached its end. Its beginning is designedly simple, so as to make one ask what the point of it is at all. If one is in the slightest interested (and of course the poet risks that one will not be) then one is held. It is difficult to *stop* reading (or quoting):

> You are already
> asleep. I lower
> myself in next to
> you, my skin slightly
> numb with the restraint
> of habits . . .

And so on. There is no obscurity to repel one: only a continuous creation of suspense in the passage from one line to another, a sufficient stimulus to curiosity to reach the end, and, all the way through, an evocation of the sort of situation which is or will be part of the life of almost all of us. Like touch, it seduces us into an awareness of what it is we share with everyone—what we all have in common.

As the 'patina of self' gives way to consciousness of the other person's living, physical presence, so the speaker's world opens up to include the domain of others. It has already been suggested that this is a characteristic move in Gunn's poetry, particularly in the books succeeding *The Sense of Movement*. It is worth drawing attention to the fact also that here, as in many other poems, 'real' life is imagined as a place. Gunn does not evoke an *object* like the bird in Yeats's 'Byzantium', nor is his place enclosed, as Eliot's rose-garden; it is wide open, a place for infinite meetings. (It cannot be said that Yeats's Byzantium gives us that sense either.)

Consequently, the 'real' world into which the poem opens, to which it leads us, is notably unspecific. It evades precise definition. It 'seeps from our touch'; one might almost say that it flies from our touch, that because it exists only in immediate experience it cannot be defined; we are only aware of it when it *has been*. The same mysterious quality is implied in the phrase 'continuous creation'; to be continuous, creation can never be complete, and so, in a sense, is never properly creation. The paradox is familiar, but the form of Gunn's poem realises it afresh for us. And this is his task: to help us realise our lives, and our worlds, as giving us space in which to encounter imaginatively, among others, the poet himself. It is a task performed by his making the poem the act by which he himself realises the world as a place of shared possibilities.

The same movement and the same paradox appear, for example, in 'The Goddess', in which a life-force is imagined travelling upward from the earth's centre to men and women:

> Goddess,
> Proserpina: it is we,
> vulnerable, quivering,
> who stay you to abundance.

The force is *stayed* by us, but *abundance* gives the lie to this temporary halt. We *stay* her, because both *we* and *she abound*, and so exist in a relationship never truly halted. (It is a pity that this poem is spoilt by what I feel to be a dreadful wrong note— the line 'her dress tight across her ass', which just does not fit in with the language of the rest.)

'Flying Above California', from an earlier volume (*My Sad Captains*) depends on this kind of contradiction too. It is a poem about the 'richness' of the Californian landscape, a richness which includes the 'cold hard light' of fogless days, 'that reveals merely what is'.

> That limiting candour,
>
> that accuracy of the beaches,
> is part of the ultimate richness.

To see the point of the poem you have to feel a conflict between *limiting* and *richness*. *Ultimate richness* should be a richness without limit; here, the limit, which should mark the outward bound of a thing, is mysteriously included inside the thing itself, and is *part* of the ultimate richness. It is as though Gunn were saying that he knew there were things that we called limits and that we respected as such, but that ultimately, though real and existent, they ceased to count. We experience the circular and limited world as limitless (particularly, of course, when flying above it).

'Touch', 'The Goddess', 'Flying Above California', are all different from 'Lines for a Book' in that they are more or less seductive in technique where 'Lines' is aggressive. This difference corresponds to one between the two early books *Fighting Terms* and *The Sense of Movement* and the rest, and the transition is marked by the substitution of W.C. Williams and Marianne More for Yeats as poetic models. The imitation of Yeats involved the use of more or less strict and obvious forms:

> I put this pen to paper and my verse
> Imposes form upon my fault described . . .
> ('A Plan of Self Subjection')

The early poems could often be spoken of, not inappropriately, as objects, as things made rather than words spoken. If one were to use the analogy of space, one would call them places where the walls seem to press in—cells or prisons. A kind of cheerless order has been imposed. A poem in *Touch* called 'In the Tank' takes up the prison metaphor in a way that reflects interestingly on 'Flying Above California' and also on the poetry of the first two books. In this poem 'the ultimate richness' again figures in contrast to a 'limiting candour'. A prisoner sits in his cell and sees 'all that there was to see':

> And then he knew exactly where he sat.
> For though the total riches could not fail
> —Red weathered brick, fountains, wisteria—yet
> Still they contained the silence of a jail,

The jail contained a tank, the tank contained
A box, a mere suspension, at the centre,
Where there was nothing left to understand,
And where he must re-enter and re-enter.

'Tank' is a slang term for both prison and cell; it is a useful word
for Gunn because a tank functions as a container, something necessarily *limiting*. The difference between this poem and 'Flying
Above California' lies in the point of view taken; there, one was
above the limiting factor which was to be included in a greater (and
by implication unlimited) whole: but here, the prisoner is *within*
limits. 'The total riches' do not *fail*; they continue to exist , and
to exist as richness, yet they exist as part of a symbolic relationship of which the other part is poverty and imprisonment. The
totality which prison and riches add up to can be defined by
either term in the relationship. It depends on the point of
view.

Both poems are concerned with attitude, not with the social
and political processes that go to form it. The man in the tank is
simply a 'felon', and the extent of his responsibility for his
situation is not examined. There is, however, a parallel
relationship between his physical and his mental situation. The
'box', 'a mere suspension', at the centre of the cell is the *cell* of
his own thoughts, his thought-tank, and it is, like the cell,
empty but for the man himself, or rather, the man's consciousness of himself. In this way, 'In the Tank' takes up a theme of
one of the crucial poems in *The Sense of Movement*, 'Merlin
in the Cave: He Speculates Without a Book':

What could I do but start the quest once more
Toward the terrible cave in which I live,
The absolute prison where chance thrust me before
I built it round me on my study floor . . . ?

The cave in which Vivien imprisons Merlin is also the prison-
cell of his own thoughts, a self-consciousness which could not

commit him to the 'quick illogical motions' which are the evidence that 'lovers move and live'.

The relevance of existentialist thought to an understanding of Gunn's poetry has often enough been remarked on—by John Mander, for example, in his interesting essay on the poet in *The Writer and Commitment*. The positive influence on Gunn is best illustrated by 'The Corridor' in *The Sense of Movement* which depends directly on a passage in Sartre's *L'Être et le Néant* (the section on 'le regard'). Existentialist theory is obviously relevant to the subject-matter of 'Flying Above California' and 'In the Tank'. The poems present contrary points of view, the physical situation (plane, cell) figuring as a metaphor for the mental. The question is: how is the transition made from one point of view to another? The answer would seem to lie in the realm of the act of faith, the existentialist leap, another version of the 'quick illogical motions' which proved to be beyond the reach of Merlin in the cave.

In existentialist philosophy the idea of personal freedom figures largely. It is felt to be implicit in the self's ability to project itself in time and to be conscious of its own potentiality. Emmanuel Mounier in his *Introduction aux Existentialismes* puts the matter in this way:

'. . . the human existent is always more than what he is (at a given moment), although he may not yet be what he will become. He is, according to Sartre, the "being who is not what he is, and who is what he is not". This conception of existence as forward-looking is opposed by Heidegger to inertia, to the totally determined nature of classical *existentia*, of substance, or at least of the degraded image which is often offered in its place.'*
The quotation is useful to us, incidentally, because it points to another influence than that of Yeats at work in 'Jesus and his Mother', but it is here principally because it introduces an important pair of contraries, Heidegger's inertia and the projection into possibility which is its complement. The prisoner of 'In the Tank' could well exemplify inertia, just as

*Mounier, *Introduction aux Existentialismes*, Paris, 1947, p. 40. My translation.

the air-traveller of 'Flying Above California' could be said to look at the world from a point of view of projection.

There seems to be an ambiguity in existentialist thought about the extent to which the self's consciousness of its own potentiality or freedom is voluntary or not. On the one hand, human consciousness may be viewed as determined by the polarity of inertia and its opposite, and in this case the sense of freedom seems to be something more or less involuntary, something inherent in the human situation; on the other, since the consciousness of potentiality is actually threatened by the dead weight of inertia, it would seem necessary that it be kept alive by an effort of the will. This ambiguity is present in the idea of *risk* which crops up frequently in existentialist thought. A risk involves calculation and choice, the assent of the will, and also a submission to its consequences which must overrule the will. Mounier here describes Kierkegaard's notion of risk, but much the same sort of thing is to be found in other thinkers in this tradition. Man is free, rises above inertia, in the act of risking to choose:

'The constitution of a man made in order that he should choose can only be that of a being who takes *risks*. Am I sure, you say, when I engage in such and such a course of action, that such and such a reward in eternity, or even in history, awaits me? If you were sure, replies Kierkegaard, you would not be exactly engaged in an action of an eternal order, you would be making a profitable speculation.'*

The essence of a risk is that it is a voluntary commitment to the irrational.

Gunn's poetry is centred on the irrational. In his early work there is an emphasis on the will and consequently on the act of choosing risk, like the motor-cyclists in 'On the Move'; this gives way to the less intimidating view that the world of freedom and possibility remains in a sense perpetually available, with a consequent reduction of anguish. Although life is still most fully lived at moments only, it does not lapse into the kind

* Mounier, p. 46.

of non-being posited by such a poem as 'Wind in the Street': 'The same faces, and then the same scandals . . . ' Now, life outside the moments of fullness is sustained by a faith in the availability of that fullness.

Faith is not certainty, is not rational. The leap from the imprisoning self is a mysterious and irrational act, like the one by which the central character of 'Misanthropos' rejoins the world of others. He has believed himself the sole survivor of some universal catastrophe for some long period of time, until a party of other survivors appears. He hides: but when one of the others is scratched by a briar and bleeds:

> he performs an action next
> So unconsidered that he is perplexed,
> Even in performing it, by what it means—
> He walks around to where the creature leans.

The risk is not consciously taken, as it would have been by the speaker of almost any poem in *The Sense of Movement*. Gunn's existentialism now draws on the view of life as *necessarily* (that is, *naturally*) dependent on the polarity between inertia and choice, the leap out into the world where possibilities are realised.

The poetry of *Fighting Terms* and *The Sense of Movement* is just as irrational in principle as the rest. A poem like 'Lazarus Not Raised' is set out in an ostentatiously lucid manner; it is orderly, but what it describes is nevertheless mysterious and impervious to reason. This seems the expressive function of what would otherwise be an unnecessary complication in the following lines: the repetition of the word *rest* at so close an interval with opposite meanings which all the same coincide is quite as puzzling as the decision by Lazarus not to be raised:

> He chose to spend his thoughts like this at first
> And disregard the nag of offered grace,
> Then chose to spend the rest of them in rest.

As Gunn rewrites the Bible story, Lazarus so perfectly exemplifies the force of inertia that he is not even raised from the
grave in order to return to it. Although he is said by the poet to
choose, he is not seen to choose on a rational basis. The *rest* of
his thoughts are spent in *rest:* they seem to exemplify a natural,
necessary and inexplicable relationship to inertia, which is in
ironic contrast to the orderly form of verse used throughout the
book in which the poem appears.

The complementary figure to that of Lazarus in *Fighting
Terms* is the soldier in 'Incident on a Journey', whose commit-
ment to a life of action is no more rational than the choice of
Lazarus not to be raised:

> And always when a living impulse came
> I acted, and my action made me wise.

There is nothing in the early style quite like the 'seductive-
ness' of 'Touch' and its companions. In some ways the early
style is more complex in intention and effect than the later.
Partly it works as an ironic counterpart to the highly subjective
nature of the experiences recorded in the poems; but partly, too,
it stands for an orderliness to which the speaker in the poems
would often aspire. It is the imposed order of a victorious army.
In this way the style reflects Gunn's interest in the anti-self of
Yeats—it is an aesthetic reflection of Yeats's general observation that
'if we cannot imagine ourselves as different from what we are,
and try to assume that second self, we cannot impose a discipline upon ourselves though we may accept one from others'.
Much of the weakness of the early poems is her accounted for.

However, it seems to me that the main effect of the early
style is felt neither as an achieved irony of tone nor as the
successful or unsuccessful attempt to don a mask of complete
control over a subjective and irrational content, but rather as an
agonized consciousness of the gap between what is said and
the manner of saying it. A poem like 'Carnal Knowledge' works

by giving a sense of the difference between the polish of manner and the extremity of the situation discussed. It is not enough to describe the poem as ingenious; the play on words is more emotionally exhausting than intellectually dazzling:

> Even in bed I pose: desire may grow
> More circumstantial and less circumspect
> Each night, but an acute girl would suspect
> My thoughts might not be, like my body, bare.
> I wonder if you know, or knowing, care?
> You know I know you know I know you know.

Surely one is struck in this poem by the incongruity of its style; the situation demands a cry from the speaker, and not the deliberation of speech which Gunn supplies and which, I think, we may legitimately describe as a stifled or inhibited cry. Precisely what seems not quite polished enough to be consistent with the rest is here the most potent part of what is said—the pairing of *More circumstantial and less circumspect*, which seems pointless, is especially effective for that very reason: it emphasizes the total pointlessness of the attempt at 'poise' in such a situation (which, incidentally, bears a clear relation to Sartre's account of the psychology of love in *L'Être et Le Néant*).

This point is worth labouring because it brings us back to something we have looked at earlier, the element of submissiveness in Gunn's poetic character. In the early poems one is most acutely aware of a tendency to think in terms of a divided self, illustrated by 'The Secret Sharer', 'Lofty in the Palais de Danse' or, a poem excluded from the revised *Fighting Terms*, 'A Village Edmund'. The duality in the protagonist's nature in these poems seems to correspond to that between subject-matter and style in 'Carnal Knowledge', and to that between sub-missiveness and self-willed, self-justifying action in the poetic character of this poet. What has been said of 'Lines for a Book' would also make it possible to phrase the duality in terms of stasis and action, or in Heidegger's way, in terms of inertia and projection.

What seems to happen in the development of Gunn as a poet is that the stifled cry of 'Carnal Knowledge' becomes progressively apparent in poems like 'The Beaters', 'Julian the Apostate' and 'Jesus and his Mother', culminating in the 'one convulsion' of 'Saul becoming Paul' in the beautiful poem 'In Santa Maria del Popolo'. From this point on, the poetry becomes increasingly *persuasive* in intention, and the semblance of reasonableness ('I circle because I have found/That tracing circles is a useful spell/Against contentment' and so on) becomes less and less significant. In this way the books so far written describe one single action.

Many poets regard their art as lying in an ordering of significance, a making sense of what we find in everyday life intractable for one reason or another. I don't think that this is true of Thom Gunn, whose poems ask rather for an act of faith on our part. They do not help us to understand experience, they help us to believe in certain kinds of experience—the ultimate richness of 'Flying Above California', the spiritual poverty of 'In the Tank' (which is analogous to that of 'Carnal Knowledge'), and the gaps between them. The poems exist primarily to be experienced, secondarily to be understood; and what there is to be understood is not necessarily new in the context of Gunn's poetry, or conceptually very astonishing. 'Lights Among Redwood', for example, is not a poem that makes any extraordinary statement; it simply calls the reader into the experience described, so that the experience becomes his own. One might say that the poet's aim is to make his reader feel 'This is beautiful' rather than 'This is true', except that 'beautiful' suggests static perfection of a work of art whilst his poem is about a movement, and is movement, action, itself:

> Calm shadow! Then we at last
> remember to look upward . . .

'Lights Among Redwood' like 'Touch' depends for its success on a syntactic movement across lines:

> And the streams here, ledge to ledge,
> take care of light. Only to
> the pale green ribs of young fern
> tangling above the creek's edge
> it may sometimes escape, though
> in quick diffusing patterns.

Ledge to ledge describes the sinuous course of the literal sense as it trickles here from line to line. 'Quick diffusing patterns' describes the minimal effect of the rhymes, whose impact is diffused because neither rhythm nor meaning permits that they should be dwelt on. 'Elsewhere it has become tone,/pure and rarified', we are told, concerning the light; but up to the moment when we look upward with the speaker the poem is entirely an illustration of 'tone', particularly in its avoidance of a personal pronoun. This delayed entry of the personal element ('we at last/remember to look upward . . . ') works by contrast with the indefiniteness of mere 'tone'; *we* are not *pure and rarified* but stand embodied in the shadowy forest scene and in contrast to it. Furthermore, the oblique course by which the reader is made, first to enter the tonal *dimness* of the poem and then to encounter the pronoun, encourages his identification with it. *We* refers not simply to 'I speaking in the poem and my companion', or to 'anyone happening to be in the same situation as I speaking in the poem', but also to 'I speaking in the poem and you reading it'. The place described is like that in 'Touch', a place where imaginative encounter is possible in a given experience:

> constant, to laws of size and
> age the thick forms hold, though gashed
> through with Indian fires. At once
> tone is forgotten: we stand
> and stare—mindless, diminished—
> at their rosy immanence.

This is the experience towards which the rest of the poem leads us: our sense of diminishment before the actually defined and other. The trees distinguish themselves from mere tone; they are permanent and substantial. *Hold* is a word felt to relate to *laws of size and age*, but is also felt absolutely: the trees hold, where everything else tangles or is muted. They are *thick* forms, not Platonically ideal. But why are we diminished, made mindless by them? Their very size makes us feel small, but also, and especially, their *immanence*. The word is used by Kierkegaard, who took it, in his turn from Hegel, in order to disagree with him. Outside a specific philosophical context, the word is therefore ambiguous, as it is here. The word implies a paradox of the kind we have already seen in 'Touch'; it means firstly the actual existence of these trees in this world shared by the speaker and the reader of the poem, and in this sense a supernatural quality is implied but not stated—the trees are like God, who is immanent in the universe, not apart from it. At the same time the word has a meaning in conflict with this first one. Their *immanence* is then the trees' quality of fulfilling or having fulfilled intrinsic purposes which do not connect with our world at all. This is the N.E.D.'s sense 2 for *immanent*:

'Immanent act (action): an act which is performed entirely within the mind of the subject, and produces no external effect: opposed to a *transient* or *transitive* act.'

In this sense the trees' *immanence* is completely unobservable: it is something we intuit, that the trees exist in total indifference to us. And so we are made to feel two different things at once, *diminished* both because we recognize something marvellous, akin to religious feeling, in the discovery of the substantial reality of the world in which we live (we are then *mindless* because no longer prisoners of our own minds, no longer in the situation of, let us say, the speaker in 'Carnal Knowledge'), and also because we are apart from and less than the world outside us, which continues whether we like it or not, and according to its own *laws* (we are then *mindless* because our sense of the trees' indifference to us temporarily extinguishes our consciousness of ourselves).*

One thing more: it is a *rosy* immanence. It has the health of rosy cheeks, the promise of rosyfingered dawn. Contradictory though the experience is, it is also salutary: it puts us where we have to begin again, to give ourselves again a mind, a consciousness. This sense of promise as inherent in our condition of life is what Gunn wishes to give us—to give us, not to prove.

The poem illustrates how Gunn has brought the two sides of his poetic character into harmony; the submissiveness is present in the way the experience is recorded, in which the charm of 'tone' is expressed equally with the overpowering definition of the trees' 'immanence', and yet so is the quality of action, of guiding, of swaying, the reader.

One activity in particular requires a willingness to submit to experience in equal proportion to the ability to shape it, and that is the explorer's. Gunn's poetry seems truly to be exploratory, with an exactitude of meaning one can rarely achieve.

That is what, ultimately, distinguishes him from Byron:

> His touch
> Was masterful to water, audience
> To which he could react until an end.
> Strong swimmers, fishermen, explorers: such
> Dignify death by thriftless violence—
> Squandering with so little left to spend.
>
> ('Lerici')

Byron 'squandered with so little left to spend'; he was, like

*What the poem seems to be getting at in this use of the word 'immanence' could be well expressed in Heidegger's account of the dual aspect of 'being': ' "Being" meant for the Greeks: permanence in a twofold sense:

1. standing-in-itself (In-sich-stehen) in the sense of arising (Ent-stehen, standing-out-of) (*physis*),

2. but, as such, "permanent" (ständig), i.e. enduring (*ousia*).' (Martin Heidegger, *An Introduction to Metaphysics*, translated by Ralph Manheim, New York: Doubleday, 1961, p.52).

the speaker in Gunn's early poems, a *poseur*. The paradox which applies to him is obvious and strained, and calls on no qualities held in common with the reader. By contrast, Gunn's later poems proceed with a sinuous and plastic grace, far from the rigidity of *pose*, and suggest not a death dignified by violence, but a life that manifests, like his best poetry, a sense of inexhaustible vitality, of what Mounier calls 'cet être qui jaillit de l'être', 'that being which wells up out of being'. The notion of an energy not to be defeated, figured by the persistence of some deep well, a continual bubbling forth, is perhaps too facile as a description of the various action of Gunn's poetry; but in its general emphasis it is also, perhaps, the necessary one.

DONALD DAVIE

The Black Mountain Poets:
Charles Olson and Edward Dorn

THE name 'Black Mountain', as it is attached to the poets I
am going to discuss, derives from Black Mountain College, an
institution in North Carolina, now long defunct, where several
of the most prominent members of the group first came together
in the early 1950s. The history of Black Mountain College is
itself of great interest, though it isn't my concern at this
moment. Suffice to say that it was in most ways the earliest
instance of something that is now much in the public eye, which
is to say, 'the anti-university'. It was founded by disaffected
teachers from an American university, who despaired of effect-
ing what they understood as 'education' in the institutionalized
places of higher learning in their country, smeared and distorted
as those places were by the prevailing ideology of the national
society. In the last years of its brief but eventful history, Black
Mountain College was directed by Charles Olson, who at the
age of 41 came from a career in politics and government service
to serve as rector of the college from 1951 to 1956. Olson, who
did not publish his first poem until he was 35, was at that time
known in literary circles chiefly as the author of a monograph
on Herman Melville's *Moby Dick*, a book entitled *Call Me
Ishmael* which first appeared in 1947 and is still the best introduction to his thought. But the exceptionally discerning reader
of poetry might have noted also, published in a New York
poetry magazine in 1950, Olson's essay-manifesto, *Projective
Verse*, which has since been reprinted several times and is
available most readily as a 'Statement on Poetics' in an appendix

216

to D. M. Allen's anthology, *The New American Poetry: 1945–1960*. Allen's sadly indiscriminate anthology, which came out in 1960, was the means by which the so-called Black Mountain group of poets came to be recognized as, for good or ill, a feature of the Anglo-American literary scene. And this delay in the group's establishing itself was no accident. For just as Black Mountain College repudiated the institutionalized organization of higher education in the U.S.A. (and so repudiated the normal, high-powered channels of publicity for itself), so the members of the Group for many years shunned the normal channels of publication, the well-established and soundly-financed magazines, and the New York publishing houses. Their own magazines, shoddily produced in small printings and distributed privately, often for free, are now already collectors' items; as are their slender booklets and pamphlets, often produced on private printing-presses. Even now, when in many cases the reputations can be said to be firmly established, the collections are brought out by small and sometimes fugitive publishing concerns; they are very seldom reviewed, and hardly ever in the expected places; and they are hard to come by except through a few booksellers, whether in New York, in San Francisco, or in London.

This distinguishes the Black Mountain poets from a group which externally looks similar, with which they have had, and still maintain for the most part, friendly relations. I mean, the so-called Beatnik poets centred on San Francisco in the late 1950s, of whom the most familiar names are doubtless Allen Ginsberg, Gregory Corso, Jack Kerouac, Lawrence Ferlinghetti. The Beatnicks were always, and remain, very astute self-publicists, whereas the serious Black Mountaineers have shunned publicity very effectively.

So much for general information: now for the poetry. But at once I must warn you that there is a disappointment in store for you. I have chosen no specimen poems to dissect for your benefit. No, on consideration I have decided against this. For that procedure smacks altogether too strongly of precisely the milieu for poetry that the Beatniks and Black Mountaineers alike want to avoid: the graduate seminar class which spends a happy hour winkling out the symbols and the ambiguities from a dozen lines of Allen Tate or Robert Lowell or Ted Hughes. The poems of Charles Olson, of Ed Dorn and Robert Creeley, are not written for that sort of reading, any more than are the poems of Allen Ginsberg or Walt Whitman. As Olson's treatise makes clear, they are written very insistently for the speaking voice, and for the speaking voice of the poet himself; and they are composed so as to be performed, live, before a live audience, by the poet in person. It need not be the bravura performance before massed microphones of an Allen Ginsberg; on the contrary, Creeley's poems in his way, and Dorn's in his (I haven't heard Olson read) are meant to be given a very soft-voiced performance, hesitant and deliberate, intimate and personal. And equally, it does not mean with Creeley and Dorn as it seems to do with Ginsberg that the text of the poem is a slack and colourless 'score', which comes to life only in the charismatic presence of the bard. The poems have much to give to the solitary and silent reader, as I hope to show. (And the scoring for the speaking verses is in some cases, notably Creeley's and Duncan's, extremely punctilious and exact.) But they are not meant to be mulled over excitedly, and tugged this way and that, in earnest discussion. And in fact, of course, we too seldom remember how few poems ever were written with that sort of reading in mind; how very special and peculiar is this sort of treatment of poems, which we tend to regard as normal.

But there is another reason why it isn't appropriate to approach the Black Mountain poets by close reading of selected specimens. Some of their poems can be submitted to that sort of inspection, and can survive it, as can the poems of Milton or Ezra Pound. But in Olson's case and Dorn's, as in Pound's case and Milton's, such an experiment is in any event wide of the mark. With these poets it is not the case that the poem in isolation, if only you scrutinize it closely enough, will reveal to

you everything you need to understand it and enjoy it. Even of
T. S. Eliot and Robert Lowell, Allen Tate and Ted Hughes,
this is not true; for all these poets, like all poets there ever
were, expect the reader to bring something to the poem—and
something more than just receptivity, sympathy and alertness.
The reader is expected to bring to the poem a certain body of
information, and certain assumptions. In the cases of Olson
and Dorn, Milton and Pound, this is more than usually important; for the stock of information, and the body of assumptions,
which you are expected to bring to the poem are not those that
you would normally come by as part of the equipment of a
normally well-educated person. Poets like the four I've named
have followed a wayward and eccentric path through the records
of human experience; they have read books that aren't on the
normal curriculum, and they set more store by these than by
some which *are* on the curriculum; as a result, when they do
encounter a monument of the curriculum, an acknowledged
'classic' (Homer, for instance) they find their way into him as it
were from an unexpected angle, they are interested in things
about him that are not the things usually singled out for attention, they place the emphasis in places we do not expect and are
not prepared for and which, often enough, we consequently fail
to recognize. As a result, with poets like these, there is a lot of
spadework for us to do before ever, as it were, we open their
books. They are very learned poets, who write very learned
poems; and they have come by their learning in out-of-the-way
places. What's more, they are not interested in making their
poems self-sufficient, sailing free like so many rockets from the
learning that was accumulated only as it were to assist take-off;
on the contrary the poems depend on the learning, they emerge
from it only to burrow back into it again, the poems depend
upon—and are themselves *part of*—the lifelong addiction of the
poet to the business of educating himself, i.e. the business of
understanding the world that he and we are living in. The poems
differ in degree but not in kind from the excited letters that the
poets write to each other and to their admirers, or from the

reviews and articles they write for each other's magazines. And so the poems have, quite deliberately, the sort of untidiness and hastiness that we associate with lecture-notes and reading-lists.

This is very different indeed from the fastidious impersonality that T. S. Eliot sought for and attained in his poems, or Wallace Stevens in his. And in fact what gets in the way of most of us apart from the very young, when we attempt to approach these poets at the present day, is precisely our experience of Eliot's poetry and the way we have nearly all been conditioned, more than we realize, to regard Eliot's procedures in poetry, and Eliot's sort of poetry, as the norms for poetry in English in the present century. This is the point of insisting on the name of Pound. For Olson and his followers derive from that side of Ezra Pound on which Pound is most unlike his esteemed colleague and one-time protégé, T. S. Eliot. To put it more exactly, these poets, as Americans, use Pound so as to bypass Eliot, because only by bypassing Eliot can they re-establish contact with the great American poet of the last century, Walt Whitman. (The line of descent from Pound to Olson can be traced in more detail through two other American poets—William Carlos Williams and Louis Zukofsky.) Not only Eliot, but also the poets of the past whom Eliot taught several generations to esteem afresh (for instance John Donne and Andrew Marvell) are stumbling-blocks if we want to get into the world of Black Mountain poetry; and this is true of the Black Mountain poets as of no other poet considered in this book. Far more useful, if as British readers we want a British name—far more helpful and worth remembering is the name of D. H. Lawrence, and not just Lawrence's poems either. Olson's most Lawrencian book is his *Mayan Letters*, written from Central America to Robert Creeley, when Olson was pursuing archaeological researches into the Maya civilization. And Dorn is at his most Lawrencian in *The Shoshoneans*, his prose book on the Amerindian peoples of the part of America he has made his own.

After what I have said, it will not surprise you that I think the best thing for me to do in the space that I have is to introduce you to some of the preoccupations that Dorn and Olson share. (For these are the two poets I'm really concerned with.) These preoccupations appear in—indeed, they are the substance of—many of the poems that these men write; but in order to recognize them when they appear in the poems, you need to be acquainted with them beforehand—in other words they are part of that stock of information and assumptions which you have to bring to the poems. The ones that I want to isolate turn around the notion of 'geography'. And as good a way as any of beginning to show how important this has been, and is, for Dorn and Olson, is by quoting from one of their acknowledged forerunners, William Carlos Williams, writing a manifesto in 1930:

'To what shall the mind turn for that with which to rehabilitate our thought and our lives? To the word, a meaning hardly distinguishable from that of place, in whose great virtuous and at present little realized potency we hereby manifest our belief.'

The portentousness of the phrasing here should not prevent us from recognizing that this is the sort of thing that has been said often before. The crucialness of a grasp on *locality*, the imaginative richness for poetry of a sense of *place*—this is no novel perception. We need go no further back than to the generation preceding that of Williams; to Yeats saying, 'And I, that my native scenery might find imaginary inhabitants, half-planned a new method and a new culture.' And so it should not surprise us if *The Maximus Poems* of Charles Olson, the only poetic enterprise of the present day in English which appears to be planned on a scale to challenge comparison with Williams's *Paterson* and Pound's *Cantos*, should be geographical rather than historical in its focus. *The Maximus Poems* aspire to give in language a *map*, a map of one place, the town of Gloucester, Massachussetts. This town, Olson's home-town, is otherwise known to twentieth-century literature only by way of Rudyard Kipling's *Captains Courageous*. And the Portuguese-speaking fishermen of Gloucester, embodied by Spencer Tracy in the film that was made of Kipling's story, figure repeatedly in the poems that Olson has made about his home place. For the poems do not, by concentrating on the geography of Gloucester, thereby *ignore* its history. Quite the contrary. The great geographer Alexander von Humboldt remarked that 'In classical antiquity the earliest historians made little attempt to separate the description of lands from the narration of events the scene of which was in the areas described. For a long time physical geography and history appear attractively intermingled'. And of course this is true; the ancient Herodotus is the father of geography but also the father of history, and he fathers the one by virtue of fathering the other. Crucial terms from Herodotus, as well as the name of Alexander von Humboldt himself, figure in Pound's *Cantos*. Yet it was probably not in Pound that Olson found the grounds for the veneration of Herodotus which he has repeatedly professed. A more likely source is an American geographer of the present day, Carl Ortwin Sauer, whose name figures in a pamphlet that Olson published some years ago, called *A Bibliography on America for Ed Dorn*.

(The slangy in-group flavour of that title, incidentally, as of much of the excited telegraphese prose which it introduces, is something that you may well find tiresome; but it is inevitable, given a movement which defines itself as all that organized society is not. Such a movement is an open conspiracy, which is only another word for a coterie, though an unusually ambitious and serious one. The same set of social circumstances produces the equally tiresome and not dissimilar telegraphese idiom of Ezra Pound's letters.)

At any rate Sauer's essay of 1925, 'The Morphology of Landscape', makes the same point about the ancient geography of Herodotus that we have just seen Alexander von Humboldt making: 'The *historia* of the Greeks, with its blurred feeling for time relations, had a somewhat superior appreciation of areal relations and represented a far from contemptible start in geography.' Dorn dutifully learned his lesson, from Olson's reading list, and uses the very word, 'areal', in the poem he has addressed to Olson, called 'From Gloucester Out':

To play areal as particulars, and out of the span
of Man, and as this man
does,
     he does, he
   walks
     by the sea
in my memory
and sees all things and to him
are presented at night
the whispers of the most flung shores
from Gloucester out.

The same emphasis—on the home-base, on the local terrain as
needing to be securely grasped by the imagination before it can
afford to look further abroad—is in Dorn's similarly entitled
poem 'Idaho Out', in his third collection with the significant
programmatic title, *Geography*. (The poem is now available in
a booklet by itself.) These poems by Dorn, like many of
The Maximus Poems by Olson which they emulate, may be
regarded as investigations of just what it means to have 'a
standpoint'—the place on which you stand, on which you take
your stand, the place which necessarily conditions everything
which you see when you stand on that place and look from it.

Olson recommends the geographer Sauer's writings as a
whole. But he specifies as particularly important an essay by
Sauer called 'Environment and Culture during the last Deglacia-
tion'. And it's easy to see why Olson does this. For this particular essay by Sauer takes up, and applies to North America
particularly, a thesis which Sauer argued in another paper
called 'Agricultural Origins and Dispersals'. Both these essays
argue that the culture-hearth of agricultural man, which is to say
of Neolithic man, is not, as is still most generally supposed, in
South-West Asia, but in South-East Asia; and this for the
reason that (so Sauer maintains) the breakthrough to agriculture
made by Neolithic man came from a fishing culture rather than
a hunting culture. Only if this precarious and disputed thesis is

DONALD DAVIE

true can Olson in his *Maximus Poems* use his chosen standpoint,
Gloucester (which is primarily a *fishing* community), in the
way he wants to do—as a vantage-point for surveying and
understanding human society however various, and human
mythology however archaic.

This, it may well be thought, is an instance of how poetry
may become entangled with geography too much for its own
good, an ambitious poetic enterprise perilously dependent upon
a particular disputed geographer's thesis. But the point is
important, because otherwise we might think that Olson chose
to concentrate on Gloucester simply because it happened to
be the poet's home-town, out of some familiar Romantic notion
of mystical properties available for a man in his native origin,
his 'roots'. This is not the case; Olson *chose* to make Gloucester
his standpoint, there was no mystical compulsion upon him to
do so. This is where it's instructive to remember his essay on
Melville, with its title 'Call me Ishmael'. Ishmael—the archetypal nomad and wanderer. And in fact Olson's argument about
Melville's *Moby Dick* shows once again with what desperate
seriousness he takes the matter of geographical location; for his
argument is that the greatest character in Melville's great and
strange romance is the Pacific Ocean, that the book as a whole
celebrates the imaginative discovery and appropriation by
Western man, specifically by American man, of that great waste
of waters in the West, the Pacific—one more territory which
the pioneers could light out into when they had crossed the
entire continent and found themselves faced by the sea. The
standpoint which Olson, and more consistently Dorn, are concerned to investigate is not characteristically a fixed point, the
place where roots are sunk; it is a moving point, the continually
changing standpoint of a man who is on the move across con-
tinents and oceans. Thom Gunn exhorts us to be 'on the move',
but Dorn's poem 'Idaho Out', *gives us* this man moving, and
moving by automobile, from Idaho into Montana and back again,
his standpoint changing as he moves, yet conditioned by the
terrain it moves through and over, as much as by the conscious-

224

ness which occupies the moving point. One might compare the novels of a prose-writer, Douglas Woolf, who has published in the same magazines with Olson and Dorn; in particular his wittily entitled *Wall to Wall*, the fictional narrative of a trans-continental journey by car from the Pacific Ocean to the Atlantic.

But one could compare equally a much earlier poem by a quite different kind of poet, Yvor Winters's 'The Journey', which is like Dorn's poem in nothing except in being a very Western poem about the experience of moving over the vast distances of the American West. The America of these poems has nothing whatever in common with the Atlantic seaboard America of Robert Lowell, John Berryman, or indeed Charles Olson. (For Olson's slim little volume, *West*, is an exception for him, and to my mind not distinguished.)

Edward Dorn and Yvor Winters, neither of them Westerners by birth, choose to live in the West and to celebrate it in their poems, not at all because they had chosen to sink their roots there (as Wordsworth chose to root himself in the English Lake District), but because the history of the Western States— both the brief recorded history, and the much longer unrecorded history of the indigenous Indian peoples—is a history of human *movement*; and the still largely empty landscapes of those territories are images of nomadic life, an arena for human life to which the imaginative response is still (as it always has been) to *move*, to *keep moving*. Moreover, because the human history of those territories is so short and scant, and because they are still so empty, the spectacle of them—like the spectacle of the oceans when one travels on them—teases the imagination into conceiving that human migrations across these spaces are only the last chapter of a history of non-human migrations, a history which is read out of geology and climatology. This is what Olson says in a recent poem:

> in successive waves basically NW
> as in fact the earth's crust once—and mantle or at least

the depth of the asthenosphere broke
apart and went
    itself mid-

                 north north West
    150,000,000 years ago to that,
    definitely now established by
    J. Tuzo Wilson as well as other
oceanographers and geographers who have paid
                    attention to the
    fit of the Earth's continental shelfs
        on either shore of each
ocean—including runs right down the middle
                such as when
   India ground a path for herself traveling
from an original place as African about where
                 Mozambique
and sometimes about 150,000,000 years ago
went off to where she now is, attaching herself to
Eurasia—as if Tethys went under Ocean to
    maka the love with him
      a love with

                near Crete

    on the water's
      surface at or about
    Gortyna

             migrations

    turn out to be
  as large as
bodies of earth and of
    stories

              and primaries
of order which later is taken for granted are
such as the Atlantic migration which filled America.*

* Charles Olson, 'An Essay on Queen Tiy'. *The Wivenhoe Park Revue* 2 (1967),
pp. 38–39.

And this same area of human learning—where geography and geology, oceanography and climatology, anthropology and archaeology and prehistory meet—is the area which Dorn's imagination explores; not didactically like Olson (who in this respect is much nearer to Pound), but more freely and provisionally, as a sort of serious make-believe. Dorn is not committed to this field for imaginative speculation, as Olson is. On the dustjacket of his latest collection, he says for instance:

'In *The North Atlantic Turbine*, the poems since *Geography*, I have tried to locate another hemisphere. And I want this collection to be the last necessity to work out such locations.'

That is to say, his explorations of geographical space are now over; as he says elsewhere in the same blurb:

'That non-spacial dimension, intensity, is one of the few singular things which interest me now.'

The element of make-believe, of merely *provisional* belief in the primacy of geography, shows up in Dorn's humour, which is much more in evidence and also more various and shifting than in Olson. Olson's jokes (like 'maka the love with him') are hearty, but bluff and simple-minded. Dorn's humour is much harder to pin down, and also much harder to take—particularly in *The North Atlantic Turbine*, the latest collection, where it seems to be often raucous and sick, a sort of snarl. This is particularly hard for the British reader to take, because *The North Atlantic Turbine*, Dorn's fourth collection, consists of the poems he has written in England since he came here, to the University of Essex, in 1965; and the image he gives of England, often in this languid snarling tone, is decidedly unflattering. He is no more flattering to his own country, the United States. But then . . . he refuses to take nation-states (the U.K. vs. the U.S.) seriously. That indeed is the meaning of his title. His subject is the North Atlantic, as Herman Melville's (so Olson argued) is the Pacific. The tide of human migration long ago crossed the North Atlantic, and left it behind; and so the only movement left in it is rotation, a 'bind' or circular swirl;

it is now to all intents and purposes a landlocked ocean, and the swirl around in it (imaged as the pulse from a dynamo at its centre) locks together and makes virtually identical, in one pointless round of activity, all countries that have a North Atlantic seaboard—the U.K., the U.S., Canada, France, Spain.

The North Atlantic Turbine contains a long poem in six parts on 'Oxford'. The most immediately accessible and engaging of these is Part II, in which we see Oxford through an eye which refuses to be daunted by the historical patina on that or any other city of the Old World, insisting instead on 'locating' it for the imagination in a way which is natural for territories like Idaho, Montana, or the Dakotas—by way, that is, of the geological structure of the land mass which supports it:

> The sands of the Cotswolds
>   line the streets, the stone portals
> a light of light brown brilliance
> when the suns of May
>   cast a black swatch
> by Radcliffe Camera
>   solitary as
>   any Baptistry encrusted
>   or a product
>   of the sea.
>   However the streams of thin
>   elegance come down past the town
>   it is the linear strip
>   of the beautiful Jurassic lias
> running from Flixborough in Lincolnshire
> hanging from there
>   this liana falls, lier
> as the most springing joint
>   of England
>   to Bristol

But more challenging, and less palatable, is for instance 'Oxford Part V':

    England beware
        the cliff of 1945
    turns a natural insularity
    into a late, and out of joint
    naturalism of inbred
    industrial indecision. The hesitation
    to hard sell small arms
    to backward countries and
    'if we must, can't the man
    be more civilized' of a man
    who only knows his business
    be it selling washing machines
    or machine guns: un 'produit
    de l'industrie moderne'.
            White Sunday,
    the day of the Big White Sale.
    We speak of payments as
            balanced
Oxford, the dull if sometimes
            remote
      façade
    is balanced in limestone, the
    Bodleian has as a copyright
    every book,
        Lincoln College
      has high on the wall
        in the first court
    a small bust of John Wesley, fellow
    there is in Merton an Elizabethan
    stretch of building and beyond
    that, under a passage
    the treed lawn where only fellows
    and there is the garden where Hopkins
    as at Cambridge the tower

where Byron's Bear near
　　the rooms of Coleridge
　or Shelley's notebook in the
case at the Bodleian, the Lock
of His Hair, his glove, in a case.
not two gloves as he must
have had two hands to cover
but that hip thing
one glove you can do something
　　　　　　with
in terms of those and these brown spectacular
times, two
of course are a boring reminder
we are the animals we are
a lovely glove admittedly
but not so lovely as Shelley.

I walked back from Merton
with two lads who spoke of the police
and their perilous adventures
in Oxford's streets of explanations
'I shall climb up a drain pipe—
'But won't that disturb the authorities?
'it shall disturb them more
'if you wake them to report me
and thus we walked along—
there were more great names
than you'd care to hear
But at one point one of them said
it's impossible to write of it
every substantive fit
to name and celebrate has been spoken
and named. Then there was
a turning, we entered another street which
I'm more used to a grid,
swore to myself I'd never reenter,

but once I loved the idea of such narrow places.
And the easy talk of obscure things
I must admit I envied
    those children
because I love the dazzle of learning
and I am only concerned
when I think the strings
have gone loose.
    if I weren't an intelligent man
I'd share the attitude
    of my president
'Education is a wonderful thing.'

        But I said *everything?*
has been talked about
around Oxford. I was assured
it had been. I didn't *say* while walking
but I thought well then make up!
something! Because baby if you don't
they's gonna take all your wine away
they's gonna turn you into a state
institootion and you'll all be working
for the state just like in America
and you'll have to *prove*
you're useful, the most *useless*
sort of proof you'll ever have to make
. . . .
    Thus those children
could start by naming themselves and the rocks
in a larger than
national way and then more intimately,
if only for a more hopeful world
say what hope this 'rock
from which the language springs'
can be in the world. Can't
you tell yourselves it is time

Oxford stopped having a place
in English life as sanctuary,
World War II was *not* ended
in Europe because you failed
to take up the language
—not *the* language
oh you still have *that*, you
are stuck with that, that's
all you have,
because you so desired
to be the English Race
you so much wanted the courses
to come in their proper order
'where's the fish' you said
you were so impatient
and now
all you have is a few people you consider
problems anyway who won't even bother to speak
your language
and all they want to do is beat
your unemployment schemes, the best
of them have gone off
to Katmandu, the best of them
aren't even interested, except Tom
    Pickard
  who still makes his own sense
      in Newcastle, but he's a northerner.
   and will steal and resell
 every book Calder and Boyars prints
God bless him.

Part IV is introduced by 'An Epistolary Comment: knowing none of it accurately, the world can be surveyed'. And this ought to tell us the sort of poem we are dealing with: a poem in which concern for locality and for 'locating', so far from leading to localism or regionalism, lends itself on the contrary to vast and rapid panoramas. This poetry sets up the tourist as hero, and would persuade us that the only trustworthy eye is the travelling eye, casual and disengaged. In this *The North Atlantic Turbine* is like 18th-century poems such as Goldsmith's *The Traveller*, or Thomas Gray's *Education and Government*, or the prose-poetry of Burke's speech 'On Conciliation with the Colonies'. For those 18th-century works were similarly inspired by geography, indeed by a geographer—the French thinker, Montesquieu. The difference is that Montesquieu's bird's-eye view nourished a buoyant sense of diversity and plenitude. He argued that differences of climate and terrain made for different national temperaments, and hence that the form of government evolved by one people would not be appropriate for another differently located. Some of this buoyancy and eagerness appears in Olson. But Edward Dorn's space-capsule eye reports on the contrary that none of the differences matters, that one 'turbine', pumping out trade-cycles of production and consumption, governs and defines us all—the Communist East set on the same objectives as the Capitalist West, the negro American indeed different from the white American in (alas) no more than the pigment of his skin. The only valid and total alternative is the *Red* American.

POSTSCRIPT

In his latest work, *Gunslinger*, Dorn has reached the 'spiritual address' which he announced he was setting out for after *The North Atlantic Turbine*. Departing from geography and moving across 'that non-spacial dimension, intensity' (its colouring that of the American Southwest, but not literally located anywhere), Dorn has beautifully recovered his good humour. Of the verbal horse-play which carries the surreal narrative on a steady ripple of comedy ('horseplay' is exact—a talking horse occasions much of it), a broad and therefore quotable example is when in Book II we notice, as do the more-than-human travellers in the poem, that the first person has disappeared from the narration. Lil, archetypal madam of a Western brothel (but of much else—she practised 2000 years ago in Smyrna) is first to notice:

> What happened to I she asked
> his eyes dont seem right.

The Poet, another of the company, reports, 'I is dead', and is reproved: 'That aint grammatical, Poet'. Lil responds:

> Oh. Well I'll be . . .
> We never knew anything much
> about him did we. I
> was the name he answered to,
> and that was what he had
> wanderin around inside him
> askin so many questions
> his eyes had already answered . . .

Gunslinger himself, archetypal Westerner but also Greek, sun-worshipper and solar deity like Alexander the Great, explains:

> Life and Death
> are attributes of the soul
> not of things. The Ego
> is costumed as the road manager
> of the soul, every time
> the soul plays a date in another town
> I goes ahead to set up
> the bleechers, or book the hall
> as they now have it,
> the phenomenon is reported by the phrase
> I got there ahead of myself
> I got there ahead of my I
> is the fact
> which not a few anxious mortals
> misread as intuition. . . .

Since among the areas of language drawn upon for ambiguities is the dialect of drug-takers ('acid', for instance, and 'grass'), this questioning of personal identity is serious and comical at the same time. At once comic and profound, narrative and piercingly lyrical, the form and idiom of *Gunslinger* transcend completely the programmes of Black Mountain, just as they transcend (dare one say?) any programme so far promulgated or put into practice in Anglo-American poetry of the present century.

© Donald Davie 1970

A Reading List

NOTE

THE suggestions for reading that follow are selective, but an attempt has been made to list all the important *poetic* publications of the authors discussed, as well as a certain amount of secondary material, such as details of books edited, and of some critical articles where this seemed relevant. In addition, all works *on* the authors concerned mentioned in the body of the book, whether in approbation or not, have been included, together with other recommendations for reading on these poets. Reponsibility for the reading list remains that of the editor entirely, although it has been compiled in consultation with contributors. The list has been divided into sections corresponding to those in the book as a whole.

M.D.

I

The following anthologies of poetry together give a useful view of the whole scene in England and America since about 1950:

New Lines, edited by Robert Conquest, London: Macmillan and Co.; New York: St. Martin's Press, 1956.

> (The anthology which has come to define, though not by intention, the poetry of the English 'Movement'.)

The New Poets of England and America, edited by Donald Hall, Robert Pack and Louis Simpson, New York: Meridian Books, Inc., 1957.

The New American Poetry: 1945-1960, edited by D. M. Allen, New York: Grove Press, 1960.

> (A substantial selection of Black Mountain and beat poetry, with a section of prose statements on poetry by the poets concerned.)

New Poets of England and America, Second Selection, edited by Donald Hall and Robert Pack, Cleveland and New York: The World Publishing Co. (Meridian Books), 1962.

Contemporary American Poetry, edited by Donald Hall, London: Penguin Books, 1962.

> (An excellent anthology now out of print.)

The New Poetry, edited by A. Alvarez, London: Penguin Books, 1962; revised and enlarged, 1966.

> (Primarily English poetry.)

A Controversy of Poets, edited by Paris Leary and Robert Kelly, New York: Doubleday and Co., Inc. (Anchor Books), 1965.

> (American poetry. The book covers an exceptionally wide

range of poets, and has useful biographical and bibliographical information.)

A bibliography of the works of Charles Olson will be found in
section VIII of this reading list. A partial bibliography of the
other poets discussed in the first essay in this book follows:
James Dickey, *Poems 1957–67*, New York: Random House;
London: Rapp and Carroll Ltd., 1967.
> (Contains nearly all his poetry to date; one book of his had
> previously been published in England, by Longmans in
> 1964—*Helmets.*)

—— *Babel to Byzantium*, New York: Farrar, Straus and
Giroux, 1968.
> (Reviews and essays on poetry, containing nearly all of
> his earlier book, *The Suspect in Poetry*, Madison, Minne-
> sota: The Sixties Press, 1964.)

Robert Bly, *Silence in the Snowy Fields*, Middletown, Conn.:
Wesleyan U.P., 1962; enlarged, London: Jonathan Cape,
1967.

—— *The Light around the Body*, New York: Harper and Row,
1967; London: Rapp and Whiting, Ltd., 1968.
James Wright, *The Green Wall*, New Haven, Conn.: Yale
University Press, 1957.

—— *Saint Judas*, Middletown, Conn.: Wesleyan University
Press, 1959.

—— *The Branch Will Not Break*, Middletown, Conn.: Wesleyan University Press; London: Longmans, Green and Co.,
1963.

—— *Shall We Gather at the River*, Middletown, Conn.:
Wesleyan University Press, 1968; London: Rapp and
Whiting Ltd., 1969.
> (Bly and Wright have also published, separately, together,
> or with others, mostly through the Sixties Press, Madison,
> Minnesota, selections from the following poets in transla-
> tion: Gunnar Ekelöf, Juan Ramon Jimenez, Pablo Neruda,
> Georg Trakl and César Vallejo.)

Three poets of our time not discussed in this book are specially recommended to the reader—Donald Davie, Geoffrey Hill and Thomas Kinsella.

Donald Davie: [*Poems*], Swinford: The Fantasy Press (The Fantasy Poets), 1954.

—— *Brides of Reason*, Swinford: The Fantasy Press, 1955.

—— *A Winter Talent*, London: Routledge and Kegan Paul, 1957.

—— *The Forests of Lithuania*, Hull: The Marvell Press, 1959. (Derived from Mickiewicz's poem, *Pan Tadeusz*.)

—— *A Sequence for Francis Parkman*, Hull: The Marvell Press (Listenbooks), 1961.
(Issued with a record of the poet reading his poem.)

—— *New and Selected Poems*, Middletown, Conn.: Wesleyan University Press, 1961.

——*Events and Wisdoms*, London: Routledge and Kegan Paul, 1964; Middletown, Conn.: Wesleyan U.P., 1965.

—— *Essex Poems*, London: Routledge and Kegan Paul, 1969. (Donald Davie has also written several books of literary criticism, including *Purity of Diction in English Verse*, *Articulate Energy*, *The Heyday of Sir Walter Scott*, and *Ezra Pound: Poet as Sculptor*. He has translated, with a commentary, *The Poems of Doctor Zhivago* by Boris Pasternak.)

Geoffrey Hill: [*Poems*], (Fantasy Poets No. 11), Oxford: Oxford University Poetry Society, 1953.

—— *For the Unfallen*, London: Andre Deutsch, 1959; Chester Springs, Pa.: Dufour Editions Inc., 1961.

—— *King Log*, London: Andre Deutsch; Chester Springs, Pa.: Dufour Editions Inc., 1968.
(Includes all the poems in the pamphlet *Preghiere* (1964), and the new poems from the selection in *Penguin Modern Poets 8* (1966).)

Thomas Kinsella: *Poems*, Dublin: The Dolmen Press, 1956.

—— *Another September*, Dublin: The Dolmen Press, 1958.

—— *Poems and Translations*, New York: Atheneum Publishers, 1961.

—— *Downstream*, Dublin: The Dolmen Press; London: Oxford University Press, 1962.

(Includes a revised version of the sequence *Moralities*, Dublin: The Dolmen Press, 1960.)

—— *Nightwalker and Other Poems*, Dublin: The Dolmen Press; London: Oxford University Press; New York: Alfred Knopf, 1968.

(Includes a revised version of the sequence *Wormwood*, published in a limited edition by the Dolmen Press in 1966. The title-poem was published separately as *Nightwalker* in 1967, also by the Dolmen Press.)

Works mentioned in the first essay of this book include:

'Poets in Public', *The Times*, 25 January 1969.

Introduction to Poetry, edited by Louis Simpson, New York: The Macmillan Co., 1968; London: Macmillan and Co., 1969.

Soren Kierkegaard, *The Present Age*, translated by Alexander Dru, London: William Collins (The Fontana Library), 1962.

(A convenient paperback edition. This essay is published in America as a Harper Torchbook.)

John Bayley, *The Romantic Survival*, London: Constable and Sons, 1957; New York: Essential Books, 1959.

F. R. Leavis, *New Bearings in Modern Poetry*, London: Chatto and Windus, 1932; enlarged, 1950; New York: George W. Stewart, Inc., 1947; enlarged, 1950; Ann Arbor: University of Michigan Press, 1960.

II

Philip Larkin: *The North Ship*, London: The Fortune Press, 1945; enlarged, with an introduction, London: Faber and Faber, 1966.

—— *XX Poems*, 1951.

(Printed at the author's expense when he was living in Belfast. The additional poem in the 1966 edition of *The North Ship* comes from here; most, but not all, of the others are in *The Less Deceived*.)

—— [*Poems*], (Fantasy Poets No. 21), Swinford: The Fantasy Press, 1954.

(A pamphlet.)

—— *The Less Deceived*, Hull: The Marvell Press; New York: St. Martin's Press, 1955.

—— *The Whitsun Weddings*, London: Faber and Faber; New York: Random House, 1964.

He has made two records:

Philip Larkin reads The Less Deceived, Listen Records, 1958.

Philip Larkin reads and comments on The Whitsun Weddings, Listen Records, 1965.

(Reprints Christopher Ricks's *New York Review of Books* piece on its jacket.)

He has also published two novels:

Jill, London: The Fortune Press, 1946; revised, with an introduction, London: Faber and Faber; New York: St. Martin's Press, 1964.

A Girl in Winter, London: Faber and Faber, 1947; New York: St. Martin's Press, 1963.

He has brought together writings on jazz in:

All What Jazz?, London: Faber and Faber, 1970.

The following anthologies to which he has contributed are of interest:

Poetry From Oxford in Wartime, edited by William Bell, London: The Fortune Press, 1944.

New Lines, edited by Robert Conquest, London: Macmillan and Co.; New York: St. Martin's Press, 1955.

Poets of the 1950's: An anthology of new English verse, edited by D. J. Enright, Tokyo: Kenkyusha Ltd., 1955.

(Includes a note on his poems by Larkin.)

A READING LIST

Poet's Choice, edited by Paul Engel and Joseph Langland.
(Larkin comments on the poem of his own that he likes
best.)

See also:

Philip Larkin, 'Not the Place's Fault', *Umbrella*, Vol. 1, No. 3,
Summer 1959.

Christopher Ricks, 'A True Poet', review of *The Whitsun
Weddings*, *New York Review of Books*, 14 June 1965.

Christopher Ricks, review of *The North Ship*, *The Sunday Times*,
25 September 1966.

Christopher Ricks, on 'Love Songs in Age' by Philip Larkin,
The Sunday Times, 7 January 1968.

Ian Hamilton, 'Four Conversations', *The London Magazine*,
N.S., Vol. 4, No 8, November 1964.
(A conversation with Larkin.)

III

Robert Lowell: *Land of Unlikeness*, with an introduction by
Allen Tate, Cummington, Mass.: The Cummington Press,
1944.

—— *Lord Weary's Castle*, New York: Harcourt, Brace and Co.,
1946.
(A number of poems here are from *Land of Unlikeness*. In
The Poetic Themes of Robert Lowell, Jerome Mazzaro
quotes various passages which did not find their way from
the one volume to the other.)

—— *Poems 1938–49*, London: Faber and Faber, 1950.
(All *Lord Weary's Castle*, and *The Mills of the Kavanaughs*,
except the title poem, which is printed as an appendix to
Faber's *Robert Lowell: The First Twenty Years*, by Hugh B.
Staples.)

—— *The Mills of the Kavanaughs*, New York: Harcourt, Brace
and Co., 1951.

—— *Life Studies*, London: Faber and Faber, 1956; enlarged edition, New York: Farrar, Straus and Giroux, 1959; London: Faber and Faber, 1968.

(The 1959 edition was enlarged because it contained the prose reminiscence '91 Revere Street', which had not appeared before.)

—— *For the Union Dead*, New York: Farrar, Straus and Giroux, 1964; London: Faber and Faber, 1965.

(The English edition is a lithographic reprint.)

—— *Selected Poems*, London: Faber and Faber, 1965.

(A paperback selection.)

—— *Near the Ocean*, New York: Farrar, Straus and Giroux; London: Faber and Faber, 1967.

(The American edition has illustrations by Sidney Nolan.)

Robert Lowell has written three one act plays in verse, which are published as:

The Old Glory, New York: Farrar, Straus and Giroux, 1965; London: Faber and Faber, 1966.

He has published versions of foreign poetry in some of the collections of poetry already listed and in:

Imitations, New York: Farrar, Straus and Giroux, 1961; London: Faber and Faber, 1962.

J. Racine, *Phaedra*, London: Faber and Faber, 1963.

(This version was first published in *The Classic Theatre*, edited by Eric Bentley, Vol. IV: *Six French Plays*, New York: Doubleday and Co. (Anchor Books), 1961. It was later published with Jacques Barzun's translation of Beaumarchais's *Figaro's Marriage*, New York: Farrar, Straus and Giroux, 1964.)

'*Prometheus Bound* . . . derived from Aeschylus', *New York Review of Books*, 13 July 1967.

(In prose.)

Olga Carlisle, *Poets on Street Corners*, New York: Random House, 1968.

(Includes Lowell's versions of Osip Mandelshtam.)

A READING LIST

The Voyage, London: Faber and Faber, 1968.
(Versions of Baudelaire reprinted from *Imitations* with illustrations by Sidney Nolan.)

Robert Lowell has edited (with Peter Taylor and Robert Penn Warren):
Randall Jarrell, 1914–1965, New York: Farrar, Straus and Giroux, 1967.

He has written introductions for:
Ford Madox Ford, *Buckshee*, Cambridge, Mass.: P.Y.M. Randall Press, 1966.
Sylvia Plath, *Ariel*, New York: Harper and Row, 1966.
(Not in the English edition, which preceded this.)

Other miscellaneous pieces are:
'Hopkins' Sanctity', in: The Kenyon Critics, *Gerard Manley Hopkins*, Cleveland: The World Publishing Co.; New York: New Directions; London: Dennis Dobson Ltd., 1949.
'William Carlos Williams', *Hudson Review*, Vol. XIV, No. 4, Winter 1961–62.
(Reprinted in: *William Carlos Williams*, edited by J. Hillis Miller, Englewood Cliffs, New Jersey: Prentice Hall, Inc. (Twentieth Century Views series), 1968.)
'Randall Jarrell 1914–1965: An Appreciation', in Randall Jarrell, *The Lost World*, London: Eyre and Spottiswoode, 1966.
(Not in the earlier American edition. First printed in the *New York Review of Books*.)

See also:
Randall Jarrell, 'From the Kingdom of Necessity', *Poetry and the Age*, New York: Alfred Knopf, 1953; London: Faber and Faber, 1955.
'The Art of Poetry III: Robert Lowell', *Paris Review*, No. 25, Winter-Spring 1961.
(Reprinted in *Writers at Work* (*Second Series*), New York: Viking Press; London: Secker and Warburg, 1963.)
Hugh B. Staples, *Robert Lowell: The First Twenty Years*, London: Faber and Faber, 1962.

(Reprints the title-poem of *The Mills of the Kavanaughs* as an appendix.)

Ian Hamilton, 'Robert Lowell', *The Review*, No. 3, August/September 1962.

(Reprinted in *The Modern Poet*, edited by Ian Hamilton, London: Macdonald, 1969.)

'The Poet and his Critics: III', *New World Writing*, No. 21, 1962.

(A symposium on Lowell's 'Skunk Hour', with a contribution by the poet himself, edited by Anthony Ostroff.)

'Robert Lowell in conversation with A. Alvarez', *The Review*, No. 8, August 1963.

(Reprinted in *The Modern Poet*—see Hamilton above.)

Jerome Mazzaro, *The Poetic Themes of Robert Lowell*, Ann Arbor: University of Michigan Press, 1965.

Denis Donoghue, 'Edward Arlington Robinson, J. V. Cuningham, Robert Lowell', *Connoisseurs of Chaos*, New York: Macmillan, 1965; London: Faber and Faber, 1966.

Thomas Parkinson, *For the Union Dead*, Salmagundi, I.4, 1966–67.

(This number of the magazine was entirely devoted to Lowell.)

Norman Mailer, *The Armies of the Night*, Cleveland: The World Publishing Co.; London: Weidenfeld and Nicolson, 1968.

IV

John Berryman: *Poems*, New York: New Directions (Poet of the Month Series), 1942.

(A pamphlet.)

—— *The Dispossessed*, New York: William Sloane Associates, Inc., 1948.

—— *Homage to Mistress Bradstreet*, New York: Farrar, Straus and Co., 1956; London: Faber and Faber, 1959.

(The American edition contains the title-poem only; the English edition follows it with the poet's own selection of his other poems. See *Short Poems* beneath.)

—— *77 Dream Songs*, New York: Farrar, Straus and Co.; London: Faber and Faber, 1964.

(The first instalment of *The Dream Songs*.)

—— *Berryman's Sonnets*, New York: Farrar, Straus and Giroux, 1967; London: Faber and Faber, 1968.

(Written in the 1940's.)

—— *Short Poems*, New York: Farrar Straus and Giroux, 1968.

(The text is identical with that of Faber's *Homage to Mistress Bradstreet*, without the title-poem, and with the addition of a 'Formal Elegy on the Death of President Kennedy'.)

—— *His Toy, His Dream, His Rest*, New York: Farrar, Straus and Giroux, 1968; London: Faber and Faber, 1969.

(The conclusion of *The Dream Songs*.)

Poems by Berryman appeared in the following two anthologies at the beginning of his career:

New Poems: 1940, edited by Oscar Williams, New York: Yardstick Press, 1941.

('An anthology of British and American verse, introduced by George Barker'.)

Five Young American Poets, New York: New Directions, 1941.

(The other poets were: Mary Barnard, Randall Jarrell, W. R. Moses and George Marion O'Donnell.)

Berryman has written one critical book:

Stephen Crane, New York: William Sloane Associates, Inc., 1950; London: Methuen and Co., 1951.

(Reprinted by The World Publishing Co. (Meridian Books), 1962.)

He has written introductions for:

M. G. Lewis, *The Monk*, New York: Grove Press, 1952.

Thomas Nashe, *The Unfortunate Traveller*, New York: G. B. Putnam's Sons, Inc. (Capricorn Books), 1960.

(Berryman edited the book as well.)

A READING LIST

The following miscellaneous prose pieces are of interest:

'The Lovers', *Kenyon Review*, Vol. VII, No. 1, Winter 1945.
(A story.)

'The Imaginary Jew', *Kenyon Review*, Vol. VII, No. 4, Autumn 1945.

(This story was reprinted in *Horizon*, Vol. XVI, Nos. 93–4, October 1947, and reprinted in *The Golden Horizon*, edited by Cyril Connolly, London: Weidenfeld and Nicolson, 1953; New York: University Books, Inc., 1950.)

'F. Scott Fitzgerald', *Kenyon Review*, Vol. VIII, No. 1, Winter 1946.

'The State of American Writing, 1948: Seven Questions', *Partisan Review*, Vol. XV, No. 8, August 1948.

(Berryman's reply is one of several.)

'The Poetry of Ezra Pound', *Partisan Review*, Vol. XVI, No. 4, April 1949.

'Shakespeare at Thirty', *Hudson Review*, Vol. VI, No. 2, Summer 1953.

'Thursday Out', *The Noble Savage*, No. 3, May 1961.
(On the Taj Mahal.)

Contribution to: 'The Poet and his Critics: III', a symposium on Robert Lowell's 'Skunk Hour', edited by Anthony Ostroff, *New World Writing*, No. 21, 1962.

See also:

Robert Lowell, review of 77 *Dream Songs*, *New York Review of Books*, 28 May 1964.

Ian Hamilton, review of 77 *Dream Songs*, *The London Magazine*, N.S., Vol. 4, No. 11, February 1965.

Gabriel Pearson, 'John Berryman—Poet as Medium', *The Review*, No. 15, April 1965.

(Reprinted in: *The Modern Poet*, edited by Ian Hamilton, London: Macdonald, 1969.)

Poets on Poetry, edited by Howard Nemerov, New York: Basic Books, 1966.

(Berryman's reply to Nemerov's set of questions, proposed

to a number of poets, was also printed in *Shenandoah*, Vol. XVII, No. 1, Autumn 1965.)

Review of *His Toy, His Dream, His Rest, Times Literary Supplement*, 26 June 1969.

V

Ted Hughes: *The Hawk in the Rain*, London: Faber and Faber; New York: Harper and Bros., 1957.

—— *Lupercal*, London: Faber and Faber; New York: Harper and Bros., 1960.

—— (and Thom Gunn), *Selected Poems*, London: Faber and Faber, 1962.

(A paperback selection from the two poets.)

—— *Recklings*, London: Turret Books, 1966.

—— *The Burning of the Brothel*, London: Turret Books, 1966. (A comic ballad.)

—— *Wodwo*, London: Faber and Faber; New York: Harper and Row, 1967.

—— *Scapegoats and Rabies*, London: Poet and Printer, 1967. (A pamphlet. The poem was also published in the *New Statesman*.)

—— *Five Autumn Songs for Children's Voices*, Bow, Devon: Richard Gilbertson, 1969.

—— Poems from the sequence in progress provisionally entitled 'Crow Lore' have appeared in *The Listener*, 25 January and 26 September, 1968.

Ted Hughes has written the following books for children:

Meet My Folks!, London: Faber and Faber, 1961.

How the Whale Became, London: Faber and Faber, 1963; New York: Atheneum, 1964. (Prose.)

The Earth Owl and Other Moon-People, London: Faber and Faber, 1963.

Nessie, The Mannerless Monster, London: Faber and Faber, 1964.

The Iron Man, London: Faber and Faber, 1968.
(Prose.)

Ted Hughes has edited the following books:
Here Today, London: Hutchinson and Co., 1963.
(An anthology of contemporary verse for schools. Two records were issued in association with it.)
(and Thom Gunn), *Five American Poets,* London: Faber and Faber, 1963.
(Selections from Edgar Bowers, Howard Nemerov, Hyam Plutzik, Louis Simpson and William Stafford.)
Keith Douglas, *Selected Poems,* London: Faber and Faber; New York: Chilmark Press, 1964.
(The introduction by Hughes was also published in *The Critical Quarterly,* Vol. 5, No. 1, Spring 1963.)
Poetry in the Making, London: Faber and Faber, 1967.
(A selection from Hughes's work for B.B.C. radio schools programmes.)
A Choice of Emily Dickinson's Verse, London: Faber and Faber, 1968.

He is also an editor of the magazine *Modern Poetry in Translation,* and has written an introduction for:
Vasko Popa, *Selected Poems,* translated by Anne Pennington, London: Penguin Books, 1969.
He has translated and adapted:
Seneca's 'Oedipus', London: Faber and Faber, 1969.

See also:

C. J. Rawson, 'Ted Hughes: A Reappraisal', *Essays in Criticism,* Vol. XV, No. 1, January 1965.
C. Ingli James, 'The Animal Poetry of Ted Hughes: A Devaluation', *The Southern Review* (Adelaide), Vol. II, No. 3, 1967.

VI

Sylvia Plath: *The Colossus,* London: William Heinemann, 1960, Faber and Faber, 1967; New York: Alfred Knopf, 1962.

(The American edition is slightly different from the English.)

—— *Ariel*, London: Faber and Faber, 1965; with an introduction by Robert Lowell, New York: Harper and Row, 1966.

(The American edition is slightly different from the English).

—— *Uncollected Poems*, London: Turret Books, 1966.

—— *Three Women*, London: Turret Books, 1968.

(Two extracts from this radio play were printed in *The Critical Quarterly*, Vol. 10, No. 3, Autumn 1968.)

—— *The Art of Sylvia Plath*, edited by Charles Newman, London: Faber and Faber, 1970.

(Contains otherwise inaccessible material, as well as essays on her work.)

—— *The Bell Jar*, London: William Heinemann, 1960, Faber and Faber, 1966.

(First published under the pseudonym 'Victoria Lucas'. Her only novel.)

—— *American Poetry Now*, Critical Quarterly Poetry Supplement, No. 2 [1961].

(A pamphlet anthology edited by Sylvia Plath.)

Some of Sylvia Plath's last poems, not otherwise easily available, will be found in *The Review*, No. 9, October 1963 and in *Encounter*, XXI.4, October 1963.

Triquarterly No. 7, Fall 1966, contains a selection of Sylvia Plath's poems, and the following articles about her:
Charles Newman, 'Candor is the only wile'.
A. Alvarez, 'Sylvia Plath'.

(First printed in *The Review*, No. 9, October 1963, and reprinted in *The Modern Poet*, edited by Ian Hamilton, London: Macdonald, 1969. Mr. Alvarez wrote a postscript for the essay's appearance in *Triquarterly*, and this is reproduced along with it in his own book of essays and reviews, *Beyond All This Fiddle*, London: Allen Lane, The Penguin Press, 1968.)

Ted Hughes, 'The Chronological Order of Sylvia Plath's Poems.'

Anne Sexton, 'The Barfly Ought to Sing'.

Lois Ames, 'Notes towards a Biography'.

All this material is reproduced in *The Art of Sylvia Plath*, edited by Charles Newman, London: Faber and Faber, 1970, which also contains a comprehensive bibliography.

The Cambridge Review, Vol. 90, No. 2187, 7 February 1969, contains four poems from the early unpublished manuscript *Two Lovers and a Beachcomber*, as well as the following articles:

A. Alvarez, 'Sylvia Plath: The Cambridge Collection'.

George Steiner, 'In Extremis'.

David Holbrook, 'Sylvia Plath and the Problem of Violence in Art'.

Eric Homberger, 'I am I'.

M.W.C., 'Remembering Sylvia'.

See also:

David Holbrook, 'The 200-inch distorting mirror', *New Society*, 11 July 1968.

David Holbrook, 'R. D. Laing and the Death Circuit', *Encounter*, Vol. XXXI, No. 2, August 1968.

A. R. Jones, 'Necessity and Freedom: The Poetry of Robert Lowell, Sylvia Plath, and Anne Sexton', *The Critical Quarterly* Vol. VII, No. 1, Spring 1965.

VII

Thom Gunn: [*Poems*] (Fantasy Poets, No. 16), Oxford: Oxford University Poetry Society, 1953.

(A pamphlet.)

—— *Fighting Terms*, Swinford: The Fantasy Press, 1954; revised, New York: Hawk's Well Press, 1958; further revised, London: Faber and Faber, 1962.

(The Faber edition is closer to the first version of the book than to that of 1958.)

A READING LIST

—— *The Sense of Movement*, London: Faber and Faber, 1957; Chicago: University of Chicago Press, 1959.

—— *My Sad Captains*, London: Faber and Faber; Chicago: University of Chicago Press, 1961.

—— (and Ted Hughes), *Selected Poems*, London: Faber and Faber, 1962.

(A paperback selection.)

—— (and Ander Gunn), *Positives*, London: Faber and Faber; Chicago: University of Chicago Press, 1966.

—— *Touch*, London: Faber and Faber; Chicago: University of Chicago Press, 1968.

—— *Poems 1950–66*, London: Faber and Faber, 1969.

(A paperback selection.)

Thom Gunn has edited:

Poetry from Cambridge 1951–52, London: The Fortune Press [1952].

(and Ted Hughes), *Five American Poets*, London: Faber and Faber, 1963.

(Selections from Edgar Bowers, Howard Nemerov, Hyam Plutzik, Louis Simpson and William Stafford.)

Selected Poems of Fulke Greville, London: Faber and Faber; Chicago: University of Chicago Press, 1968.

Thom Gunn has done a good deal of reviewing, notably for *The London Magazine* and *The Yale Review*. The two pieces following are of special interest:

'William Carlos Williams', *Encounter*, Vol. XXV, No. 1, July 1965.

'Interpenetrating Things', *Agenda*, Vol. 4, Nos. 3–4, Summer, 1966.

(A review of Gary Snyder's *A Range of Poems*.)

See also:

New Lines, edited by Robert Conquest, London: Macmillan; New York: St. Martin's Press, 1956.

John Mander, *The Writer and Commitment*, London: Secker and

Warburg; Chester Springs, Pa.: Dufour Editions Inc., 1961.

John Fuller, 'Thom Gunn', *The Review*, No. 1, April–May 1962.
(A review of the revised *Fighting Terms*; reprinted in *The Modern Poet*, edited by Ian Hamilton, London: Macdonald, 1969.)

Alan Brownjohn, 'The Poetry of Thom Gunn', *The London Magazine*, N.S., Vol. 2, No. 12, March 1963.

Ian Hamilton, 'Four Conversations', *The London Magazine*, N.S., Vol. 4, No. 8, November 1964.

Martin Dodsworth, 'Thom Gunn: Positives and Negatives', *The Review*, No. 18, April 1968.
(The inclusion of poems from *Positives* in Gunn's *Poems 1950–66* may invalidate some of the argument here.)

In connection with Gunn's existentialist interest, it may be helpful to read:

Emmanuel Mounier, *Introduction aux Existentialismes*, Paris: Éditions Denoël, 1947.

J.-P. Sartre, *L'Être et le Néant*, Paris: Gallimard, 1943; *Being and Nothingness*, translated by Hazel E. Barnes, London: Methuen and Co., 1957.

VIII

Charles Olson's principal publications have been:

Call Me Ishmael, New York: Reynal and Hitchcock, 1947; London: Jonathan Cape, 1967.
(An essay on *Moby Dick*, reprinted in America in 1958 by Grove Press, and in 1967 by City Lights.)

Mayan Letters, edited, with a preface, by Robert Creeley, Palma de Mallorca: Divers Press, 1953; London: Jonathan Cape, 1968.
(Included in Olson's *Selected Writings*.)

The Maximus Poems (*Jargon* 24), New York: Jargon/Corinth Books, 1960.
(The first 37 letters.)

A READING LIST

The Distances, New York: Grove Press, 1960.
    (Poems.)

Human Universe and Other Essays, edited by Donald Allen, San Francisco: Auerhahn Press, 1965.
    (Includes 'Projective Verse'; reprinted by Grove Press, 1967.)

Selected Writings, edited, with an introduction by, Robert Creeley, New York: New Directions [1966].
    (Includes *Mayan Letters*, *Apollonius of Tyana*, 'Projective Verse' and other essays, with a selection of the poems.)

Maximus Poems IV, V, VI, London: Cape Goliard Press, 1968.
    (A continuation of *The Maximus Poems*.)

Letters for Origin, 1950–1956, edited by Albert Glover, London: Cape Goliard, 1969.

Olson has published many pamphlets and books through small presses; the reader is referred, for full details, to:

G. F. Butterick and A. Glover, *A Bibliography of Works by Charles Olson*, New York: Phoenix Bookshop, 1967.

Here, however, is a short list of Olson's miscellaneous publications; it has not been possible to give full details in every case, and, whilst accuracy has been striven for, it cannot be guaranteed:

To Corrado Cagli, New York: Knoedler Gallery, 1947.

Upon a Moebius Strip, New York, 1947.

Portfolio V, Paris, 1947.

y & x, Paris: Black Sun Press, 1948.

The Sutter-Marshall Lease with the Yalesumney Indians for Monopoly of the Gold-Bearing Lands, with introductory notes by Charles Olson, California: 1948.

Projective Verse, New York: Poetry, New York, 1950.
    (Reprinted in many places: with 'Letter to E. B. Feinstein' as *Projective Verse Vs. The Non-Projective*, for which see below; in *Human Universe and Other Essays*; in *The New American Poetry*, edited by Donald Allen, New York;

Grove Press, 1960; and in *Modern Poets on Poetry*, edited by James Scully, London: Collins (Fontana Books), 1966.)

Letter for Melville, Black Mountain, N.C., 1951.

This, Black Mountain, N.C.: Black Mountain College Graphics Workshop, 1952.

Apollonius of Tyana, Black Mountain, N.C., 1952.

(A 'dance with some words, for two actors', in prose, reprinted in *Human Universe* and *Selected Writings*.)

In Cold Hell, In Thicket (*Origin*, Series 1, No. 8), Palma de Mallorca: Divers Press; Dorchester, Mass.: Origin Press, 1953.

(Poems; reprinted by the Four Seasons Foundation, 1967.)

Maximus 1–10 (*Jargon 7*), Stuttgart; Highlands, N.C., 1953.

Anecdotes of the Late War (Jargon Broadside No. 1), Highlands, N.C. [1956].

Maximus 11–22 (*Jargon 9*), Stuttgart; Highlands, N.C., 1956.

O'Ryan 2, 4, 6, 8, 10, San Francisco, 1958.

Projective Verse Vs. The Non-Projective, New York: Totem Books, 1959.

(See *Projective Verse* above.)

Maximus from Dogtown I, with a foreword by Michael McClure, San Francisco: Auerhahn Press, 1961.

A Bibliography on America for Ed Dorn, San Francisco: Four Seasons Foundation, 1964.

Signature to Petition, Berkeley, California, 1964.

O'Ryan 1–10, San Francisco: Oyez Press, 1965.

Proprioception, San Francisco: Four Seasons Foundation, 1965.

(A pamphlet of essays and notes.)

Stocking Cap, San Francisco: Four Seasons Foundation, 1966.

(A short story which first appeared in *The Montevallo Review*, Vol. 1, No. 2, Summer 1951.)

Causal Mythology, San Francisco: Four Seasons Foundation, 1969.

West, London: Goliard Press, 1966.

Reading at Berkeley, Los Angeles: Coyote Books, 1968.

A READING LIST

See also:

Robert Creeley, 'Some Notes on Olson's *Maximus*', *Yugen*, No. 8.

Edward Dorn, *What I See In* The Maximus Poems, Ventura, California: Migrant Pamphlet, 1960.
> (Reprinted in *Kulchur*, No. 4, 1961.)

Robert Duncan, 'Notes on Poetics Regarding Olson's Maximus', *The Black Mountain Review*, No. 6, 1956.
> (A revised version of this essay appears in *The Review*, No. 10, January 1964.)

Edward Dorn: *The Newly Fallen*, New York: Totem Press, 1961.

—— *Hands Up!*, New York: Totem Press, in association with Corinth Books, Inc., 1964.

—— *From Gloucester Out*, London: Matrix Press, 1964.

—— *Idaho Out*, New York: Matter Books; London: Fulcrum Press, 1965.

—— *Geography*, London: Fulcrum Press, 1965.
> (Dorn's first full-length book of poems. It includes *Idaho Out*.)

—— *The North Atlantic Turbine*, London: Fulcrum Press, 1967.

—— *Gunslinger*, Books 1 and 2, two volumes, Los Angeles: Black Sparrow Press, 1968 and 1969; one volume, London: Fulcrum Press, 1970.

Edward Dorn has also published:

What I See In The Maximus Poems, Ventura, California: Migrant Pamphlet, 1960.
> (Reprinted in *Kulchur*, No. 4, 1961.)

Rites of Passage A Brief History, Buffalo: Frontier Press, 1965.
> (A novel.)

The Shoshoneans, with photographs by Leroy Lucas, New York: William Morrow and Co., Inc., 1967.
> (An essay on the Shoshonean Indians today.)

A READING LIST

He has translated, with Gordon Brotherston:

Our Word: Guerrilla poems from Latin America, London: Cape
Goliard Press, 1968.

He has also translated:

Tree Between Two Walls, by José Emilio Pacheco, Los
Angeles: Black Sparrow Press, 1969.

'Edward Dorn reads from The North Atlantic Turbine' is a
record issued in 1967 by Intersound Recordings, London, and
subsequently by Stream Records, London.

See also:

R. D. Gooder, 'The Work of a Poet', *The Cambridge Quarterly*,
Vol. 3, No. 1, Winter 1967–68.

(A review of *The Shoshoneans.*)

For a simple introduction to the history of Black Mountain
College, the reader is referred to:

Alasdair Clayre, 'The Rise and Fall of Black Mountain College',
The Listener, 27 March 1969.

A representative selection of Black Mountain Poetry will be
found in *The Review*, No. 10, January 1964, a number specially
edited by Charles Tomlinson. For further bibliographical
information on these poets, the back pages of *A Controversy of
Poets*, edited by Paris Leary and Robert Kelly (New York:
Doubleday and Co. (Anchor Books), 1965) will be found very
helpful.

The quarterly journal *Form* carried a series of articles on
Black Mountain College in 1968 and 1969. Michael Weaver
has a book on the College in preparation.

116741

Ohio Dominican College Library
1216 Sunbury Road
Columbus, Ohio 43219

DEMCO